# THE BEF IN FRANCE 1939-1940

DESPATCHES FROM THE FRONT
The Commanding Officers' Reports From the Field and At Sea.

# THE BEF IN FRANCE 1939-1940

**Manning the Front through to the Dunkirk Evacuation**

Introduced and compiled by
Martin Mace and John Grehan
With additional research by
Sara Mitchell

Pen & Sword
**MILITARY**

First published in Great Britain in 2014 by
Pen & Sword Military
an imprint of
Pen & Sword Books Ltd
47 Church Street
Barnsley
South Yorkshire
S70 2AS
Copyright © Martin Mace and John Grehan, 2014

ISBN 978 1 78346 211 7

The right of Martin Mace and John Grehan to be identified as Authors of this Work has been asserted by them in accordance with the Copyright, Designs and Patents Act 1988.

A CIP catalogue record for this book is available from the British Library. All rights reserved. No part of this book may be reproduced or transmitted in any form or by any means, electronic or mechanical including photocopying, recording or by any information storage and retrieval system, without permission from the Publisher in writing.

Printed and bound in England
By CPI Group (UK) Ltd, Croydon, CR0 4YY

Pen & Sword Books Ltd incorporates the Imprints of
Pen & Sword Aviation, Pen & Sword Family History,
Pen & Sword Maritime, Pen & Sword Military, Pen & Sword Discovery,
Pen & Sword Politics, Pen & Sword Atlas, Pen & Sword Archaeology,
Wharncliffe Local History, Wharncliffe True Crime, Wharncliffe Transport,
Pen & Sword Select, Pen & Sword Military Classics, Leo Cooper,
The Praetorian Press, Claymore Press, Remember When,
Seaforth Publishing and Frontline Publishing.

For a complete list of Pen & Sword titles please contact:
PEN & SWORD BOOKS LIMITED
47 Church Street, Barnsley, South Yorkshire, S70 2AS, England
E-mail: enquiries@pen-and-sword.co.uk
Website: www.pen-and-sword.co.uk

# Contents

| | |
|---|---|
| Introduction | vii |
| List of Illustrations | xix |
| The Despatches | |
|    1. Despatches on operations of the British Expeditionary Force, France and Belgium, 3 September 1939 to 31 May 1940, by General the Viscount Gort | 1 |
|    2. Operation *Dynamo* – the evacuation of the Allied armies from Dunkirk and neighbouring beaches by Vice Admiral Bertram Ramsay | 101 |
|    3. Despatches on operations of the British Expeditionary Force, France from 12 June 1940 to 19 June 1940, by Lieutenant-General Sir Alan Brooke | 165 |
| Appendix - The British Expeditionary Force Order of Battle as organised on 10 May 1940 | 176 |
| Abbreviations | 185 |
| Index | 187 |

# Introduction

Britain had fully expected to send a large expeditionary force to France in the event of war being declared in 1939 and the very day after Prime Minister Chamberlain's dreaded announcement of war with Germany the first units of the BEF, under the command of General John Gort, were shipped across the Channel. Six days later, on 10 September, the main force began its move to France.

This deployment was different from that of August 1914 in that because of the risk of air attack upon the ships, which was not a factor in the early years of the First World War, the troops were shipped to Cherbourg with their stores and vehicles being sent even further south to Nantes, Saint-Nazaire and Brest.

From these ports the men and equipment had to be transferred all the way to the Belgian border and to the sector allocated to the BEF, which was from Maulde to Halluin, with its left flank following the line of the River Lys as far as Armentières. The French 51st Division was added to Gort's command and this was placed slightly in the rear of Gort's left front covering the towns of Roubaix and Tourcoing.

In 1914 the Germans had advanced through Belgium and because France had invested heavily in the magnificent fortifications of the Maginot Line it was expected that, should the Germans decide to attempt an invasion of France, they would have little choice but to repeat the same strategy.

Because the Belgians would not participate in the Maginot Line, and because France did not want to isolate Belgium by extending the Maginot Line along its border with it, it was only this part of the French frontier and that which bordered Luxembourg that was not powerfully fortified. An advance by the Germans through Luxembourg, however, was discounted because of the heavily-wooded Ardennes hills which extended along this region of the border. The BEF was therefore placed at what was likely to be where the main German attack would be met.

As soon as the British troops arrived on the Belgian border they found that French engineers had already built an almost continuous anti-tank ditch covered by concrete blockhouses equipped with anti-tank guns and machine-guns. It had been agreed earlier that the French engineers would continue to add to these defences in conjunction with the BEF. A massive building programme of reinforced concrete pillboxes and trenches began in earnest. The BEF was digging in.

This saw the start of the "Phoney War", or the "Bore War" as it was sometimes called, with the Germans showing no sign of risking an attack upon France or Belgium. As the months passed by with no indication of movement by the enemy, discussions were even held about reducing the strength of the BEF and transferring the troops to other theatres where they would be of more use.

On either side of the BEF there were French divisions and most of these were no more gainfully employed than their British counterparts. It was only those positioned along the Saar front, ahead of the Maginot Line, that came into contact with the enemy. The French actually undertook an offensive along this sector in 1939 in a bid to draw German troops away from their attack on Poland. However, the French had little interest in provoking the Germans and the operation was called off after just five days. The French troops returned to their positions along the Maginot Line.

Whilst no further large-scale operations took place, the Saar front was not completely quiet. Engagements between the French and the Germans were not uncommon though few risks were taken by either side, the troops being quite content to stay safely within their own lines.

Nevertheless, there were calls for the British troops to take their share of the limited fighting on the Saar and in response to this call the 3rd Brigade of the BEF's 1st Division of I Corps was selected to be the first British brigade to go into the Maginot Line.

Not only was this an opportunity for the men to gain combat experience but it would also counter the German propaganda taunts that "Britain would fight the war to the last Frenchman". By putting these troops in the front line it would show the French just what the British were capable of and help overcome the morale-sapping effects of indefinite inaction in the waterlogged defensive positions on the Belgian border.

On 27 November 1939, the 1st Battalion of the King's Shropshire Light Infantry, along with the 1st Battalion Duke of Wellington's Regiment, the 2nd Battalion Sherwood Foresters, and the 3rd Infantry Brigade Anti-Tank Company, were transferred to Metz, before moving up to the Maginot Line itself.

They were now in Lorraine and as the Shropshires' commanding officer pointed out to his men, the older Frenchmen in whose farms and houses they were billeted in had served in the First World War as conscripts for the German Army.

Indeed, some people in this border region were still clearly pro-German as this incident shows which is recorded in the battalion's written history: "The attitude of some inhabitants was not quite what was expected, for instance an ex-Uhlan NCO deliberately drove his sheep into one of the company billets saying he preferred they should be comfortably accommodated rather than the British troops!"

The Shropshires' first impression of the Maginot Line defences was a mixed one. "We were all astonished at the 'Maginot Line'," wrote one officer. "As I drove through I hardly noticed anything more than a strong anti-tank obstacle of rails, several strong belts of barbed wire and a few pillboxes, so well were the main forts concealed in our sector. The forts were tunnelled out of a small line of hills. The inside of the forts resembled a battleship, each having engine rooms, living accommodation, kitchen, command post and control rooms, turrets, magazines, hospital and so on."

Another Shropshire officer made quite a different observation: "We were given a lecture by the French divisional commander on the infantry dispositions – the line of contact, the line of 'recoil', the line of reserve. In fact we discovered none of these lines had been prepared in any way – no trenches, no wire, nothing."

The 3rd Brigade was placed under the command of the French 42nd Division and when the Shropshires moved up to the front the French troops offered the British plenty of advice – but only on how to avoid trouble. This included removing a vital part from each Bren gun just in case someone was stupid enough to fire one at the Germans! The British troops were also advised never to fire at enemy patrols unless they were actually cutting the wire in front of the Allied trenches, just in case the Germans fired back.

Although the French were reluctant to leave the security of the *ligne de contact*, the line of contact, the most advanced of the Maginot Line's defences, the BEF was there to fight – indeed, the Army's first gallantry medals of the war were won on the Maginot Line. The battalions in the line of contact sent out "battle" patrols at night to engage the enemy. It was later found that large patrols were difficult to control in the dark and twelve seems to have become established as the best number of men for these missions.

A number of men in each patrol were armed with sub-machine guns, the rest carried grenades, rifles and bludgeons. They blackened their faces, wore cap comforters and long, leather sleeveless Army jerkins. It was, declared one man from another brigade, like playing Boy Scouts.

There was, of course, a serious side to this deadly game of patrol and skirmish, trap and ambush amongst the deserted houses and empty fields of No Man's Land. It was on one of these patrols that Corporal Thomas William Priday met his death, the first British soldier to die in combat in the Second World War.

"As soon as dark fell the khaki-clad patrols climbed over the parapet and crawled out through the gaps in the wire into the unknown", ran one report. "They moved here and there, searched houses and villages whose civilian population had long since been evacuated, ever on the lookout for traces of the passage of their opposite numbers in the German ranks. Always they had to be on the very tip-top of alertness, with hands ready to shoot and eyes keen for the slightest suggestion of a well-placed 'booby trap' such as both sides delighted to plant."

Sadly, it was one of those devices, in fact a British booby trap, which detonated and killed Priday near the small village of Monneren. Some accounts state that he was leading a patrol out, others that the men were returning.

Priday was buried with full military honours. During the ceremony the French divisional commander gave a long address, saluting Priday as "*Le premier soldat qui est mort pour France*". Unfortunately the coffin was dropped upside down into the grave with the Union Flag and the accoutrements underneath. Both had to be retrieved and the entire process repeated again from the start.

Following the publication of the BEF's first casualties on 30 January 1940, the French issued a communiqué: "The British now have their wounded and even their dead on French soil once again."

However, the French Prime Minister M. Daladier was keen to play down the events on the Saar front. "Military operations have not yet developed with that violence and that vast and brutal extension over wide fronts which they seemed likely to assume," he told the French National Assembly. "But we ought not to take this initiative. This war is to us a war for our security and our liberty. Our rule for those who defend us is economy in blood and economy in suffering."

The economy in lives which the French premier sought certainly seemed valid at that stage of the war when compared with the Great War twenty-five years earlier. Up to December 1939, less than 2,000 British and French Army personnel had lost their lives; by the first Christmas of the First World War that figure had been more than half-a-million.

Altogether nine British brigades served on the Maginot Line until, in April 1940, it was decided that the British commitment to the defence of the Line would be increased to divisional strength. The unit chosen for the first – and last – divisional tour of duty on the Maginot Line was the 51st (Highland) Division.

Commanded by Major General Victor Fortune, the 51st (Highland) Division was a powerful, self-contained formation. It was comprised of three infantry brigades, the 152nd Brigade (2nd and 4th Battalions Seaforth Highlanders, 4th Battalion Cameron Highlanders), 153rd Brigade (1st and 5th Battalions Gordon Highlanders, 4th Battalion Black Watch) and 154th Brigade (1st Battalion Black Watch, 7th and 8th Battalions Argyll & Sutherland Highlanders), with an Armoured Reconnaissance Regiment of light tanks and Bren carriers, plus three regiments of field artillery and one anti-tank regiment.

To this force were attached another two artillery regiments, two machine-gun battalions and two battalions of Pioneers. General Fortune also had a composite squadron of the RAF under his command, one flight of which was fighters, the other a flight of Westland Lysander

Army Co-operation aircraft. The entire force totalled around 21,000 men.

The comparative inactivity which had persisted all through the winter along the Saar front continued during the early days of the 51st Division's occupation of the Line. When the Scots moved up to the *ligne de contact* they found that the French had settled into a comfortable routine of doing nothing that would upset the Germans. When Major James Grant of the 2nd Seaforths suggested a joint patrol against the German lines to his French counterpart, the French officer almost fainted!

Things appeared to change at night, however. "Punctually at 21.00 hours the fun began", recalled Sergeant John Mackenzie. "The whole valley was filled with an ear-splitting volume of sound. Things banged, boomped, screeched, whee-ed, whistled, and thumped. Light flickered from gun-flash and shell-burst. Out in front sped line upon line of tracer, looking like red-hot bees, down and across the valley." But this drama was an act played out for the generals and the newsreels, the bullets and the shells flying harmlessly over the heads of the men sheltering safely in their trenches. There was no real intention of doing harm.

Towards the end of April, German patrols became increasingly active against the *ligne de contact*. There was some intense fighting in which the artillery of both sides joined in. Then from the beginning of May this activity died down and an "uncanny" quiet descended upon the Highlanders' sector of the Line.

This period of calm ended on 6 May 1940, when the German artillery shelled the British positions. Then, on 10 May, less than a month after the 51st (Highland) Division had arrived on the Maginot Line, the great German offensive began. The following day, the Highlanders again came under fire but the German attack was not pressed home. On the 13th, however, the battle began in earnest against the Hackenberg sector of the Maginot Line held by the Highlanders.

The *ligne de contact* was held from left to right by 4th Cameron Highlanders, 1st Black Watch and 4th Black Watch. At around 14.00 hours the German attack began against the French troops on both flanks of the Highlanders. This was then followed by a heavy artillery barrage across the entire Hackenberg front, which was the prelude to further infantry attacks against the *ligne de contact*.

In response, the artillery attached to the Highland Division began its defensive fire plan but the German infantry continued to exert pressure all along the contact line throughout the night. There was close-quarter fighting for several hours on the northern edge of the British sector. The Highlanders forward line held, despite mounting casualties (particularly amongst the Black Watch), until the evening of 13 May when the German forces disengaged.

The relative peace on the following day evaporated just before dawn on the 15th when the German artillery opened fire once more. At 06.00 hours Germany infantry stormed the positions vacated by 4th Black Watch, which were now being held by the 5th Gordons. The attack was repulsed but this led to a renewal of the artillery barrage, which persisted for three hours.

Continuing pressure against the Allied troops holding the *ligne de contact* forced a general withdrawal to the second, or recoil line at dusk that evening. But the Germans did not pursue the retreating Highlanders nor follow up their attack.

As a result, for the remainder of their time on the Maginot Line, the 51st (Highland) Division had to deal only with the occasional enemy patrol. Further north beyond the Maginot Line, however, the rest of the BEF was in serious trouble.

For the men of the 51st Division, the first indication that things were not going to plan was when, on 17 May, the French formation holding the Line to the south of the Hackenberg sector – the 42*eme* Division – was withdrawn and sent north to help stem the German advance.

The next development occurred three days later when General Fortune was informed that the 51st Division was being transferred from the Third Army to go into reserve under the direct control of the French High Command. On 22 May 1940, the Highlanders marched away from Hackenberg and the Maginot Line to be dragged into the ever-spiralling vortex of what General Gamelin, the French Commander-in-Chief, called France's "struggle to the death".

\*

On the morning of 10 May 1940, the Germans launched their predicted invasion of Belgium, and a message was issued from French Headquarters to implement 'Plan D'. This plan called for the BEF to move into Belgium to take up a position on the River Dyle. It meant that the Germans had violated Belgium neutrality, and Britain was treaty-bound to march to her defence.

The formulation of this plan had occupied the minds of Gort and the French commanders, General Georges and General Gamelin, throughout the first months of the war. Between them they had at first decided that, in the event of a German attack, the BEF should continue to hold the frontier defences, pushing forward mobile troops to the line of the River Escaut, while the French 7th Army on the British left were to delay the enemy on the line of the Messines Ridge and the Yser Canal. This plan was soon discarded, however, in favour of moving the BEF up to the Escaut, where they would hold the line of the river from the point at which it crosses the frontier at Maulde northwards to the neighbourhood of Ghent where the Belgian Army was concentrated.

This plan was also abandoned because, in Gort's words, "as information became available regarding the defences of the Belgian Army, and its readiness for war, the French High Command formed the opinion that it would be safe to count on the Belgian defence holding out for some days on the Eastern frontier, and the Albert Canal".

The Belgians had, in fact, been building considerable defensive structures which, though not on the scale of the Maginot Line, were still impressive. It was accepted that the Belgians would be unable to stop the Germans on the frontier, so they decided to build a fortified line in the heart of the country. The time taken for the Germans to advance into Belgium up to the fortified line would allow the army to fully mobilise and dig in – and for Belgium's Allies to come to its help.

The fortified line, then, was intended to run from Antwerp in the north through Leuven and Wavre along the River Dyle, and then on to Namur and Givet (France) along the Meuse. Unfortunately it was incomplete when the Germans attacked, with the vital stretch from Namur to the French border still devoid of fortifications.

Nevertheless, the strength of the Belgian fortifications encouraged Gort and Georges to put together their third scheme which was for the

BEF to move up to the River Dyle. According to Gort, the line of the Dyle was, from the military point of view, a better one than that of the Escaut. "It was," he explained, "shorter, it afforded greater depth and its northern portion was inundated, in addition, it represented smaller enemy occupation of Belgian territory." This latter was not merely a political move. The district that would be saved included Belgium's industrial heartland.

What such a move up to the Dyle meant was that the positions on the border which the British and French had been strengthening all winter would be abandoned. It also meant that the moment the Allies were informed of the German invasion of Belgium, the BEF would have to rush some sixty miles up to the Dyle to get there before the Germans and to occupy positions which the troops were unfamiliar with. Of possibly even greater significance was that this move left a large gap in the Allied front around Gembloux where there was no natural anti-tank obstacle. Earmarked to fill this gap, was France's strongest force, the First Army supported by a full half of its armoured reserves.

As we now know, the attack by the Germans into Belgium, though conducted with very heavy forces, was only part of the German operation. As planned, as soon as the news of the German invasion reached Allied Headquarters, Gamelin ordered his troops forward. But, with the BEF and the First Army holding off the German attacks and the French Second and Third armies manning the Maginot Line and associated areas, there was little to halt the German Panzer divisions when they entirely unexpectedly penetrated the Ardennes and broke into France.

Despite all the planning, no arrangements had been made to counter an attack through the Ardennes, nor had any plans been made for the withdrawal of the Allied forces from Belgium, as it was expected that the German attack would be stopped in that country. The result was chaos.

On 15 May 1940, just five days after the start of the German onslaught, the new French Prime Minister, Paul Reynaud, rang his recently installed counterpart in London, Winston Churchill, to announce that: "We have been defeated. We are beaten; we have lost the battle."

Though Churchill tried to reassure the French Government, it soon became clear that the French commanders and soldiers held the same view as the politicians. The French were on the run and the unprecedented speed of the advances made by the Germans through northern France seriously endangered the BEF's communications. Though the new French commander General Weygand urged the armies in the north to fight their way south, on 23 May the decision was made to try and save the BEF by evacuating it back to the UK.

Gort's despatches from France end at midnight on 2/3 June with Major-General Alexander and the Senior Naval Officer Captain W.G. Tennant making a tour of the beaches and harbour of Dunkirk in a motor boat. No more British troops could be seen on the shore and so the last ship left for the UK. Though it had been forced to abandon almost all of its equipment, somehow the BEF had been saved from almost certain disaster.

The evacuation of the BEF from France, Operation *Dynamo*, was led by Vice Admiral Ramsay. His is the second despatch in this compilation. This operation, admitted Ramsay, "took the shape of a forlorn hope to rescue the maximum number, say up to 45,000 before the whole force was to be overwhelmed by the enemy". It was, as many have said since, nothing short of a miracle that by the time Alexander and Tennant turned for home on 3 June 1940, 330,000 men had been rescued.

The story of Dunkirk is too well known to require repeating here. Ramsay's despatch, however, contains a wealth of precise detail not given in other publications. Though it does not contain the dramatic eye-witness accounts usually associated with the Dunkirk evacuation, it includes signals sent to and from Ramsay which provide a mounting drama of their own as events unfold on the beaches and in the Channel.

It is interesting to note Ramsay's observations in his conclusion that "the earlier parties were embarked off the beaches in a condition of complete disorganisation. There appeared to be no Military officers in charge of the troops, and this impression was undoubtedly enhanced by the difficulty in distinguishing between the uniforms of such officers as were present and those of other ranks. It was soon realised that it was vitally necessary to despatch Naval Officers in their unmistakable uniform with armed Naval beach parties to take charge of the soldiers on shore."

The final despatch is that of Lieutenant General Alan Brooke who was given the impossible task of supporting the French with a second British expeditionary force. The evacuation of the BEF from Dunkirk was not intended to be the end of Britain's involvement in the defence of France, merely to rescue the British Army from encirclement by the Germans so that they could be deployed further south along with the remaining French armies. However, almost every gun and every item of equipment had been left behind at, or on the road to, Dunkirk and the British Army was in no state to continue fighting.

Churchill hoped to keep the French armies in the field by sending whatever equipped units could be found in Britain over to France under Brooke. However, upon his return to France, Brooke found General Weygand entirely dispirited and disillusioned. "He spoke most frankly and explained the situation to me," wrote Brooke, "He said that the French Army was no longer capable of organised resistance."

Though there was a scheme proposed in which the British and the remnants of the French Army would attempt to hold the Brittany peninsula, Brooke knew that there was no point in risking the lives of any more British troops and he ordered a final withdrawal of all the British forces from France.

When the last of those men sailed from Cherbourg on 18 June 1940, the Germans were only three miles away. Had Brooke not decided to evacuate as quickly as he did, the uplifting story of the BEF and the "miracle" of Dunkirk might have had an entirely different ending.

Gort's, Brooke's and Ramsay's despatches are reproduced here in the form that they were originally published. They have not been edited, added to or truncated in any way. We have not commented on them or attempted to interpret them. That is not the purpose of this book.

Similarly, any peculiarities in grammar or spelling have been left as they were in the original document. This includes the use of the Roman numeral I, which was used throughout the despatches instead of the Arabic 1. The only change we have made is in the manner in which the footnotes are displayed. In the original despatches they were placed at the bottom of each relevant page. It has not been possible to do this in a book of this nature and so they have been numbered and placed at the end of the despatch. This apart, they are reproduced here just as they were when they were first made public some seventy years ago.

*Martin Mace and John Grehan*
Storrington, 2013

# List of Illustrations

1 Field Marshal John Standish Surtees Prendergast Vereker, 6th Viscount Gort, was given command of the British Expeditionary Force in September 1939. John Gort had fought in the First World War, during which he was Mentioned in Despatches eight times, was awarded the DSO with two Bars and received the Victoria Cross for his actions at the Battle of the Canal du Nord in September 1918. In 1939 the BEF had been placed under the orders of the French high command but when Gort saw the rapid collapse of the French forces in the second week of May 1940, he took the bold decision to disregard those orders in order to save the BEF.

2 A head and shoulders portrait shot of Admiral Sir Bertram Ramsay who, on 24 August 1939, as a Vice-Admiral, was given command of the Dover area of operations in which position he had responsibility for the Dunkirk evacuation. This photograph was taken at his London Headquarters in October 1943.

3 Lieutenant General Alan Brooke, later Field Marshal Lord Alanbrooke, was in command of the BEF's II Corps and distinguished himself in the handling of his corps during the retreat to Dunkirk. On 29 May he was ordered to return to the UK, being told that he was to be given the task of "reforming new armies". In his diary he described his journey back to the coast: "Congestion on roads indescribable. French army became a rabble and complete loss of discipline. [French] troops dejected and surly and refusing to clear road, panicking every time a Boche plane came over." Understandably Brooke had no confidence in the French and, after consulting with General Gamelin, the French commander, he ordered the withdrawal of all remaining British troops from France.

4    Troops of the British Expeditionary Force pictured upon their arrival in France. The first deployment was completed by 11 October 1939 at which point 158,000 men had been transported to France. The Secretary of State for War, Leslie Hore-Belisha, said: "158,000 had been transported across the Channel within five weeks of the commencement of the present war. Convoys had averaged three each night and the BEF had been transported intact without a single casualty to any of its personnel." (HMP)

5    British soldiers from the 51st Highland Division pass over a drawbridge into Fort de Sainghin on the Franco-Belgian Frontier, 3 November 1939. Though this and the other images in the series claim that this shows British troops on the Maginot Line, this is in fact not correct. Built in 1878, Fort de Sainghin was occupied by a garrison and armed with forty-four guns until it was overrun by the Germans in 1914. After the First World War it served as an ammunition depot and did not form part of the Maginot Line. Because of the perceived need for secrecy, the French permitted no photographs of the Maginot Line to be published. In contemporary reports all that was ever allowed were generic drawings. (HMP)

6    A view looking out from the top of Fort du Hackenberg on the Maginot Line. The positions seen here, and those nearby, dominated the open countryside on the approaches from the German border, which is just out of the shot to the right. This area is part of that which would have been patrolled by troops of the BEF serving on the Maginot Line during the winter of 1939/1940. (HMP)

7    A soldier from the Cameron Highlanders, part of the 51st Highland Division, looks through a periscope in Fort de Sainghain, 3 November 1939. (HMP)

8    HM King George VI visits a bunker on the Maginot Line during December 1939. There is a story about the king's visit to the Maginot Line which is still frequently recounted by locals. The story goes that it had been arranged for the king to have lunch in the great Fort du Hackenberg. However, General Gamelin, who was accompanying him, had other ideas: "Mais, non, mon Roi,

the chef there is not very good, we go to Fort des Welches, the food there is much better!" (HMP)

9   The junction between the main tunnel in Fort du Hackenberg and the branch to the vast underground ammunition stores (on the left). General Alan Brooke wrote the following about the Maginot Line in December 1939, comments which were to prove highly prophetic: "There is no doubt that the whole conception of the Maginot Line is a stroke of genius. And yet! It gave me but little feeling of security, and I consider that the French would have done better to invest the money in the shape of mobile defences such as more and better aircraft and more heavy armoured divisions than to sink all this money into the ground." (HMP)

10  Another anecdote about the British Army's occupation of the Maginot Line concerns the now-disused Army barracks at Veckring (one of the entrances to which is seen here). Veckring is the closest village to Fort du Hackenberg and part of this was used as a British hospital by medical units attached to the BEF troops occupying this part of the front. It is said that a direct telephone link was established between the Officers' Mess in the fort and the hospital. The reason for this is that when the British officers, having sampled too much of the local beverages, were incapable of returning to their billets, a call would be made to the hospital and an ambulance would be sent to pick up the inebriated officers! (Courtesy of Mark Khan)

11  More than 10,000 men of the 51st (Highland) Division were taken prisoner at Saint-Valéry-en-Caux and surrounding area – the men in this picture forming a small part of that number. The Scots also suffered over 5,000 casualties, including 1,000 killed. (US Library of Congress)

12  Soldiers of the BEF pictured at their post on the front line in France during the cold winter of 1939-1940. An intelligence report by the German IV Army Corps written in the summer of 1940 included the following comments about the men of the BEF: "The English soldier was in excellent physical condition. He bore his own wounds with stoical calm. The losses of his own troops he discussed with complete equanimity. He did not complain of

hardships. In battle he was tough and dogged. His conviction that England would conquer in the end was unshakeable ... Certainly the Territorial divisions are inferior to the Regular troops in training, but where morale is concerned they are their equal." (HMP)

13  An official announcement in December 1939 reported that "the first British soldier killed in action" during the Second World War had lost his life on 9 December 1939. That man was 27-year-old Corporal Thomas William Priday of the 1st Battalion King's Shropshire Light Infantry – seen here. He was, the press reported, killed in action "while leading a patrol towards the German lines". Roughly four-and-a-half miles from the Franco-German border, it was near the village of Monneren that Corporal Priday's patrol was located when he was killed. (© The Shropshire Regimental Museum)

14  A wounded French soldier is taken ashore on a stretcher at Dover following his evacuation from Dunkirk. He is one of 338,226 British, French and Belgian troops brought back from the French coast.

15  Posted ahead of the Maginot Line the men of the 2nd Battalion Royal Norfolk Regiment were determined that the Germans would not be allowed to rest easy in their positions less than 1,000 yards to the east. During the night of 4/5 January 1940, 'A' Company's Captain Francis Peter Barclay duly led a patrol out from the British line near the village of Waldwisse into No Man's Land. For their actions in the hours that followed, Barclay and another member of the patrol, Lance Corporal H. Davis, would be awarded the BEF's first gallantry medals of the Second World War. The following was published on 13 January 1940: "For his conspicuous gallantry, coolness and resource Captain F.P. Barclay has received from Lord Gort the Military Cross and Lance Corporal H. Davis, who shared his hazardous adventure, has been awarded the Military Medal." The other members of the patrol, Second Lieutenant C.R. Murray Brown, Lance Corporal A. Harris and Lance Corporal A. Spooner, were Mentioned in Despatches.

Captain Barclay, on the left, can be seen in this staged photograph that was taken on 26 January 1940. (HMP)

16   This bridge marks the very spot near the Franco-German border where Captain Barclay's patrol clashed with German soldiers on the night of 4/5 January 1940. The British front line was some 1,000 yards beyond the slope at the back of this view. One of the metal stanchions on the bridge, the angled one on the far side of the structure, still displays what appears to be evidence of the fighting when Barclay's patrol clashed with enemy troops – a number of bullet marks and holes. As well as being awarded the BEF's first gallantry medals of the Second World War, the 2nd Battalion Royal Norfolk Regiment achieved another notable "first" during the same night. A second patrol, this time led by Second Lieutenant Patrick Everitt, actually crossed the border into Germany itself. (HMP)

17   This drawing was created at the request of the Ministry of Information for propaganda purposes during the Second World War. It depicts Captain Harold Ervine-Andrews, The East Lancashire Regiment, during the action for which he was awarded the Victoria Cross. On the night of 31 May/1 June 1940, the company commanded by Captain Ervine-Andrews was heavily outnumbered and under intense German fire near Dunkirk. When the enemy attacked at dawn and crossed the Canal de Bergues, Ervine-Andrews, with volunteers from his company, rushed to a barn and from the roof engaged the enemy with a rifle and a Bren gun. When the barn was set alight, he sent the wounded to the rear and led the remaining eight men back, wading for over a mile in water up to their chins. The group of eight travelled through rough enemy lines to the blood-soaked beaches and finally escaped back to the UK on 4 June 1940. (HMP)

# 1

# Despatches on Operations of the British Expeditionary Force, France and Belgium, September 1939 to May 31 1940

### By General the Viscount Gort, Commander-in-Chief, B.E.F.

#### FRIDAY, 17 OCTOBER, 1941

*War Office,*
*March, 1941.*

The following Despatches have been received by the Secretary of State for War from General the Viscount GORT, V.C., K.C.B., C.B.E., D.S.O., M.V.O., M.C., Commander-in-Chief, British Expeditionary Force. (France and Belgium 1939-40.)

## FIRST DESPATCH
(Covering the period from 3rd September, 1939, to 31st January, 1940).

*General Headquarters,*
*British Expeditionary Force,*
*25th April, 1940.*

Sir,

1. I have the honour to submit a report on the employment of the British Expeditionary Force in France from 3rd September, 1939, the date I assumed command, until 31st January, 1940.

2. The move of the Force to France began as a whole on 10th September, although small advanced parties and technical personnel had been arriving since 4th September. The success of the initial operation was due primarily to the many detailed and complex plans carefully prepared under conditions of absolute secrecy in peace time. The perfection of these plans, the ready co-operation of the Board of Trade, the complete arrangements made by the Admiralty for the safety of ships while at sea, and the willing help of the French Naval, Military, and Civil authorities all combined to ensure the successful landing of the British Troops in France.

3. The plans for the despatch of the Force differed in two important respects from those of August, 1914.

The possibility of attack by sea and air made it necessary to use the Western ports of France instead of the Channel ports, while the total replacement of animals by mechanical vehicles, which had been completed by 1939, presented a new problem in transportation.

The troops were landed at Cherbourg and their stores and vehicles were despatched to Nantes, St. Nazaire, and Brest.

This plan entailed the early despatch of staff with the proper complement of units of the Docks and other Transportation Services. The personnel of these Services were in the main recruited from the Port Authorities in Great Britain at the outbreak of war.

These units were operating to full capacity the berths allotted to the Force, within forty-eight hours of landing, and the programme was carried out according to the time table throughout the whole period of the disembarkation of Ist and 2nd Corps. This I regard as a feat deserving of the highest praise.

4. On landing the fighting troops were passed rapidly through transit camps and their vehicles were cleared at once to Vehicle Marshalling Parks, whence they were despatched in convoys, while troops left by rail on the same day as they landed.

Since the troops and their vehicles were landed at different ports they had to be collected in an assembly area which had been chosen in the vicinity of Le Mans and Laval. The assembling of troops by rail and vehicles by road took about six days. The resource of individual drivers was tested by changes of programme, inevitable in an operation of this kind, by the damage which some vehicles had sustained during the sea passage and by mechanical failures. Drivers and vehicles were on the road for long periods, but their duty was lightened by the hospitality of the French inhabitants, which all ranks will recall with gratitude.

5. On I3th September I moved my headquarters from the War Office to Camberley, where General Headquarters was forming. On the following day, accompanied by Lieutenant-General (now General) Sir John Dill, Commander of Ist Corps, and by my personal staff, I embarked in H.M.S. "Skate," and, landing at Cherbourg, left by motor car for the Château de la Blanchardière, Le Mans, which the French Government had kindly placed at my disposal.

6. On 2Ist September the concentration of the General Headquarters Staff and of the essential Lines of Communication units was complete. The next day the advanced elements of Ist Corps and of General Headquarters Troops arrived, the former moving to an area around Laval and the latter to an area around Le Mans. Units were given a minimum of one week in which to assemble and reorganise and although some of the units of Ist Corps were still incomplete, the limited accommodation available in the assembly area made it essential to begin the move forward before 26th September when the leading units of 2nd Corps were due to arrive.

7. During these early weeks the maintenance of the Force presented a problem which called for the greatest resource and initiative on the part of my Quarter-Master-General, Lieutenant-General W.G. Lindsell, his Staff and Services.

In the units of the Royal Army Service Corps were many officers and men fresh from civil life who were constantly called upon to surmount unforeseen difficulties. By their unflagging energy and the assistance of the French authorities the Force was maintained without any failure of supplies. It should be added that with the exception of eleven regular officers, the personnel of the Movement Control organisation was built up from Supplementary Reserve officers and men.

The administrative staff were obliged to deal with the day-to-day work of landing troops, their vehicles and current supplies, and to undertake the equally important task of building up reserves of ammunition, supplies, and ordnance stores. Covered accommodation was difficult to obtain and temporary dumps of non-perishable stores had to be established wherever the necessary space could be found in the vicinity of the ports of entry.

8. In these early days the Staff met for the first time the problem arising from the wide dispersion imposed by the necessity to guard against air attack.

The towns of Le Mans and Laval were fifty miles apart, and the base ports were on an average one hundred and fifty miles from the assembly area. Helpful though the French authorities were, the unfamiliar conditions made telephone communication difficult, apart from the danger of breach of security which it entailed. Since many despatch riders spoke no French it was often found that control could only be properly maintained by personal visits; Commanders and their staffs were therefore forced to spend many hours on the road.

The dispersion dictated by the possibility of aerial bombardment greatly increases demands upon signal communications and transport and thus lengthens the time which must elapse between the issue of orders and their execution.

**The Move to the Belgian Frontier.**
9. On 22nd September, I left Le Mans for Amiens. Arriving at Mantes-sur-Seine, I was handed a telegram from General Georges, Commander of the French Front of the North-East, which read as follows:-

"Pour Général Commandant, B.E.F.

"Limite envisagée prévoit front de B.E.F. droite à MAULDE gauche à MENIN ou gauche à AUTRYCHE-SUR-ESCAUT. Général GEORGES désirerait avoir accord 22 Septembre."

In the meantime, however, General Gamelin had proceeded to London to discuss with His Majesty's Government the frontage which was to be held by the British Expeditionary Force.

After I had made a reconnaissance on 24th and 25th September of the sector which it was proposed to allot to the British Expeditionary Force I visited General Georges at Grand Quartier General on 26th September, in the company of my Chief of the General Staff, Lieutenant-General H.R. Pownall. I then agreed to accept the sector offered by General Georges to the British Expeditionary Force. This sector was from Maulde exclusive to Halluin inclusive, and thence a defensive flank along river Lys/Armentières. General Georges placed 5Ist French Division (Général de Brigade Gillard) under my command, and I decided to employ it in my left sector, covering the towns of Roubaix and Tourcoing.

I0. It had been originally intended that formations, as soon as they had completed their reorganisation in the assembly area, should move to a concentration area in the North of France, and remain there in readiness to occupy the line not earlier than 5th October. General Georges decided, however, that it was inadvisable to await the arrival of the whole British Expeditionary Force in the concentration area and expressed a wish that Ist Corps should move without delay into the sector north of Maulde. I accordingly informed General Georges that Ist Corps would take over its sector on 3rd October and that 2nd Corps would be able to go into the line about I2th October.

Ist Corps began the two hundred and fifty-mile move from the assembly area on 26th September.

Tanks, tracked vehicles, and slow moving artillery proceeded by train and the remainder of the force advanced on three parallel routes.

Three days were allotted for the move of each formation. Two staging areas were arranged on each road, south of the rivers Seine and Somme respectively, and anti-aircraft defence was provided at these river crossings. The weather was fine throughout the whole period of the move.

The first stage was one hundred and twenty miles. An average of five hundred vehicles moved daily over each stage of the route, maintaining a distance of one hundred yards between each vehicle as a precaution against air attack. A halt of one day for maintenance purposes was made after the first day's move.

In the initial stages of the move, the Provost service were responsible for the regulation of traffic, but on entering the French Zone des Armees, columns came under the direction of the French road control (Regulatrice Routiere) organisation, which gave valuable help in marking detours and in directing traffic through towns. A French-speaking British officer was established in Amiens to ensure liaison between my headquarters and the French authorities.

Breakdowns and accidents were few, which reflects great credit on the drivers, who were unaccustomed to long hours at the wheel and to driving on the right-hand side of the road. Among the many important lessons which were learnt during the largest road movement ever undertaken with motor transport by any British Army were the need for early reconnaissance of staging areas, for control at the dispersal points, and for allowance for unforeseen delays.

11. The move forward continued without incident or interruption, and on the agreed date, 3rd October, Ist Corps took over from the French the sector Maulde-Gruson on the Belgian frontier. This sector lay between that of the Ist French Army and of the I6th French Corps, with 2nd Division (Major-General H.C. Loyd) on the right and Ist Division (Major-General Hon. H.R.L.G. Alexander) on the left.

General Headquarters opened in and around Habarcq (8 miles west of Arras) on 2nd October.

On I2th October, 3rd Division of 2nd Corps (Major-General B.L. Montgomery) moved into the line between Bouvines and Lannoy, relieving the left brigade of Ist Corps and the right regiment of the French 5Ist Division. 4th Division of the same Corps (Major-General D.G. Johnson, V.C.) was located in General Headquarters reserve.

The initial occupation of the line by the British Expeditionary Force was thus completed and the organisation of the position was undertaken at once.

### *The Organisation of the British Positions.*

I2. In allotting sectors the geographical features of the pronounced salient occupied by the British Expeditionary Force had to be considered. East of the Tournai-Orchies road the country is flat, much wooded and intersected by small streams. Further to the north lies open and undulating agricultural land which lends itself to artillery observation and to the movement of armoured fighting vehicles. Further north again the sector is for the most part on the fringe of a highly industrial and mining district.

When Ist Corps arrived in the sector assigned to the British Expeditionary Force in the first week in October, an almost continuous anti-tank obstacle already existed in the form of a ditch covered by concrete blockhouses built to mount anti-tank guns and machine guns. In accordance with plans prepared in peace time certain French technical troops continued to work in the sector under the command of the French Commander of the Defensive Sector of Lille, Colonel (now Général de Brigade) Bertschi.

While defences continued to develop on the lines of the original plan, based on the close defence of the frontier, it was also necessary to organise the position.

The priority of work envisaged the eventual construction of three positions in the forward area, and a Corps reserve position was sited across the base of the Lille salient formed by the frontier. Further in rear, a second position had been sited, following the line of the Haute Deule, Sensée and La Bassée canals.

The whole scheme involved the immediate construction of field defences and the duplication of the anti-tank obstacle in the forward zone.

It was consequently necessary to construct at an early stage reinforced concrete "pillboxes" to afford protection to those weapons which formed the backbone of the fire defence throughout the whole depth of the position. In order to save time standard designs were prepared to accommodate both British and French weapons.

I3. Work on these "pill-boxes" was begun by the Royal Engineers, assisted by other arms. Early in November a specially constituted force composed of twelve field companies of the Royal Engineers drawn from Territorial Army Divisions at home, and known as "X Force," arrived in the British Expeditionary Force area. This force had its own transport and special plant for the construction of reinforced concrete "pill-boxes" by mass production methods. It was accompanied by companies of the Auxiliary Military Pioneer Corps.

A special Excavator Company, equipped with mechanical excavators of various types, arrived at the same time as X Force. It has been employed in digging anti-tank ditches, burying signal cables, constructing breastworks, and other tasks.

A creation of such a defensive system demanded a quantity and variety of engineer stores far exceeding pre-war anticipations.

Bad weather in October and November, and a succession of frosts later, considerably delayed the work, but by the end of the period covered by this despatch the position had been developed in considerable depth. A large number of concrete "pill-boxes" had been completed and many others were under construction; new wire had been erected and existing wire strengthened, buildings had been reinforced, and many miles of anti-tank ditch dug.

## *The Saar Detachment.*

14. In November, 1939, I arranged with General Georges that a British infantry brigade should take its place in the line on the Saar front, under the command of a French Division.

The brigade took over the sector from the French 42nd Division on the 4th December without enemy interference and during the period under review conditions were quiet.

Since that date infantry brigades of the British Expeditionary Force have successively completed short tours of duty in this sector, and junior leaders have thus had valuable training in their day to day duties when in contact with the enemy.

The fortifications of the Maginot Line in the sector concerned continued to be manned by French fortress troops, the British battalions being disposed in depth in advance of the fortified line. The enemy positions were on the average one thousand five hundred yards distant from our foremost posts.

The British Army contains to-day very few regimental officers and other ranks who fought in the last war; much that was common knowledge and accepted practice then, must therefore be learned again. Nevertheless, events on the Saar front have proved beyond doubt that the young officer and his men, once they have had experience of active service, will be in every way worthy of their predecessors.

## *The Completion of the First Contingent.*

15. During October and November, 15th and 17th Infantry Brigades were sent from home, and placed under command of 1st and 2nd Corps respectively. 13th Infantry Brigade was also relieved on the Lines of Communication by 25th Infantry Brigade.

On 1st and 2nd December, the French 51st Division was relieved by 4th Division and 17th Infantry Brigade, and withdrawn from my command: I was sorry to part with them and with their commander, who at all times gave me loyal support.

The plans for the despatch of the Force had envisaged that two divisions of the Territorial Army would be sent from home as soon as they were sufficiently trained. Since three regular infantry brigades had by now arrived, however, I decided on 27th October to form the 5th Division under the command of Major-General H.E. Franklyn. On the night of 29th-30th December the division took over a sector on the left of the 4th Division.

At this time the five divisions of the British Expeditionary Force were all in the line.

During the month of January the 48th Division (Major-General A.F.A.N. Thorne) arrived in France, and by 23rd January had completed its move forward. It was placed under 1st Corps, but held in G.H.Q. reserve.

By the end of January the Force, therefore, consisted of two corps, each of three divisions, with corps and army troops. The first stage in the development of the Force was thus concluded.

The strength of the British Expeditionary Force at the end of January stood at two hundred and twenty-two thousand two hundred, all ranks, not including the men of the Air Component and of other units of the Royal Air Force for whose maintenance I am responsible.

## *Air Forces and Anti-Aircraft Defence.*

16. Although development of the Air Forces and of the Air Defence organisations proceeded simultaneously with the despatch of the Force

and with its subsequent moves, I have thought it convenient to describe this development separately.

The composition of the Force included Component of the Royal Air Force under the command of Air Vice-Marshal C.H.B. Blount, Royal Air Force, consisting of two Army Co-operation Wings, one Fighter Wing and one Bomber Reconnaissance Wing.

The aircraft were flown to France according to plan at the outbreak of hostilities and came under my command from the dates of the disembarkation of their ground units. Later other units were added, and the Air Component now comprises, in addition to Headquarters, one Fighter Group Headquarters, eight Wings, a Communication Squadron, and certain administrative and other detachments.

The ground echelons were moved in advance of Ist and 2nd Corps to the aerodromes in the region to be occupied. In the early stages they were largely dependent on the assistance given to them by the French Région Aérienne under the command successively of General Jeauneaud and General Armengeaud.

On I4th and I5th September, the anti-aircraft units disembarked at the base ports and, in conjunction with fighter units of the Royal Air Force, undertook the task of protecting the disembarkation of the two Corps and their forward moves.

Once the concentration was complete, the available anti-aircraft resources were divided between forward defences and Lines of Communication. Besides the normal provision for the defence of headquarters and railheads, arrangements were made to protect certain important French installations in the British zone and a searchlight zone was also established as a protection against enemy night bombing.

On all occasions, the Air Officer Commanding has been greatly helped by General d'Astier, commanding the French Air Forces with the northern group of French Armies.

During the period under review, enemy air activity has been almost entirely confined to reconnaissance flights at great heights.

*Air Reconnaissance.*

I7. The strategical plans for air reconnaissance were worked out in conjunction with the Air Ministry and with General Mouchard, commanding the Air Forces with the French Armies of the North East.

In accordance with these plans many reconnaissances have been carried out both by day and night. Much photography has been undertaken with useful results, both in information obtained and in experience gained in photographic and survey methods.

The work of the units of the Royal Air Force engaged in air reconnaissance deserves the highest praise, since it has been performed, as a rule, in the face of enemy opposition. Pilots have often been called on to carry out flights to the full limit of the range of their aircraft, flying over long and circuitous routes to avoid neutral territory; this rigorous duty has been boldly and cheerfully undertaken.

## *The preparation of Aerodromes.*

I8. It had been decided, before mobilisation, that the maintenance and construction of all aerodromes used by the Royal Air Force in France, as well as their signal communications, should be the responsibility of the British Expeditionary Force.

Many aerodromes and landing grounds had been placed at our disposal by the French authorities, but it soon became evident that the problems of construction and maintenance were far greater than had been contemplated before the war. A new policy had, therefore, to be formulated and comprehensive plans prepared. In most parts of France, permanent pasture does not exist, and this fact, in view of the weight of modern aircraft, has made it necessary to construct concrete runways, often of considerable extent, on the principal aerodromes in use. A number of special units of the Royal Engineers had consequently to be raised, and a large amount of plant, grass seed and materials had to be provided.

## *Frontier Control.*

I9. The sector of the frontier occupied by the British Expeditionary Force presented a very difficult control problem. There were initially over ten thousand Belgians working on the beet harvest in the British zone and on the average considerably more than twenty thousand local inhabitants passed the frontier daily on their normal business.

The strength of the frontier organisations charged with the control of the frontier traffic had been seriously reduced on mobilisation. It was therefore essential to supplement the normal machinery of control.

The system devised in co-operation with the Ist French Region and the commander of the fortified sector of Lille included a primary control on the frontier proper and a secondary control on the line of the foremost anti-tank obstacle wherever the latter did not coincide with the frontier.

Co-operation with the French authorities has been close and harmonious throughout. The Field Security Police have played an important role in this unusual and difficult task and have contributed largely to the success of the organisation.

## *Intelligence.*

20. Conditions on the operational side of intelligence work in the field have naturally been abnormal. Much valuable preliminary work and re-organisation has been carried out and full advantage has been taken of the unusual situation, to complete the training of the Intelligence staffs. Co-operation with the French Intelligence service has been close and cordial.

It became apparent at an early date that the staff and organisation provided for dealing with wireless intelligence were inadequate for this increasingly important branch of operational intelligence. The expansion of the wireless intelligence units is now, therefore, in progress. Closest co-operation has been maintained with the French Wireless Intelligence Service.

It has been necessary to increase the air intelligence section of the Intelligence branch at General Headquarters, which has performed valuable work in the collection and distribution of information.

The problem of security has presented many unusual difficulties. This has been largely due to the long period of inactivity, the geographical position of the Force, the length of the Lines of Communication, and the congestion in the rear areas owing to the presence of evacuees. The French authorities have co-operated most closely in the matter of civil security and have throughout given all the assistance in their power.

## *Censorship.*

The postal censorship discipline of the British Expeditionary Force is on the whole good. Very considerable increases in personnel have been found necessary in order to impose the requisite selective censorship on the abnormally large number of letters now despatched daily. Extremely useful reports on the outlook of the British Expeditionary Force as a whole and on its relations with the local French inhabitants are produced periodically. These are based largely on information supplied by the censorship organisation supplemented by reports from the Field Security Police.

## *Publicity and Propaganda.*

The section of the Intelligence branch dealing with publicity and propaganda has worked in close co-operation with the organisations concerned both in England and France, and has fulfilled a rôle which has assumed far more importance than in previous campaigns. Much has been done to counter German propaganda. Material has been provided for the Miniform Committee in Paris in this connection, and information bulletins are issued periodically to all units of the British Expeditionary Force.

## *Cipher Personnel.*

Up to date the whole of the cipher work in the Force has been carried out most efficiently by Army Educational Corps personnel. This personnel is now required to revert to its normal duties in the United Kingdom and is being replaced.

## *Press.*

2I. The significance and requirements of the Press and of the press and cinematographic publicity in the field in modern war have proved greater than was appreciated prior to the outbreak of hostilities. Shortly after mobilisation a Public Relations unit was hastily formed and incorporated in the Intelligence branch of General Headquarters.

Since its formation in October this unit has administered and arranged facilities for a total of some fifty-five War Correspondents permanently accredited to the British Expeditionary Force, besides representatives of the principal newsreel companies. Some sixty visiting editors, correspondents, broadcasters and cinematographers, in addition to selected representatives of the neutral Press, have been given facilities for visiting the Force.

There has also been a small unit of the British Broadcasting Corporation with the Force since October, and facilities have been provided for selected official photographers to meet the requirements of the British Press.

The Newspaper Proprietors Association generously makes a large supply of papers available free daily for the Force. In the matter of distribution, close touch has been kept with them and with the "Continental Daily Mail," which supplies the troops with their latest news.

The Press and photographic censorship is now working efficiently and co-operation with the French is close and harmonious.

## *Development of the Rearward Services.*

22. The work of the administrative staffs and services in back areas has in many respects been fully as heavy as it would have been if fighting had been in progress. It was their duty, while maintaining a continually growing force, to make and put into execution long term plans in preparation for the arrival of future contingents.

The initial scheme provided for the formation of temporary maintenance depôts near the ports of Brest and Nantes, but it was soon evident that, with so long a line of communication, an advanced base was required.

The use of the port of Havre had at first been considered undesirable owing to certain geographical and technical difficulties in the air defence of the docks. These were, however, overcome in mid-November, and an Advanced Base area is now being established near this port with the co-operation of the French authorities, while Field Supply Depôts are being set up further forward. By mid-December, the staff of the Movement Control were working some ninety stations, while fourteen ports were in use for landing personnel, animals and stores. Through these ports, a quarter of a million men, forty-five thousand mechanical vehicles and a monthly tonnage varying from sixty to one hundred thousand tons of stores of all kinds were imported and distributed to their various areas and reserve depôts.

Works projects of great magnitude have been in progress from the outset, and the problems of accommodation have been many and complex. An extensive programme of building and hutting for depôts, hospitals and reinforcement camps was put in hand, together with installations for electric light and power, the bulk storage of petrol and so on. A vast amount of minor work in connection with accommodation has been carried out by the Royal Engineers.

Railway construction at depôts and aerodromes has been undertaken by the Transportation Services under very adverse weather conditions.

The complicated nature of modern military equipment has added greatly to the work of the Royal Army Ordnance Corps, as regards both storeholding and repair. Great difficulty has been experienced in finding suitable accommodation for depôts and workshops at the bases, more especially since the whole of the resources of France are engaged at high pressure on her own war industries. New installations have therefore been planned and are now under construction.

The maintenance of mechanical vehicles has received constant attention and the number of road accidents, and consequently of repairs, has been greatly reduced through measures taken by the Provost Service to enforce road discipline.

The labour problem bids fair to become one of great magnitude, and its solution may be difficult. As no adequate labour force was available on mobilisation, the gap was filled by the temporary use of cavalry and infantry reservists. Later, the Auxiliary Military Pioneer Corps absorbed the various labour units already in France. This Corps has carried out cheerfully and efficiently the important, but often unexciting tasks allotted to its units.

I am grateful to the Government of India for the high standard of the animal transport units sent to France, which have proved their usefulness on many occasions.

Major General P. de Fonblanque, General Officer Commanding, Lines of Communication Area, has under his command the greatest part of the undertakings described above. They now cover almost one third of France, stretching from Dunkirk to Brest and from Cherbourg to Marseilles.

## *The Welfare of the Force.*

23. The health of the Force has been good and the number of troops in the care of medical units has never exceeded 2·8 per cent. of the strength of the Force, despite the unusually severe weather conditions in December and January.

I wish to express my appreciation of the work of the Royal Army Medical Corps under my Director of Medical Services, Major General J.W.L. Scott.

The arrangements for leave came into force on 18th December. The numbers permitted to be absent on leave at any one time are based on the percentage of strength which can be spared from the Force. By the end of January ten days' leave home had been granted to some sixty thousand of all ranks and compassionate leave had also been granted in deserving cases.

The question of leave was worked out in great detail by the Adjutant General, Lieutenant General Sir Douglas Brownrigg, and the members of his staff.

The Expeditionary Force Institutes have now established some ninety institutes open on the Lines of Communication and bulk stores have been established in forward areas to enable units to replenish their own canteens. The same organisation is providing concert parties and mobile cinemas, and a proportion of the troops are able to visit each week one of the entertainments provided by the Entertainments National Services Association.

I am likewise grateful to those organisations which have co-operated so whole-heartedly with the Royal Army Chaplains Department in attending to the welfare of the troops.

Amongst these are the Catholic Women's Guild, The Army Scripture Readers' Association, The Church Army, The Church of Scotland, Toc H, The Salvation Army, The Young Men's Christian Association, and the Young Women's Christian Association.

The despatch and delivery of mails takes place with regularity, and more than nine thousand bags of mail have been handled in one day by the Postal Service. The necessity for censorship is fully realized, but there has been no delay in the time taken in the transit of mail for an ever increasing force.

The great distances between forward troops and the base made it necessary to depart from the old established procedure whereby the 2nd Echelon of the Adjutant General's Branch has always been located in the theatre of war. This office is now established in Margate, and the move has been fully justified by the increased speed with which matters are now handled.

### *Training and Organisation.*

24. The absence of fighting has afforded opportunities to continue the training of the Force. Weapon training has been possible for almost every unit, and thanks to the co-operation of the French Army, artillery practice camps have been held and other training facilities provided. Exercises with troops involving road movement on a large scale have been held and much progress has been made in the technique of co-operation with the Royal Air Force.

About eight hundred and fifty officers and non-commissioned officers have been sent home as instructors to assist in the training of new formations, while an equal number have been attached to the Force, for instruction, from units at home.

Despite the almost complete absence of battle casualties the supply of officers has caused me concern. Over four hundred candidates have been sent home for training as officers, while a further four hundred have been recommended for immediate commissions.

These have been drawn to a large extent from Warrant Officers Class III.

A large number of War Establishments, particularly for the Intelligence Corps and for units on the Lines of Communication, were found to need adjustment and steps have been taken to this end.

The existing War Establishment of an infantry battalion, which was not designed for Continental warfare, has called for modification and I am grateful that my recommendations for an increase have been accepted.

The Royal Corps of Signals has been put to great strain in providing communications not only for the Army, but for the whole of the Air Forces in France. The degree of dispersion required in modern warfare has materially added to their difficulties.

The success with which these demands have been met is due not only to the spirit in which the personnel of that Corps have faced and overcome difficulties, but to the successful arrangements for co-operation with the French military and civil organisations, and with the General Post Office. The Wireless Intelligence Staff have done valuable work, and the cipher duties of the Force have been most efficiently performed by personnel of the Army Educational Corps.

The Survey Directorate has been called upon to carry out a great deal of work under difficult conditions and has fulfilled all the demands made upon it.

## *Liaison with the French.*

25. On the arrival of the British Expeditionary Force in France a French Military Mission was established at my headquarters to deal with French military and civil authorities and to act as a link with Grand Quartier Général. In addition, officers and non-commissioned officers of the French Army are attached for liaison duties to the headquarters of each formation and unit as it arrives.

I wish to express my sincere gratitude to the chief of the Mission, Général de Division Voruz, and to all his staff for their ever ready help to the British Army on all occasions.

Thanks to their efforts, matters relating to billeting, hire of land, and local purchase of material have been handled without friction. To them is due, in large measure, the friendliness of the relations which exist between the French population and the troops, and also as between French and British staffs and regiments.

A British Military Mission under Brigadier J.G. des R. Swayne was established with the Headquarters of General Georges under whose immediate command the British Expeditionary Force is serving.

## *Distinguished Visitors.*

26. On 4th December His Majesty The King visited his troops in France and was received everywhere with enthusiasm. During the three days tour His Majesty was able to make a detailed inspection of forward and rear areas. On his return to England, His Majesty was graciously pleased to send a message to his Army which was warmly appreciated by all ranks.

The President of the French Republic has spent a day with the British Expeditionary Force.

The Prime Minister and other members of the War Cabinet, the Ministers from the Dominions, many members of the Army Council and seven Field Marshals are amongst those who have visited my Headquarters at various times.

### *Honours and Awards.*

27. I am submitting separately the names of officers and other ranks whom I wish to recommend for reward or to bring to your notice for gallant or distinguished service.

I have the honour to be,
Sir,
Your obedient Servant,
GORT.
General,
Commander-in-Chief,
British Expeditionary Force.

## SECOND DESPATCH†

(Covering the period from Ist February, 1940, to 31st May, 1940, with an Appendix covering operations of Ist Corps from 6 p.m. 31st May, to midnight 2nd/3rd June).

† 1. The narrative portions of this despatch have been compiled from the war diaries and other records of the General Staff at G.H.Q. These have been supplemented by war diaries, including those of the Swayne Mission, and by diaries, notes and records made by various commanders and staff officers at the time, or within a few days of their arrival in England. The records of the General Staff at G.H.Q. are only partially complete for the period 10th – 18th May, owing to some papers having been destroyed at Boulogne, and a portion of the records for 31st May lost at sea. Some records of less importance were burnt at Hazebrouck to avoid possible capture and others were destroyed in a lorry which caught fire near Cassel on or about 24th May.

2. The Appendix contains an account of the operations at Dunkirk from 6 p.m., 31st May, to midnight 2nd/3rd June, which may conveniently be appended to this despatch, though they were not carried out under the orders of the Commander-in-Chief. It has been compiled by the General Staff at G.H.Q., from sources similar to those used for the despatch itself.

*London,*
*25 July, 1940.*

Sir,

I. I have the honour to submit a report on the employment of the British Expeditionary Force, and on the part which it played in operations in France and Belgium from 1st February, 1940, to 31st May, 1940, on which date I gave up Command of the Force.

The period under review may be divided into two distinct and sharply contrasting phases, namely, before and after 10th May, on which date active operations began. The active operations themselves can be divided geographically into two distinct parts; on the east, the advance to the River Dyle, and the withdrawal to the frontier; on the west, the defence of Arras and the organisation of the Canal line. Later, the two parts merged into one whole in the final phase of the withdrawal and embarkation of the Force.

No such clear definition can be made in terms of time; furthermore, the two operations, on the east and on the west, were closely interdependent, and the same reserves had to serve for both. For this reason the accounts of the operations on the two fronts cannot but be intermingled at certain points in the narrative. Broadly speaking, however, three distinct phases can be distinguished. First, the advance to the Dyle from 10th-16th May; then from 17th-26th May the withdrawal from the Dyle to the Escaut, the defence of the Belgian frontier and of the southern and western flanks; and finally the withdrawal and embarkation of the Force from 27th-31st May.

2. The narrative in my first despatch dated 25th April, 1940, concluded with the completion of the first contingent of the Force.

I had been informed that the expansion of the Force was to be continued by the despatch of 3rd Corps during the early months of 1940; the Armoured Division was to follow in May, and a fourth Corps, with 1st Canadian Division, during the late Summer; furthermore, it had been decided that the Force should be divided into two Armies, as soon as the number of divisions in the field, excluding the Armoured Division, rose above eleven.

Preparation for this expansion, which had been proceeding since the previous autumn, continued steadily until 10th May.

## *Arrival of 3rd Corps in France.*

3. 3rd Corps (Lt.-General Sir Ronald F. Adam, Bt.), consisting of 42nd Division (Major-General W.G. Holmes), 44th Division (Major-General E.A. Osborne) and 51st Division (Major-General V.M. Fortune) was due for despatch to France in February and March, and 51st Division arrived during early February. The 50th (Motor) Division (Major-General G. le Q. Martel) arrived in France at the same time and was allotted to 2nd Corps. It had been arranged that the front of the B.E.F. should be extended northwards to Croix de Poperinghe on the Belgian frontier, two miles north-east of Bailleul, and that 3rd Corps should go into the line on the left of the B.E.F. taking over 5th Division from 2nd Corps, and relieving 53rd French Division, between Armentières and Croix de Poperinghe, with 51st Division. The Command of the new sector had passed to the B.E.F. at midnight 31st Jan./1st February, and the relief of the French troops was to take place about 12th February.

At this time, however, owing to the situation elsewhere in Europe His Majesty's Government found it necessary to postpone the despatch of 3rd Corps (excepting 51st Division) and also of certain anti-aircraft, administrative and labour units. I was also instructed to earmark one division for withdrawal from the B.E.F. if required; for this I selected 5th Division. It was evident that the programme of shipments of ammunition and other war material to France, on which I had counted to make up the serious deficiencies in stocks, would be severely curtailed in February and March.

4. These changes entailed a delay in the development of the Force which was naturally disappointing; moreover, it became impossible for me to take over the new sector to Bailleul, and at the same time to retain a proper proportion of divisions in reserve. I was, therefore, obliged to

obtain the consent of the French to the indefinite postponement of the relief, and to accept the resulting congestion in the area of the B.E.F.

50th Division was temporarily accommodated in an area south-west of Amiens in G.H.Q. reserve.

At the end of March, however, the 3rd Corps was finally despatched to France; 5Ist Division duly relieved the French in the new sector on 28th March; 44th Division, on disembarkation, moved into 3rd Corps reserve in the St. Pol area, and 50th Division into 2nd Corps reserve, southwest of Lille; 42nd Division, on arrival, moved to the area south-west of Amiens, in G.H.Q. reserve.

5. The German invasion of Denmark and Norway on 9th April created a new situation; leave was stopped in the British and French Armies on I0th April, and I5th Infantry Brigade of 5th Division was despatched to England, *en route* for Norway, on I5th April; certain units of 42nd Division were also retained at home, but with a few exceptions despatched later. The remainder of 5th Division was left in France, but in War Office reserve, and was accordingly relieved in 3rd Corps by 42nd Division. Reports of enemy intentions to invade Holland and Belgium were received from different sources and at different times, and between the IIth and 22nd April certain troops were placed under short notice to move. Intensified air reconnaissance was ordered in the zone allotted to the Air Component which included part of the Ruhr and the area to the west of it, but apart from small bridging activity no positive results were observed.

**The Saar Front.**

6. During this period the detachment of one infantry brigade on the Saar front was maintained; at the outset the severe cold interfered considerably with the work of improving the defences in the forward area. Much required to be done, as regards increased protection, provision of alternative fire positions, covered approaches and improved communications; the wire required thickening and its tactical lay-out improving; the thaw, when it set in, was rapid and energetic steps had to be taken to maintain a proper standard of sanitation.

The tour of duty of each infantry brigade was raised in March to three weeks, and a pioneer battalion was included in the detachment.

At the end of March it was decided to increase the Saar force to a total of one division, with attached troops, including cavalry, machine guns, and pioneers. 51st Division was selected. The Division had concentrated in the Metz area by 30th April and by 7th May had relieved 7th French Division, thus extending the British front on the Saar on either side of the front originally held to a total of 12,000 yards from Guerstling exclusive to Remeling inclusive.

51st Division remained in the Saar area and took no part in the operations in Northern France. From 10th May therefore, it ceased to be under my effective command; the Saar Force was later moved to the Rouen area, where it took part in subsequent operations.

Patrolling, both by our own troops and by the enemy, grew steadily more active during this period; early on the morning of the 5th March, the enemy carried out a successful raid, supported with a box barrage of a type familiar in the war of 1914-18, on one of our front line positions in a wood known as the Hartebusch, then held by a battalion of the 4th Division (2nd D.C.L.I.). In this and subsequent encounters the enemy regularly suffered casualties, many of them at the hands of battalions of the 144th Infantry Brigade of the 48th Division, the first Territorial Army formation to meet the enemy in this campaign.

The sub-machine gun was taken into experimental use by patrols in the Saar front: its value had already been recognised and I trust that a weapon of this type will be permanently included in the armament of the infantry.

### *Preparation for Further Expansion.*

7. In the meantime I had been preparing for the arrival of further troops, and, in particular, for the formation of Army Headquarters which were due to arrive in the latter part of June. On the assumption that the positions held by the B.E.F. were to remain the same, a lay-out had been prepared involving a move of G.H.Q. The construction of the new G.H.Q. and of the two Army headquarters was put in hand; this involved the laying of about 150 route miles of heavy armoured cable. Negotiations were in progress regarding the extension of the front of the B.E.F. on arrival of a fourth Corps, the French being anxious that this should be southwards rather than northwards.

## Development of the Defensive Positions.

8. The development of the successive defensive positions and switch lines behind the Belgian frontier was continued steadily till 10th May. By this date over 400 concrete "pill-boxes" of varying size had been completed with over 100 more under construction, while work on the improvement of field defences, wire and other obstacles proceeded continuously on the original front and in the sector north of Armentières recently taken over from the French.

Chiefly by the use of excavator machinery over 40 miles of revetted anti-tank ditch had been added to that prepared by the French army in time of peace. Machines had also been used to assist the troops in constructing earthwork defences, mixing concrete and burying signal cables.

## Training.

9. Training areas were being prepared to accommodate the Armoured Division and other formations; base reinforcement depôts were rapidly taking shape in their new locations near Rouen, and their training staffs had assembled. Corps schools had been established, principally for the training of junior leaders, and a sniping school had been set up. Practice camps, both for field and anti-aircraft artillery had been developed with the help of the French and steps taken to continue the weapon training of selected units.

The practice undertaken with anti-tank weapons, to which special attention was given, was amply to prove its value when the time came.

## The Equipment Situation.

10. The situation as regards equipment, though there was latterly some improvement in certain directions, caused me serious misgivings, even before men and material began to be diverted by the needs of operations elsewhere. I had on several occasions called the attention of the War Office to the shortage of almost every nature of ammunition of which the stocks in France were not nearly large enough to permit of the rates of expenditure laid down for sustained operations before the War.

There was a shortage of guns in some of the anti-tank regiments of the Royal Artillery, while armour-piercing shells for field guns had not, by 10th May, been provided.

There were also deficiencies in technical apparatus for light anti-aircraft requirements, such as Kerrison Predictors, signal lights, technical and specialised vehicles of many types and a number of smaller items. The same difficulties in provision of equipment were no doubt the cause of delays in the despatch of new units to the B.E.F., particularly armoured and anti-aircraft units, and while it is to some extent true that the shortness of the campaign prevented the full effect of the shortages being felt, it is I think, justifiable to assume that the presence of the Armoured Division and of a complete Army Tank Brigade would have been an invaluable aid in the difficulties with which we were faced in meeting enemy armoured formations.

## *The Administrative Situation.*

II. The development of the rearward installations had been proceeding systematically.

The medical base installations had been extended and a hospital area was in course of rapid development near Boulogne in addition to the original medical base sub-area at Dieppe.

The British Army requirements in the port of Brest, a French naval base, had been substantially reduced by the use of other ports such as St. Malo and Caen; by May, seventeen ports in all were being operated and 2,500 tons of stores were being despatched to railheads daily.

At the same time, the construction of semi-permanent depôts of all kinds in the neighbourhood of Nantes, Rennes and Rouen was in progress; this would later on have led to more efficient and economical working than was possible in the temporary accommodation taken up in September, 1939. By 10th May, seven ammunition depôts were open, in addition to railhead dumps; all these were intended, in time, to be rail served; while the construction of the regulating station at Abancourt, by French railway troops on behalf of the B.E.F., was well advanced. It opened on a limited scale in the first week of May. A supply depôt was being constructed close by so as to relieve the dangerous congestion at the ports of Rouen and Havre.

The progress of all these undertakings was adversely affected by the shortage of labour, to which I referred in my first despatch, and it was decided, in March, to send three Divisions to France to undertake labour duties and at the same time continue their training, albeit slowly. The Divisions selected were 12th (Major-General R.L. Petre), 23rd (Major-General W.N. Herbert) and 46th (Major-General H.O. Curtis). These arrived in April; 23rd Division was allotted for work on aerodromes in the forward area, and the remaining two to the Lines of Communication area.

## *Organisation.*

12. The absence of actual operations up to 10th May gave opportunities to make a number of changes in organisation.

Divisional cavalry regiments were grouped into Armoured Reconnaissance Brigades and the Lines of Communication area was re-organised into two districts.

Infantry battalions were filled up to the new and higher establishments, and action was initiated to raise the establishment of artillery units, including anti-aircraft. My Adjutant-General's branch, in conjunction with the Adjutant-General's branch at the War Office, had in hand plans for the more economical use of man-power, the elimination of fit men from sedentary or base duties and the reduction of tradesmen in War Establishments. Investigations made by the War Office, which had my full co-operation, were directed towards a more economical and more flexible system of replacement and repair of vehicles and equipment in the Force.

## *The Royal Air Force.*

13. On 15th January, 1940, Air Marshal A.S. Barratt had assumed command of the British Air Force in France, including the Air Component which, however, was to remain under my operational control. Under this arrangement, in my opinion, the control of available air forces was better allocated to meet the needs not only of the British but also of the French Army for whom considerable aerial reconnaissance was being carried out. The development of the Allied Central Air Bureau and of its communications to the headquarters of higher formations in France and to the Royal Air Force at home, was

likewise to prove its worth in the days to come as an organisation for co-ordinating information and requests for air action.

At the same time I felt that the resources of the Air Component would prove insufficient for the requirements of the Force during operations; so long, therefore, as this state of affairs existed it was of prime importance that the machinery for obtaining the allotment of additional bomber and fighter support should be as simple and as swift in operation as it could be made.

Throughout the period, construction of new aerodromes, landing grounds and communications for the British Air Force in France was proceeding as fast as resources would permit, concrete runways being constructed in the early part of the year until the season allowed for the sowing of grass. Upwards of 10,000 men were employed on this work, and forty-seven aerodromes and satellites (including 19 new aerodromes) were under development or construction. By 15th May eight of the nineteen new aerodromes were capable of use, and at least 50,000 tons of concrete had been laid. Constructional work was also undertaken on behalf of the Air Ministry at other R.A.F. installations in central France.

## *The Dyle and Escaut Plans.*

14. Very shortly after the arrival of the B.E.F. in their positions on the Belgian frontier I had been invited by General Georges, commanding the French Front of the North East, under whose Command I was, to study the part to be played by the B.E.F. in the event of an advance into Holland and Belgium, or into Belgium alone. The question of such an advance was one of high policy with a political as well as a military aspect; it was therefore not for me to comment on it. My responsibilities were confined to ensuring that the orders issued by the French for the employment of the British Expeditionary Force were capable of being carried out; and indeed events proved that the orders issued for this operation were well within the capacity of the Force.

The subject presented difficulties greatly complicated by the policy of neutrality to which the Belgian Government were wedded. The French authorities were never in a position to obtain reliable and accurate details of the plans of the Belgian General Staff for the defence of their country in the event of an invasion by Germany; staff conversations were out of the question, yet plans had to be framed in such a way that they could be put into instant operation in the event of Belgium asking for military assistance from France or Great Britain when invasion had taken place or was imminent.

Such slender contact as existed between the British and Belgian Military authorities was maintained through the Military Attaché at His Majesty's Embassy at Brussels and General Van Overstraeten, Military Adviser to the King of the Belgians.

15. Three alternative plans were decided on by the French High Command during October and November 1939, and I had agreed with General Georges on the part to be played in each of them by the B.E.F.

The first alternative was to occupy the frontier defences, pushing forward mobile troops to the line of the Escaut, while the French 7th Army on my left were to delay the enemy on the line of the Messines Ridge and the Yser Canal. This plan was soon discarded in favour of the second alternative, which was to secure and hold the line of the Escaut itself, from the point at which it crosses the frontier at Maulde northwards to the neighbourhood of Ghent where it was intended to effect a junction with Belgian forces.

Later, however, as information became available regarding the defences of the Belgian Army, and its readiness for war, the French High Command formed the opinion that it would be safe to count on the Belgian defence holding out for some days on the Eastern frontier, and the Albert Canal. It was also ascertained that the Belgians were preparing a *de Cointet* anti-tank obstacle running southwards from Wavre towards Namur.

The line of the river Dyle was from the military point of view a better one than that of the Escaut. It was shorter, it afforded greater depth and its northern portion was inundated. In addition, it represented smaller enemy occupation of Belgian territory.

On the other hand, it involved the B.E.F. in a forward move of some sixty miles against time, while it also necessitated the holding by the French on our right of the Gembloux gap which contains no natural anti-tank obstacle. This plan was twice discussed by General Georges with me on 13th October at my headquarters at Le Cauroy and again on 16th November at Folembray the headquarters of the French First Group of Armies; on this occasion there were also present General

Billotte, who commanded the Army Group, and Generals Blanchard and Corap, Commanding the French Ist and 9th Armies. At this conference it was agreed that the frontage of the B.E.F. on the Dyle position was to be from Wavre to Louvain, both places inclusive, and a formal instruction to this effect was issued to me by General Georges on the following day. From this time onward, Commanders and Staffs were studying simultaneously two alternative plans for advances to the Dyle or the Escaut; these became known as plans D and E.

Both these plans were worked out in the greatest detail, and orders and instructions kept up to date as new divisions arrived and the role of divisions changed.

The Escaut plan was by far the simpler of the two; it involved sending armoured car reconnaissances to the river Dendre to be relieved by divisional cavalry, who were later, if necessary, to fight a delaying action backwards to the Escaut; demolitions were provided for on both rivers; for the remainder of the force, however, the advance appeared likely to be an easy one, well within a day's march on foot. The Dyle plan, on the other hand, involved an advance of some sixty miles, carried out at a time when every moment was of value over roads not previously reconnoitred, perhaps crowded with refugees moving counter to the allied armies. Much too, depended on the resistance which the Belgians, and perhaps the Dutch, were able to offer to the enemy, who at such a time would certainly be making every effort to pierce the line of the Meuse and the Albert Canal.

16. The plans made in advance for the advance to the Dyle position actually worked to schedule in almost all respects. It may therefore be convenient to summarise them here.

The Allied forces were to advance to the line Namur-Wavre-Louvain-Antwerp, of which the B.E.F. Sector extended from Wavre to Louvain, both inclusive. On our right was to be the French Ist Army (Général d'Armée Blanchard) under whose command was the French Cavalry Corps, and whose task it was to delay the arrival of the enemy on the Dyle position and to block with its main forces the Gembloux gap, with the Cavalry Corps pushed forward to the line Eghezee (8 miles north of Namur)-Tirlemont. On our left the French 7th Army (Général d'Armée Giraud) was to advance to the general area Antwerp-Ghent, with the object of supporting Belgian resistance north of

Louvain. The plans of this Army included a possible advance into Holland as far as the line Turnhout-Breda, and this was actually carried out. It had been ascertained that a portion of the Belgian Army, if forced to withdraw from their frontier defences would come into line on the left of the B.E.F. on the general line from Louvain exclusive, thence northward to the fortified area of Antwerp, known as the National Redoubt.

The British front was to be occupied initially with Ist Corps (Lieutenant-General M.G.H. Barker, who had recently taken over command from General Sir John Dill), on a two-division front, on the right, and 2nd Corps (Lieutenant-General A.F. Brooke, now Sir Alan Brooke) on the left, on a front initially of one division.

The advance was to be made in four periods. In the first, I2th Royal Lancers (Armoured Cars) were to move to a general line some eight miles beyond the Dyle in observation of the approaches from the east; they were to be relieved by cavalry regiments of Ist and 2nd Corps when they arrived.

Behind them were to come, from right to left, 2nd Division (Major-General H.C. Loyd) and Ist Division (Major-General Hon. H.R.L.G. Alexander) of Ist Corps, and 3rd Division (Major-General B.L. Montgomery) of 2nd Corps. The whole of the move of these three divisions was to be made by motor transport, and troop carrying companies were allotted to Corps in such a way as to complete the move in 90 hours.

At the same time 44th Division was to march to an area north-west of Audenarde, with a view to organising the defence of the Escaut in this area.

Movement in the first phase was to be continuous by day and night. The French had decided to restrict the movements of their main bodies to the hours of darkness, but I judged the time factor to be of paramount importance and accepted the risk that our air support might be insufficient to prevent enemy interference with the move. Events proved that the risk was justifiable.

In the second period, to be completed by the end of the sixth day, 48th Division (Major-General A.F.A.N. Thorne) and 4th Division (Major-General D.G. Johnson, V.C.) were to move by march route and motor transport into Ist and 2nd Corps reserve respectively, while Ist

Army Tank Brigade consisting of two battalions was to move chiefly by rail into Ist Corps area.

The third period was to be completed by the tenth day, and included the movement of 50th Division to 2nd Corps reserve, while 4th Division moved into the line on the right of 3rd Division.

The fourth period included the forward movement of 3rd Corps. 5th Division (Major-General H.E. Franklyn) was to move to positions in G.H.Q. reserve, along the river Dendre, north and south of Grammont; 42nd and 44th Divisions to the line of the river Escaut around Tournai and to the south of Audenarde respectively, to organise bridgehead positions pending orders for a further advance.

Detailed instructions had also been issued for the preparation of defences on the three river lines of the Dyle, Dendre and Escaut, as also for the necessary demolitions and inundations. Special arrangements had been made for the control of traffic, including refugees for whom routes had been allotted; definite bodies of troops were detailed for these tasks.

## *The Belgian Anti-Tank obstacle.*

I7. Late in April and early in May, I received reports regarding the siting of the Belgian anti-tank obstacle; it appeared that, without informing either the French High Command or myself, they had sited the obstacle much further to the east than had originally been planned, namely on the line Namur-Perwez-Louvain: furthermore the obstacle was not as yet by any means completed. The matter was discussed with General Georges.

On the British front, the river Dyle was so far superior as an anti-tank obstacle to any artificial work further east which the Belgians might be preparing that I had no hesitation in urging adherence to the existing plan for the defence of the Dyle position.

On the front of the French Ist Army the situation was different: the absence of a natural obstacle forced them to rely on that prepared by the Belgians. To clear the matter up, information was demanded as to the true site of the artificial obstacle. These negotiations were begun through our Military Attaché on 8th May, but they were not destined to be concluded.

## OPERATIONS – FIRST PHASE
(10th-16th MAY)

*Belgium calls on Allies for assistance: advance to the River Dyle by British and French Armies: the Belgian anti-tank obstacle is found to be sited further forward than had been expected. The enemy penetrates the front of French 9th Army and crosses the Meuse. Action by Royal Air Force. General Billotte appointed to co-ordinate action of British, French and Belgians. The Dutch lay down arms.*

**10th May – The enemy invades Holland and Belgium.**

18. The tension which had been increasing during April had lessened somewhat during the early days of May; during this period I had received reports of enemy activity from several sources of varying degrees of reliability, culminating in a report from the Hague, but it was not until the night of 9th-10th May that information was received of exceptional activity on the frontiers of Luxembourg, Belgium and Holland. The weather was set fair, and with the exception of some heavy thunderstorms which had no effect on operations, remained so to the end of the month. At about 4.30 a.m. on 10th May, enemy aircraft appeared over my headquarters at Arras and bombs were dropped on aerodromes in the neighbourhood and on a number of towns including Doullens and Abbeville. At 5.30 a.m., a message was received from my mission with General Georges ordering "Alertes 1, 2 and 3," namely, instant readiness to move into Belgium. I at once sought, and obtained, the release of the 5th Division from War Office reserve, and henceforward it was employed under my orders. At about 6.15 a.m. I received instructions to put Plan D into effect.

It was ascertained that 12th Royal Lancers could be ready to cross the frontier at 1 p.m., and accordingly I laid down this time as zero hour.

At 1 p.m. I opened my command post at Wahagnies, midway between Douai and Lille.

1st and 2nd Corps experienced some delay in moving, due largely to the fact that owing to the short notice received, preliminary moves of transport had not taken place; apart from this, moves on this day proceeded according to plan; very little interference was experienced either from enemy aircraft or refugees and 12th Lancers reached the Dyle unopposed at 10.30 p.m.

The French armies on our right and left were reported as advancing on time.

The Belgian population received the allied armies in the most cordial manner, and in particular the leading troops were loudly cheered.

## *Operations between 11th and 15th May.*

19. On 11th May, enemy air action increased somewhat, but did not interfere with the forward movement of troops, and during the afternoon and evening, the leading infantry brigades reached the Dyle, refugee traffic being handled successfully. The original arrangements, of which the Belgian Government were aware, included the use by the B.E.F. of roads passing through the northern and southern outskirts of Brussels, but not through the centre of the city. A series of requests was however received to discontinue the use of these roads on the ground that Brussels had been declared an open town and that British troop movements would prejudice its safety, but no adequate alternative routes to the Dyle were available and I was therefore compelled to adhere to the original plan of using the outskirts of the city.

The 3rd Division, on arrival, reported that a Belgian division was holding the bridgehead at Louvain, although I had assumed that this should be a British responsibility. 2nd Corps therefore took up a narrow front on their right with a strong reserve in rear of Louvain.

5th Division, which was training in the area south-west of Amiens, was ordered to proceed by march route so as to shorten the move by motor transport in a later phase, and later occupied a position on the Senne.

The news from the Belgian army, of which King Leopold had assumed command on the outbreak of war, was not good. Belgian cyclist troops from east of the Meuse were falling back on Huy. At Maastricht, it was reported that they had been forestalled by enemy action from the rear and had been unable to demolish important bridges over the Albert Canal and the Meuse across which the enemy had begun to move. Air bombing was requested and was extremely effective, but could not altogether deny the passage of the water obstacles to the enemy. On my right the French Cavalry Corps had reached their position on the line Huy-Hannut-Tirlemont and reconnoitred the Belgian anti-tank obstacle. They reported that, as I had supposed, there was no effective obstacle on the Gembloux line and that the obstacle on the Perwez line was not only unfinished but badly sited on a forward slope. I thereupon conveyed to General Georges a confirmation of my objections to pushing forward so as to make use of the obstacle in its unfinished state, notwithstanding the Belgians' anxiety that I should do so. Later that day I was informed that he had decided that the main line of resistance was to be on the Gembloux line as planned, but that the French were to push out advanced troops to the line of the obstacle. He expressed the hope that the B.E.F. would conform, and Ist and 2nd Corps accordingly reconnoitred the anti-tank obstacles reported to exist round the forest of Meerdael with a view to pushing forward detachments with anti-tank guns. They found them complete only in places.

20. The first phase of Plan D was successfully completed by I2th May, and the French Ist Army on my right then accelerated the programme governing their forward movement by moving by day as well as by night. The enemy progress across the Albert Canal had up to now been relatively small, due to a successful counter-attack by the French Cavalry Corps at St. Trond, but larger concentrations were now reported north of the Albert Canal. Disquieting news was received from the Ardennes, where a German thrust was reported as developing on the front of the French 9th Army, with at least two armoured divisions.

On this date I requested the War Office to expedite the despatch of the Ist Armoured Division to the greatest extent possible. I also asked that they should be shipped to the nearest available port and loaded tactically with a view to operations as soon as possible after landing.

The day was one of great activity in the air, and afforded great opportunities for the Royal Air Force to impede the enemy advance; but such opportunities were of a fleeting character, since the enemy established strong anti-aircraft defences soon after his arrival, particularly in towns at which roads converged. Tactical reconnaissance became virtually impossible without fighter support, and the demands made on the fighter group of the Air Component were extremely heavy. They had been met with unfailing skill and courage, and with marked success, but by now the group was reduced to some 50 aircraft, and although I had asked for four fresh squadrons from home, only one had arrived. In three days' operations, the British Air Force in France had firm reports of the destruction of 10I enemy aircraft, mostly fighters, against a loss of 78 of our own.

That afternoon a conference was held at the Château Casteau, near Mons which was attended by the King of the Belgians, General Van Overstraeten, M. Daladier, Generals Georges and Billotte, and my Chief of the General Staff (Lieutenant-General H.R. Pownall), as my representative in my absence. The primary object of the conference was to achieve some measure of co-ordination in the Belgian theatre of war. General Billotte's command included the French Ist and 7th Armies, between which lay the Belgian Army under the independent command of their King, and the B.E.F. which, though under the command of General Georges, was not under that of General Billotte. Whatever the nature of the operations, a common doctrine was clearly necessary and when General Georges enquired if the King of the Belgians and I would be prepared to accept co-ordination by General Billotte as his representative, General Pownall said he was sure that I would agree. The King of the Belgians likewise agreed.

2I. On 13th May I moved my Command Post forward to Renaix; no event of major importance occurred during the day, but some small infantry attacks developed on the British sector. These were easily held. Movements of the main bodies of the French Ist and 7th Armies continued in accordance with their plans, and units of the latter were by now north of Antwerp on the Dutch border. It was, however, becoming increasingly evident that they would be unable to prevent the enemy occupation of Walcheren and Zuid Beveland which was developing from the north-east.

During the day and the following night the Belgian forces were in process of withdrawing their northern forces to the general line Louvain-Antwerp, and the Staff of the Belgian G.Q.G. expressed concern lest the simultaneous withdrawal of their Cavalry Corps and that of the French, north-west and south-west from their junction point at Tirlemont, would create a gap. There appeared to me to be little danger, but nevertheless I ordered I2th Lancers to watch the situation, assisted if need be by divisional cavalry regiments.

22. On I4th May I went to Brussels, where at I2 noon I met the

Commanders of Ist and 2nd Corps at the British Embassy. The Commander of 2nd Corps reported that the Belgian Ist Corps was now reforming in 4th Division area. I also discussed the organisation of the second position on the Senne canal and of a Corps reserve line east of Brussels. 5th and 48th Divisions were ordered to reconnoitre the Senne position on I5th May. That afternoon at 3 p.m. I visited H.M. the King of the Belgians and General Van Overstraeten and reached agreement that the Belgian Ist Corps should be withdrawn from the area of 2nd Corps and that the left boundary of the B.E.F. should be adjusted so as to allow the Belgians the use of the road Vilvorde-Alost for this purpose. I also stressed the importance of having fresh Belgian troops established early in position north of Louvain to continue the British line covering Brussels.

Further serious news came from the south where the enemy had crossed the Meuse between Sedan and Mézières, and further north he was reported to be surrounding the fortress of St. Héribert (4 miles S.S.W. of Namur).

The French Cavalry Corps on my right had on the previous day received orders to retire to the Perwez position whence they subsequently withdrew, according to plan, to the main position running through Gembloux.

At the request of Air Marshal Barratt I placed at his disposal for use on the French front three squadrons of fighters which I had only recently received in response to an urgent appeal to the Secretary of State for War.

23. On I5th May the Dutch Army laid down its arms; the immediate effect of this on the operations of the B.E.F. was small, for the British forces operating in Holland had at no time been under my command. I anticipated, however, that this would come as a shock to the Belgian Army.

The French 7th Army withdrew its advanced formations to the neighbourhood of Antwerp and on this day ordered divisions to move across my rear to fill the gap created further south. This move, however, did not take place till some three days later when it was accomplished, thanks to efficient traffic control, with little delay to our own movements.

On this day (I5th May) I established a command post at Lennick St.

Quentin, 6 miles west of Brussels. On the British front, the day passed quietly on the whole, Ist Corps was not attacked in strength; 3rd Division of 2nd Corps was attacked north-west of Louvain and its forward positions were penetrated, but a counter-attack successfully restored the original line. There was considerable enemy bombing of rearward areas during the day, and the movement of refugees became increasingly difficult to control. This was, in part, due to the bombing of Tournai and other towns on the routes and to the French decision to close the frontier to pedestrian and horsed traffic. Despite my requests, made as early as I0th May, the Belgian authorities had done nothing to restrict the use of private motor cars or the sale of petrol.

During the day I received a request that I should take over part of the front held by the French division on my right. To meet this request I placed under the orders of this division a brigade of 48th Division; this step proved necessary since at about 6 p.m. the enemy had penetrated the French front, thus threatening the right of 2nd Division. By this time, however, 48th Division, less one brigade, was in position in Ist Corps reserve behind 2nd Division, and I agreed with the commander of Ist Corps that the withdrawal of his right should take place to the River Lasne to join up with the French left. This movement was carried out on the night of the I5/I6 May, closely followed by the enemy.

By the night of I5th May the movements envisaged in Plan D were all running ahead of schedule. 4th Division was moving into Corps reserve behind 3rd Division; 5th Division was moving on to the Senne in place of 50th Division as originally planned, and the latter was now moving to G.H.Q. reserve along the River Dendre.

## OPERATIONS – SECOND PHASE
### (I7th-26th MAY)

*Withdrawal to the Escaut decided on; the threat to Arras and to the right flank; formation of Macforce and deployment of 23rd Division on the Canal du Nord. The enemy reaches the Somme and cuts communications with the Base; Calais and Boulogne invested: the administrative position. The organisation of the Canal line. Alternative lines discussed with French and Belgians, resulting in further withdrawal from the Escaut to the Frontier defences and fresh plans for attacks southwards in conjunction with French main forces. 5th and 50th Divisions counter-attack on 21st May. A further attack in conjunction with French planned for 26th May: this plan is abandoned owing to penetration of Belgian line on the Lys.*

**The beginning of the withdrawal *(16th-17th May).***

24. By 16th May, it became clear that a prolonged defence of the Dyle position was impracticable. The French 1st Army on my right were unlikely to make good the ground lost on the previous day, notwithstanding the support I had given them in the air and on the ground, and a further withdrawal seemed likely to be forced on them by events in the south.

On the other hand there had been no serious attack on the Belgian positions on my left; nevertheless, any withdrawal from our present positions would of necessity involve a withdrawal by the Belgian Army in the course of which Brussels, and probably Antwerp also, would be abandoned to the enemy.

Very early on 16th May therefore, I sent a representative to General Billotte who was co-ordinating the movements of the British, French and Belgian Forces; I asked that, if he intended to withdraw, he should let me know the policy and the timings at once, especially as the first bound back to the Senne canals involved a march of some fifteen to twenty miles.

At about 10 a.m. I received from him orders for a withdrawal to the Escaut, and for the occupation of the positions along that river originally planned. The operation was to begin that night (16/17 May), one day being spent on the Senne and one day on the Dendre positions; thus the Escaut would be reached on the night of 18/19 May, though the French orders did not rule out the possibility of staying for longer than one day on each bound.

That evening, I held a co-ordinating conference at 1st Corps Headquarters as a result of which I ordered 5th Division, which was on the way to join 2nd Corps, to the line of the Senne in 1st Corps reserve. Two brigades of 46th Division[1] which had been moved up from the Lines of Communication for the protection of vulnerable points, were ordered to relieve units of Ist and 2nd Corps on protection and traffic control of main routes in Belgium. Railheads, which had been advanced on 13th May to the general line Enghien-Ninove, were now moved back across the frontier.

During the night 16/17th May the withdrawal to the Senne positions began, and was successfully completed by the afternoon of the 17th. Some enemy tanks and motor cycle units had been reported on the right flank of Ist Corps, west of the forest of Soignies, and as a precaution, part of the Ist Army Tank Brigade, which had started to withdraw for entrainment, was turned about to meet the thrust.

By the time the tanks reached their entraining stations railway difficulties prevented the trucks being moved, and the remainder of the move was carried out by road; this gave rise to inevitable mechanical trouble later on.

By the early morning of 17th May the situation in the south had become grave, and enemy armoured and mobile forces were reported to have crossed the Oise. At St. Quentin the situation was obscure, and though by this time General Giraud, lately commanding the French 7th Army, had been ordered to take command of the forces in that region, it was clear from reports and from visits of liaison officers that he had not yet succeeded in establishing effective control. A gap of at least twenty miles existed south of the Forest of Mormal in which there appeared to be no organised resistance. Later in the day information was received from the French that ten enemy armoured divisions were engaged in the battle.

During the whole of this period, communication with my liaison officer at General Georges' Headquarters was maintained so as to keep in touch with events as they developed. However, I received no information through this channel of any steps it was proposed to take to close the gap, which might have affected my own command.

It was not till later, on the night of 19th/20th May, that General Billotte informed me of the action which was being taken to this end by the French Armies in the south.

## *The defence of rearward areas.*

25. Rear G.H.Q. at Arras had intensified the precautions already being taken against sabotage and air landing units, but on the early morning

of 17th May a telegram was received from General Georges ordering 23rd Division to move at once to occupy the line of the Canal du Nord, on a frontage of fifteen miles from Ruyalcourt (10 miles north of Péronne) to Arleux (6 miles south of Douai).

The division, which, like the 12th and 46th Divisions had joined the B.E.F. for work in rearward areas, consisted of eight battalions only with divisional engineers, but no artillery, and signals and administrative units in no more than skeleton form. Its armament and transport was on a much reduced scale and training was far from complete.

Nevertheless, troops of these three divisions fought and marched continuously for a fortnight, and proved, were proof needed, that they were composed of soldiers who, despite their inexperience and lack of equipment, could hold their own with a better found and more numerous enemy.

23rd Division moved to their positions during 17th May; they were provided with about forty field, anti-tank, and anti-aircraft guns from ordnance reserves.

The enemy break-through was now offering an imminent threat to rear G.H.Q., to the communications over the Somme at Amiens and Abbeville, and to the base areas. To meet this, every available man and weapon was collected and orders were issued to the commander, Lines of Communication Area, for the remainder of 12th and 46th Divisions to be despatched to the forward zone. One brigade (36th Infantry Brigade of 12th Division) arrived during the day, and the leading battalion was despatched with four field guns to cover the north-western exits from Péronne, while engineer parties, organised by the Commander, G.H.Q. Troops, were sent to prepare for demolition the crossings over the Canal du Nord between the river Somme and the right of 23rd Division at Ruyalcourt. The remainder of 36th Infantry Brigade were moved forward to Albert, and the other two brigades of 12th Division ordered to the Abbeville area. These latter, however, arrived too late to come under my effective command, and their operations on the Somme were carried out under the Commander Lines of Communication Area.

Elsewhere in the area between Corps rear boundaries and the Somme, local defence schemes were put into operation under the orders of the Commanders of G.H.Q. Troops and of "X" Lines of Communication Sub-Area[2]. Few if any of these units or their commanders had any experience in fighting, but their determination was beyond all praise.

A mobile bath unit, for example, took part in the defence of St. Pol, while, both now and later, the General Construction Companies of the Royal Engineers, and many units of the Royal Army Service Corps, set to work to place their localities in a state of defence and manned them until they were overwhelmed, relieved or ordered to withdraw. Wherever possible, transport was collected or requisitioned to enable parachute detachments to be dealt with.

These many small delaying actions all contributed to gain the time required for the withdrawal of the main forces.

The defence of the town of Arras itself was entrusted to the O.C. Ist Bn. Welsh Guards who had under his command some units of the Royal Engineers, an Overseas Defence battalion (9th West Yorks), and various details including an improvised tank squadron.

Orders were issued for all administrative troops not required for defence to move forthwith north of a line Orchies-Lens-Frévent.

At the same time to guard against a more immediate threat to my right flank a force was organised consisting of I27th Infantry Brigade of 42nd Division, Ist Army Tank Brigade, a Field Artillery Regiment and the Hopkinson Mission[3], all under the command of Major-General F.N. Mason-MacFarlane, my Director of Military Intelligence. The force was known as Macforce and its task was to cover the crossings over the Scarpe between Raches (3 miles N.E. of Douai) and St. Amand. It began to assemble at Orchies on the afternoon of I7th May.

## *Withdrawal to the Escaut begun.*

26. It had now to be decided whether or not the withdrawal from the Senne to the Dendre was to begin on the night of I7/I8 May, and the situation in the South was such that I felt that to spend a day on the Senne would be to risk being outflanked on the right and so imperil the force under my command to no good purpose. General Billotte had issued orders for withdrawal to the Dendre that night, but I had also seen an order from General Georges which envisaged remaining on the Senne for a further twenty-four hours. I therefore sent a liaison officer

to General Billotte to represent my views. In the result, General Billotte's orders stood confirmed.

By 4 p.m. on I7th May therefore Ist and 2nd Corps were on the Senne with 5th, Ist and 4th Divisions in line right to left. 48th Division was covering the right flank from Enghien to Lembecq. 50th Division was on the Dendre, to which line 2nd and 3rd Divisions were now withdrawing, whilst 3 Corps was in position on the Escaut with 42nd Division (less one infantry brigade) and 44th Division.

27. On I8th May I held a conference at the headquarters of Ist Corps at which were settled the details of the withdrawal to the Escaut. This line was to be held with six divisions, right to left Ist Corps (48th and 42nd Divisions, less one infantry brigade, with 2nd Division in reserve), 2nd Corps (Ist and 3rd Divisions with 50th Division in reserve), 3rd Corps (4th and 44th Divisions), on a front from the bridge over the Escaut at Bléharies to Audenarde, both inclusive. 5th Division was in G.H.Q. reserve.

There was little pressure during the day on the British front or on that of the Belgians to the North. Owing to the late arrival of orders the Belgian Army had started their withdrawal after the B.E.F.; they had therefore asked for and received protection to their right flank at Brusseghem up to 7 a.m. and Assche up to 8 a.m. on I8th May. On withdrawal they effected a junction with the B.E.F. on the Dendre at Alost.

Southward from their junction with the B.E.F. the French line ran through Mons and Maubeuge, and enemy tanks were attacking the front of the French Corps on my immediate right. Enemy air action had by now intensified on the front of the B.E.F. and continuous fighter support was necessary during the hours of daylight, both to enable our reconnaissances to take place and to hold off enemy bombers. The enemy did not confine his attention to troops but attacked the long columns of refugees which continued to move westwards.

### *The position on the Canal du Nord.*

28. The position on the Canal du Nord had caused some anxiety, partly on account of contradictory orders received. Shortly after orders had been issued on I7th May for the occupation of the position by 23rd Division, an order was received from G.Q.G. allotting to the B.E.F. the

sector Péronne-Ruyalcourt instead of the sector Ruyalcourt-Arleux which was now to be occupied by the French. It was not however practicable to move the 23rd Division again and G.Q.G. were informed to this effect. Yet, by next morning no French troops had appeared either on the right of 23rd Division or to relieve them. Later in the day, however, an order was received by which the commander of the French 2nd Region was ordered to fill the gap. Enquiries by a liaison officer at Amiens, where the staff of the French 7th Army was in process of taking over from the 2nd Region, established that no troops would be likely to arrive for twenty-four hours at least.

By the afternoon, however, some enemy had reached Péronne, and were in contact with 36th Infantry Brigade.

On this day Major-General R.L. Petre, commanding the I2th Division, was given command of the troops engaged on this flank, namely 23rd Division, 36th Infantry Brigade and the garrison of Arras.[4]

In the meantime an order issued by the French First Group of Armies had laid down the boundary between the French Ist Army and the B.E.F. through Maulde, Orchies, Raches and Hénin Liétard. Arras was thus excluded from the zone of the B.E.F., but its defence was necessarily continued by British troops. All troops not required for defence left on the I9th, including rear G.H.Q. which moved in two echelons to Hazebrouck and Boulogne in accordance with plans prepared on I7th May when the threat to Arras became serious.

On the evening of I8th May I moved back my command post from Renaix to its previous location at Wahagnies.

## *Moves of the Royal Air Force.*

29. On this day also, the bulk of the Advanced Air Striking Force moved from the neighbourhood of Rheims to Central France and the Air Component moved one of their main operational aerodromes from Poix to Abbeville. On the evening of I9th May enemy action obliged them to evacuate this aerodrome also. The Air Officer Commanding the Air Component then moved his headquarters to England, but an advanced landing ground was maintained at Merville until 22nd May.

From the 2Ist May onwards all arrangements for air co-operation with the B.E.F. were made by the War Office in conjunction with the Air Ministry at home. The air liaison work was carried out in England

## 44  The BEF In France 1939-1940

at Hawkinge and the targets selected in accordance with telephone or telegraphic requests from the B.E.F. so long as communications remained open, supplemented by information received from the Royal Air Force, and other sources.

*Alternative plans considered.*

30. On the night of 18/19 May, the 1st, 2nd and 3rd Corps completed their withdrawal to the line of the Escaut without interference, and prepared to defend the line of the river. Soon after arrival, however, the level of the water became dangerously low, at places less than three feet deep. It looked, therefore, as if, apart from the unusually dry weather, some of the sluices in the neighbourhood of Valenciennes had been closed in order to produce inundations in the low lying ground in that area, even if at the expense of the water on the front of the B.E.F.

The enemy had, during the previous day, penetrated as far as Amiens, and rail communication with the bases was severed at that point. Communications by road and rail over the Somme at Abbeville were still holding on 19th May and the town was being placed in a state of defence with such resources as were available, mainly, units of 12th Division. However, there was little doubt that enemy armoured forces in that area, which at the time I estimated at five armoured divisions, would shortly breakthrough to the coast.

The force could then no longer be supplied through the ports south of the Somme, and the great bulk of the reserves, which were in the rearward areas, would shortly cease to be available to the force for the purposes of maintenance or replacement. Several days' reserve had, however, for some time past been maintained north of the Somme.

The prospect of securing the reinforcement of the Armoured Division had likewise become remote. I had been advised that two Armoured Brigades, of this division would disembark at Havre on 16th May, and were to concentrate at Bolbec, and I had therefore sent instructions by the hand of a staff officer to the Commander (Major-General R. Evans). He was to move the leading brigade on disembarkation with all speed to secure the crossings of the Somme west of Amiens, from Picquigny to Pont Rémy, both inclusive, with a view to the concentration of the remaining brigade behind the Somme and the move of his division to join the main body of the B.E.F. However, in the meantime, orders had been issued locally to concentrate the Division south of the Seine, and the plan to cross the Somme and join the B.E.F. proved impossible to execute. The division therefore remained in the Lines of Communication Area and never came under my effective command.

About midnight on the l8th/l9th May, General Billotte came to see me, and gave me an account of the situation as he saw it. He also told me of the measures which were being taken to restore the situation on the front of the French 9th Army, though clearly he had little hope that they would be effective. Reports from the liaison officers with French formations were likewise not encouraging; in particular I was unable to verify that the French had enough reserves at their disposal south of the gap to enable them to stage counter-attacks sufficiently strong to warrant the expectation that the gap would be closed.

Thus, in my opinion, there was an imminent danger of the forces in the north-eastern area, that is to say the French forces next to the sea, the Belgian Army, the B.E.F. and the bulk of the French Ist Army on our right, being irretrievably cut off from the main French forces in the south.

There were three alternative courses of action open to the northern forces under General Billotte: first, in the event of the gap being closed by successful counter-attacks made simultaneously from north and south it would in theory be possible to maintain the line of the Escaut, or at any rate the frontier defences, and thence southwards on one or other of the canal lines.

Secondly, there was the possibility of a withdrawal to the line of the Somme as far as its mouth. This plan had the attraction that we should be falling back on our lines of communication and if it was successful would not entail the abandonment of large quantities of equipment. It would obviously be unwelcome to the Belgians who would be faced with the alternatives of withdrawing with us and abandoning Belgian soil, fighting on a perimeter of their own, or seeking an armistice.

So far as I am aware, the French High Command had never suggested such a movement up to that date and it is doubtful whether even had they decided on immediate withdrawal as soon as the French 9th Army front on the Meuse had been penetrated, there would ever have been sufficient time for the troops in the north to conform.

Thirdly there was the possibility of withdrawal north-westwards or northwards towards the Channel ports, making use of the successive river and canal lines, and of holding a defensive perimeter there, at any rate sufficiently long to enable the force to be withdrawn, preferably in concert with the French and Belgians. I realised that this course was in theory a last alternative, as it would involve the departure of the B.E.F. from the theatre of war at a time when the French might need all the support which Britain could give them. It involved the virtual certainty that even if the excellent port facilities at Dunkirk continued to be available, it would be necessary to abandon all the heavier guns and much of the vehicles and equipment. Nevertheless, I felt that in the circumstances there might be no other course open to me. It was therefore only prudent to consider what the adoption of such a plan might entail. On this day therefore at about 1.30 p.m. the Chief of the General Staff telephoned to the Director of Military Operations and Plans at the War Office and discussed this situation with him.

## *The Position of the French Ist Army and the British right flank reinforced.*

3I. The French Ist Army had by I9th May completed its withdrawal and was in touch with the right of Ist Corps. On the night of I9/20th May they took up positions on the line of the Escaut as far south as Bouchain; but at that point, instead of continuing to hold that river towards Cambrai (which according to my information was not held in strength by the enemy) they had drawn back westwards along the river Sensée. Thus in the quadrilateral Maulde-Valenciennes-Arleux-Douai, some nineteen miles by ten, there was assembled the bulk of the French Ist Army, amounting to three Corps of two divisions and two divisions in reserve – a total of eight divisions. The Commander of the French 3rd Corps, General de la Laurencie, remained that night in close touch with General Mason-MacFarlane, at the headquarters of Macforce.

Further west the French Cavalry Corps was assembling at Oppy, north-east of Arras.

None of these forces were being seriously pressed at this stage, but since the enemy had already penetrated so deeply further south, I felt it necessary, without more delay, to strengthen the dispositions for the defence of what had become the bastion of Arras. It was also necessary to secure crossings westwards from the right of Macforce, along the line Carvin-La Bassée.

I therefore ordered 50th Division, then in G.H.Q. reserve, to send one Infantry Brigade (25th) to take up positions on the Canal on the line La Bassée-Carvin under the command of Macforce. The remainder of the division was moved that night (19/20th) to the same area, and was thus suitably placed for the counter attack in which they took part on 21st May.

I also ordered 12th Lancers with a field battery to move to Arras and carry out necessary reconnaissances south and south-westwards, and to gain touch with the outlying portions of Petreforce.

Arras was heavily bombed for the first time on 19th May, but 23rd Division, though in an exposed position, was not seriously attacked. However, at 5 a.m., 6th Royal West Kent, of 36th Infantry Brigade, on the Canal du Nord north-west of Péronne, had been attacked by enemy tanks and had been withdrawn to Sailly on the road to Albert.

General Petre that night issued orders for 23rd Division to withdraw from the Canal du Nord to the line of the Grinchon river south of Arras to join up at La Herlière with 36th Infantry Brigade which was to hold a line thence to Doullens. 23rd Division was, however, caught by enemy aircraft when embossed and finally occupied posts on the line of the Scarpe for some six miles East of Arras.

Thus, by the evening of 19th May, the situation was somewhat relieved in that the defensive flank had begun to take shape. On the other hand, the character of the operation had now radically altered with the arrival of German troops in Amiens. The picture was now no longer that of a line bent or temporarily broken, but of a besieged fortress. To raise such a siege, a relieving force must be sent from the south and to meet this force a sortie on the part of the defenders was indicated.

## *The attack of 5th and 50th Divisions.*

32. On 20th May, the breach South of Arras deepened and widened. From indications received during the day the enemy armoured forces appeared to be directed on two main objectives; one down the valley of the Somme on Abbeville, the other by Hesdin and Montreuil, doubtless making for the Channel Ports. 12th Lancers, early in the day,

reported tanks from the direction of Cambrai approaching Arras, where they were held off by the Welsh Guards; a strong request for bomber support was therefore made through the War Office to the Air Ministry. Later in the day enemy tanks were reported to be ten miles west of Arras, and all endeavours by I2th Lancers to reach Doullens had failed. By 6 p.m. they were back on the line Arras-St. Pol.

Early in the morning General Sir Edmund Ironside, the Chief of the Imperial General

Staff arrived at G.H.Q.; he brought with him instructions from the Cabinet that the B.E.F. was to move southwards upon Amiens, attacking all enemy forces encountered and to take station on the left of the French Army. He was also to inform General Billotte and the Belgian command, making it clear to the latter that their best chance was to move that night between the B.E.F. and the coast.

Similar information was to be given by the War Office to General Georges. During the day however, it appeared that operations were actually being directed by General Weygand who later, on 23rd May, announced in a General Order that he was now Commander-in-Chief in all theatres of war.

I discussed these instructions with the C.I.G.S. at my Command Post at Wahagnies at 8.15 a.m.; I put to him my view that withdrawal to the south-westwards, however desirable in principle, was not in the circumstances practicable.

In the first place, it would involve the disengagement of seven divisions which were at the time in close contact with the enemy on the Escaut, and would be immediately followed up.

In addition to this rearguard action the B.E.F. in its retirement to the Somme would have to attack into an area already strongly occupied by the enemy armoured and mobile formations. Some of these indeed now appeared to be holding the line of the Somme whilst others were already within a short distance of the coast, and might turn northwards at any time. Thus the B.E.F. would be obliged to disengage its seven divisions in contact with the enemy, fighting a rearguard action, at the same time to attack south-westwards, and finally to break through enemy forces on the Somme. During this manoeuvre both flanks would have to be guarded.

Secondly, the administrative situation made it unlikely that sustained offensive operations could be undertaken. Communication with the bases was on the point of being interrupted. The mobile echelons of gun and small arms ammunition were full, but once they were exhausted I could not safely reckon on being able to replenish them.

Lastly, though I was not in a position to judge, I had the impression that even if I had decided to attempt this manoeuvre, neither the French Ist Army nor the Belgians would have been in a position to conform.

Nevertheless, I told the C.I.G.S. that I fully realised the importance of an attack in a southerly direction and that I already had plans in hand to counter-attack with the 5th and 50th Divisions to the south of Arras and that these divisions would be ready to attack on the following morning (2Ist May). These were the only reserves which I then had available, apart from one armoured reconnaissance brigade, and one infantry brigade of 2nd Division. To create a further reserve I had already begun negotiations with Belgian G.Q.G. for the relief of 44th Division on the Escaut, but these were not yet completed.

The C.I.G.S. agreed with this action and accompanied by the C.G.S. he left for Lens to meet Generals Billotte and Blanchard. At that interview the C.I.G.S. explained the action to be taken by 5th and 50th Divisions. General Billotte fully agreed to this plan, and said that the French would co-operate with two divisions.

On return to my headquarters, the C.I.G.S. sent a telegram to General Georges which made it clear that, in his opinion, General Billotte's Army Group would be finally cut off unless the French Ist Army made an immediate move on Cambrai or unless General Georges launched a counter-attack northwards from Péronne. My liaison officers with Generals Billotte and Blanchard conveyed a similar message from me to those commanders, making it clear that if our counter-attack was not successful the French and British Armies north of the gap would have their flank turned and could no longer remain in their present positions.

On 2Ist May I sent a formal acknowledgement of the instructions brought by the C.I.G.S. adding that, in my opinion, withdrawal to the south-west was entirely impossible until the situation had been retrieved on the front of the French Ist Army.

33. 5th Division was therefore ordered to join 50th Division in the Vimy area, and its commander, Major-General Franklyn, was placed in command of all the British troops operating in and around Arras.

Frankforce, as it was to be known, consisted of 5th and 50th Divisions (each of two brigades only), Ist Army Tank Brigade[5] (previously with Macforce) together with Petreforce and the force under O.C. I2th Lancers. Petreforce was by this time very tired and widely dispersed.

My immediate instructions to General Franklyn were to occupy the bridgeheads on the Scarpe, east of Arras and thus to relieve the remains of 23rd Division. He would then be suitably disposed to advance south and south-east of Arras on the following day in conjunction with the French.

It will be convenient to conclude the story of Frankforce here.

During the evening of 20th May, General Franklyn completed his reconnaissances for an attack on the following day to secure the line of the rivers Scarpe and Cojeul: his intention was to exploit success by moving on 22nd May to the Sensée and thence towards Bapaume and Cambrai. In these plans he had the full co-operation of General Prioux, Commander of the French Cavalry Corps, but the light mechanised divisions were much reduced in strength and probably had no more than one quarter of their tanks fit for action.

However, one of these divisions was ordered to advance on each side of Frankforce, while 12th Lancers watched the right flank on the Arras-St. Pol road. The hope was not realised, however, that the French 5th Corps would also attack southwards from Douai with two divisions in co-operation with Frankforce on the 2Ist. A conference had been arranged at 6 p.m. on the 20th at General Franklyn's headquarters but no representative from that Corps attended. Finally, at 12.30 p.m. on the 2Ist I received a letter from General Blanchard to say that the Corps Commander, General Altmeyer, thought he could move on the 22nd or the following night.

Time, however, was vital. General Franklyn adhered to his plans, and at 2 p.m. attacked with Ist Army Tank Brigade, I5Ist Infantry Brigade of 50th Division and I3th Infantry Brigade of 5th Division all under General Martel. The French Ist Light Mechanised Division co-operated, though its movements did not develop so widely to the flanks as General Franklyn had hoped.

The opposition was stronger than had been expected. Objectives for the day were reached, and in the evening there were heavy dive-bombing attacks by the enemy. Enemy tanks had been put to flight:

over 400 prisoners had been captured: a number of enemy had been killed and many transport vehicles destroyed.

The tank brigade had, however, begun to suffer severely from mechanical trouble; the tanks had been on the road continuously since they detrained at Brussels, and the mileage covered had already far exceeded the estimated life of the tracks which were now beginning to break through wear.

It was clear therefore that the attack of Frankforce would not maintain its momentum unless it was reinforced and supported by the French on its left. During 22nd May, therefore, General Franklyn held his ground, and prolonged his right flank westwards, while the French Cavalry Corps took up a position at Mont St. Eloi. All day long pressure increased round his right flank, and an observation post of I2th Lancers on Mont St. Eloi could see at one moment as many as 48 enemy tanks.

Next day (23rd May) the enemy advanced steadily north-eastwards from the high ground of the Lorette ridge, and by evening they were reconnoitring the southern outskirts of Béthune and the road from Lens to Carvin. It was clear that Frankforce was becoming dangerously hemmed in. Two roads were still available for their extrication and at about 7 p.m. I decided that there was no alternative but to withdraw Frankforce. This withdrawal had necessarily to be in an easterly direction. 5th and 50th Divisions had been engaged with the enemy all day and had inflicted very severe losses; they were now ordered to withdraw to the area around Seclin, where they would be well placed to take part in any further counter-attack to the southward which might be staged. Petreforce was withdrawn to an area north of Seclin.

Thus concluded the defence of Arras, which had been carried out by a small garrison, hastily assembled but well commanded, and determined to fight. It had imposed a valuable delay on a greatly superior enemy force against which it had blocked a vital road centre.

## 2Ist May – *The Organisation of the Canal line.*

34. The time had now come to organise, as soon as possible, the further defence of the south-western flank of the force.

The enemy advance beyond Arras had hitherto been carried out almost entirely by armoured forces, supported by motorised infantry which was doubtless increasing in numbers every day. The situation regarding the enemy's normal infantry divisions was still uncertain. It was therefore of first importance to reinforce the organisation of the line of the canals from the Escaut to La Bassée, and to continue it to St. Omer and the sea. These canals offered the only anti-tank obstacle on this flank. They were, however, crossed by numerous bridges, many of which had already been prepared for demolition by our own engineers under my Engineer-in-Chief (Major-General R.P. Pakenham-Walsh), the Commander of Macforce, and the French Commanders of the fortified sectors of Lille and Flanders (Généraux de Brigade Bertschi and Barthélémy).

It had been proved that even weak garrisons holding important road centres, such as Arras and Doullens, were of much value in imposing delay, for the initial advances of the enemy always followed the main roads. It was therefore decided to continue the policy of organising such "stops," not only along the canals but at all possible centres whether north or south of the canal line.

Macforce, which had been formed on 17th May, had been augmented on 18th and 19th by 138th Infantry Brigade (46th Division) which went into line on the canal between Raches and Carvin, and on the following day 139th Infantry Brigade of the same division joined the force. On 21st May 127th Infantry Brigade rejoined the 42nd Division and the sector from Millonfosse to St. Amand was handed over to the French.

Already on 20th May, I had ordered Major-General Curtis, Commanding 46th Division, to take command of the sector of the canals between Aire and Carvin. General Curtis' force was known as Polforce, and was to consist of four battalions of 46th Division, 25th Infantry Brigade of 50th Division (in line between La Bassée and Carvin) and one field battery, together with a number of engineer and other units of G.H.Q. troops which had been moving northwards and were collected on the Canal. It had originally been intended that part of this force should hold St. Pol, Frévent and Divion, but the railway trains in which were the remaining three battalions of 46th Division failed to reach that town in time and remained south of the Somme. The defence of these localities south of the Canal had therefore to be abandoned.

Further to the north-west the defence of the canal line was being organised by Brigadier C.M. Usher, Commander of X Lines of

Communication Sub-area. On 22nd May he reported that the enemy had already reached the left bank of the river Aa between Gravelines and St. Omer. 23rd Division had been ordered to move to this area and its leading battalion (6th Green Howards) arrived at Gravelines. Brigadier Usher therefore held the right bank of the river from St. Omer to Gravelines with this battalion and five batteries of heavy artillery used as infantry, in conjunction with certain French troops of the Secteur Fortifié des Flandres.

The front of Macforce was covered by the French, 3rd, 4th and 5th Corps, who were still in their quadrilateral on the line of the Escaut and the Sensèe. Here, however, information was frequently lacking and could only be obtained by reconnaissance.

Thus, by 22nd May, the canal line was occupied in the sense that the whole of the length of 85miles from the sea at Gravelines to Millonfosse (West of St. Amand) was divided into sectors for each of which a British commander was responsible. The total strength of the troops on the Canal line did not on this day exceed 10,000 men, and the number of anti-tank weapons was barely adequate to cover all the crossing places: certainly there could be no question of being able to keep an effective watch against small parties of infantry crossing the canal between the bridges. The barges, however, had almost all been moved away or at any rate to the bank furthest from the enemy, and bridges were fast being prepared for demolition.

## 21st May – *The Situation on the Belgian Front.*

35. On 21st May at 4.45 p.m. I met the three Corps Commanders. I told them what had happened on the southern flank and how, in order to take the initiative and encourage the French 1st Army to do likewise, I had gone to the length of committing practically the whole of my reserve.

From the Corps Commanders I learned that the line was thinly held and that attacks had taken place at several points. At Petegem on the front of 44th Division the enemy had secured a bridgehead 1,000 yards deep on a front of 3,000 yards, and at the junction with the French near Maulde on the front of 1st Division a number of enemy had crossed the river disguised as refugees, but had been detected and driven out with the bayonet. The Corps Commanders all felt that they could not now hold on for more than twenty-four hours. We discussed a withdrawal to our old frontier defences, where advantage could be taken of the existing blockhouses and trenches, and of the anti-tank ditch. This move would have little effect on the French on our right since it would pivot on the junction point, where the Escaut crossed the frontier, but would seriously affect the Belgians, who now held the line of the Escaut from Audenarde to Ghent and of the canal from Ghent to the sea at Terneuzen.

I had also to consider the pressing need to stiffen the defence of the canal line westwards to Gravelines and to form a new reserve to replace the divisions now committed to counter-attacks southward from Arras.

A provisional decision was therefore reached to withdraw to the frontier defences on the night of 22nd/23rd May, details being left until I had reached agreement with the French and the Belgians.

General Weygand had visited General Billotte during the day and the latter indicated that an attack was being planned for the following day (22nd May), northwards from the direction of Roye, with the object of closing the gap. At 8 p.m. on 2Ist May I went to Ypres where in the Burgomaster's office I met H.M. the King of the Belgians and General Billotte. There were also present General Van Overstraeten, General Champon, the head of the French Mission with Belgian G.Q.G., General Pownall and others.

I explained the situation which was developing on the Escaut about Audenarde, and the difficulty of maintaining positions there since the water in the river was so low as no longer to form an obstacle. It was then agreed that on the night of 22nd/23rd May the Escaut should be abandoned and that the Allied armies should occupy a line from Maulde northwards to Halluin, thence along the Lys to Courtrai and Ghent.

I discussed the possibility of reserves. It appeared that the available divisions of the French Ist Army were all too tired to take part in offensive operations in the immediate future. It was therefore agreed that the French should take over a further sector of the defensive positions northwards from Maulde, so that the 2nd and 48th Divisions could be withdrawn into reserve on leaving the line of the Escaut. The French took up these positions on 22nd May. On the north, 44th Division on withdrawal from the Escaut were to hold the sector

Halluin-Courtrai, but it was hoped that a Belgian formation would relieve them on the night of 23rd/24th May.

When these moves were complete the Allied line would run slightly west of north to Halluin, and then almost at right angles, north-eastwards along the Lys. It was evident that sooner or later the Belgian army would have to swing back to a line in rear, pivoting on their right of Halluin. Accordingly at the end of the conference General Billotte asked the King of the Belgians whether if he were forced to withdraw he would fall back on to the line of the Yser. His Majesty agreed, though evidently with some regret, that no alternative line existed.

On return from the meeting, orders were issued to implement these decisions, and that evening I moved my command post to the Château de Premesques, midway between Armentières and Lille.

## *The final severance of the L. of C. and the investment of Boulogne.*

36. During the 21st May the enemy penetration into the rearward areas increased and communication across the Somme was finally severed. Since the 17th May the Commander of the Lines of Communication Area (Major-General P. de Fonblanque) had been taking energetic steps for its defence, in so far as it was possible with the few and scattered troops available.

These consisted, apart from Armoured Division and 51st Division now returning from the Saar, of those portions of 12th and 46th Divisions (some nine battalions in all) which could not be despatched forward, three unbrigaded infantry battalions and the contents of the reinforcement depôts, together with troops of the Auxiliary Military Pioneer Corps and of the administrative services.

On 23rd May, however, the War Office appointed Lieutenant-General Sir Henry Karslake to command the defences on the Lines of Communication and I was not concerned in the operations which ensued. Nevertheless, I did not immediately abandon hope of the Armoured Division breaking through, and I urged the War Office to use their best endeavours to this end and to prevent its being used piecemeal in local operations at the request of the French Command.

At about 3.30 p.m. on the 21st May, I received information that an enemy column of all arms was approaching Boulogne. The rear element of G.H.Q., consisting largely of the Adjutant-General's Branch and of headquarters of Services, which had been sent to that town on 17th and 18th May, had been moved to Wimereux on 20th May as a result of enemy bombing.

All possible steps had been taken to put Boulogne in a state of defence with the troops available, consisting of labour units and the personnel of rest camps. On 19th May, an endeavour was made to bring up troops from beyond the Somme, to hold the line of the Canche; but the time for this was past and the troops could not get beyond Abbeville. The hospitals in the Etaples area were now evacuated, and on 21st May a party of Engineers, supervised by my Director of Works, Brigadier W. Cave-Browne, demolished most of the bridges over the Canche.

As soon as the news of this new threat was received, the War Office was asked for bomber support, which was at once forthcoming. Enemy tanks were located and bombed at Hesdin and Fruges, but no good targets were obtained on the coast road. The War Office was also asked to send a detachment of Royal Marines for the defence of Boulogne but had already done so. Early on the 22nd May, 20th Guards Brigade (Brigadier W.A.F.L. Fox-Pitt) of two battalions with an anti-tank battery landed, thus establishing the defence of the town and enabling those troops who were not required for the defence to be evacuated in good order.

By the evening of 22nd May, the enemy armoured forces were within nine miles of Calais. Boulogne was now isolated and its final evacuation was carried out under the orders of the War Office, being completed on the night of 23/24th May.

### *The Administrative Situation.*

37. During the whole of this period I had been kept in the closest touch with the administrative situation by the Quarter-Master-General (Lieutenant-General W.G. Lindsell). Up to 16th May the administrative arrangements which formed part of Plan D had worked well, and although enemy air action steadily intensified during the period, there was no serious interference with the maintenance of the force.

On 17th May, however, the Quarter-Master-General decided, in view of the situation south of Arras, to discontinue the use of the railway from the regulating station at Abancourt via Amiens and Arras, and to switch all traffic via Eu and Abbeville to Béthune. He also ordered forward every available trainload of ammunition to the Hazebrouck area.

On 19th May, directly after the C.G.S. had spoken to the War Office as to the possibility of enforced withdrawal, the Q.M.G. telephoned to the War Office to discuss the opening of new bases. On the same day, one of his staff officers left for London to arrange an emergency shipment programme for supplies and stores to the ports of Boulogne, Calais and Dunkirk. It was to prove none too soon, for the railway at Abbeville was cut on 21st May. A new plan had to be put into operation at once for the maintenance of the force north of the Somme, estimated at 250,000 men and requiring a daily lift of ammunition, supplies and petrol, of some 2,000 tons.

The petrol situation, fortunately, gave no cause for concern since, although the dumps forward of the Somme had been destroyed on evacuation, together with a large civil storage plant near Douai, there still remained a large army bulk filling station near Lille.

The supply situation was however, bad, and on 21st May, Corps had only three days R.A.S.C. supplies in the forward area. Matters might, at any time, have become serious had it not been for the success of the measures taken between 23rd and 26th May, to organise the supplies in Lille belonging to the Expeditionary Force Institutes and to civilian firms.

The decision to maintain the force through the northern ports was finally taken on 21st May and the headquarters of a Base Sub-Area established at Dunkirk, together with a section of Q.M.G's staff, in close touch with the British and French Naval authorities.

Rail communication in the area was by now precarious, and plans were worked out on the basis of establishing dumps, one in each Corps area, which could be wholly maintained by road. The position was, by this time, greatly complicated by the numbers of improvised forces which the quickly changing situation had made necessary: most of these, like the three divisions for pioneer duties, had no proper administrative echelons. Some were within reach of Corps, but others were not and these had to be dependent on fortuitous sources of supply, or else live for a time on the country.

The situation had grown even worse by 22nd May, when the ports at both Boulogne and Calais were out of action, and the greater part of the Railhead Mechanical Transport Companies had been captured. Furthermore a reconnaissance of Ostend had shewn that the port could not be worked for military requirements at short notice. A certain amount of rations and small arms ammunition was sent by air up to 23rd May, but from then onwards it became impossible for aircraft to land. On 23rd May therefore, on the advice of the Q.M.G., I decided to place the B.E.F. on half rations.

Dunkirk, though its water supply was destroyed, remained available for unloading supplies till 26th May, but constant air raids imposed a well nigh unbearable strain on the stevedore battalions. However, they remained at duty until, in the end, all the quays and cranes were put out of action. Thereafter supplies could only be landed on the beaches. Lighters arrived to embark troops loaded with a portion of supplies, ammunition and water, and these were unloaded and distributed by Corps. The delivery of supplies to Corps was maintained, albeit irregularly, up till 30th May when the last convoy went forward from the supply depôt on the beach at La Panne.

By 20th May all the General Hospitals had been cut off from the forward area and improvised arrangements had to be made for the evacuation of casualties. Some of the Casualty Clearing Stations had to be diverted from their normal function and used as Hospitals. Hospital ships continued to berth at Dunkirk till the night 31st May/Ist June and casualties were evacuated to them by road and by rail. Ambulance trains were running as late as 26th May.

### *Further proposals for an attack Southwards.*

38. On 23rd May the French Ist Army pushed forward some elements southwards from Douai. On the same day, 5th and 50th Divisions, which had attacked two days before, were themselves being attacked on the Scarpe and had already lost most of their tanks through mechanical wear.

The threat to their rear was increasing hourly and they were thus unable to make any further advance or to assist the French, except in so far as they were able to engage troops who might otherwise have threatened the right flank of the French advance. The French approached the outskirts of Cambrai meeting with little opposition but withdrew later on being attacked by dive-bombers.

On the same day I received a copy of a telegram from the Prime Minister to M. Reynaud, which read as follows:-

"Strong enemy armoured forces have cut communications of Northern Armies. Salvation of these Armies can only be obtained by immediate execution of Weygand's plan. I demand that French Commanders in North and South and Belgian G.Q.G. be given most stringent orders to carry this out and turn defeat into victory. Time vital as supplies are short."

I was not sure whether the situation which was developing for the allied armies in the north could be accurately appreciated except on the spot. I therefore telegraphed to Sir John Dill asking him to fly over that day.

The next day, however (24th May), the Prime Minister again conferred with M. Reynaud and General Weygand in Paris, and I received the following telegram from the Secretary of State describing that conference:-

"Both are convinced that Weygand's plan is still capable of execution and only in its execution has hope of restoring the situation. Weygand reports French VII Army is advancing successfully and has captured Péronne, Albert and Amiens. While realising fully dangers and difficulties of your position which has been explained to Weygand it is essential that you should make every endeavour to co-operate in his plan. Should however situation on your communications make this at any time impossible you should inform us so that we can inform French and make Naval and Air arrangements to assist you should you have to withdraw on the northern coast."

It will be noted that, according to the telegram General Weygand informed the Prime Minister that Péronne, Albert and Amiens had been recaptured. It later transpired that this information was inaccurate.

The Weygand plan, as it came to be known, was for a counter offensive on a large scale.

From the north the French Ist Army and the B.E.F. were to attack south-west at the earliest possible moment with about eight divisions and with the Belgian Cavalry Corps supporting the British right.

The newly formed Third French Army Group was reported to be

organising a line on the Somme from Amiens to Péronne with a view to attacking northwards.

A new cavalry Corps was assembling south of the Somme near Neufchatel and was to operate on the line of the Somme west of Amiens, in touch with the British Armoured Division on their left.

I fully appreciated the importance of attacking early before the enemy could bring up his infantry in strength, but facts had to be faced. The 5th and 50th Divisions were on this day (23rd May) still closely engaged with the enemy, and 2nd, 44th and 48th Divisions, would not become available for a further 48 hours, since the French and the Belgians, though they had arranged their relief, could not complete it earlier. The ammunition immediately available to the B.E.F. was of the order of 300 rounds per gun and with communications cut with the main base, the prospect of receiving any further supply was remote.

The French light mechanised divisions and our own armoured units had already suffered serious losses in tanks which could not be replaced. Such information as I had received of the Belgian cavalry did not lead me to take an optimistic view of the prospect of their being able to engage, at short notice, in a battle forty miles away and on French soil.

Experience had already shown the vital importance of close co-ordination of the allied armies in any operation. General Billotte had been appointed the co-ordinator at the conference at Mons on I2th May, but in practice, the measure of co-ordination fell far short of what was required if the movements of the three allied armies were to be properly controlled.

Except for the issue of orders to retire from the Dyle (obtained only after I had sent Major-General Eastwood to General Billotte's headquarters to represent my views), I received no written orders from the French First Group of Armies, though at the meetings between General Billotte and myself which took place from time to time, we always found ourselves in complete agreement. Unfortunately, however, General Billotte had been seriously, and as it turned out, fatally injured in a motor accident returning from the conference which he and I had attended at Ypres on the night of 2Ist May. General Blanchard succeeded him in command of the French First Group of Armies, and presumably succeeded to the function of co-ordination although this was never officially confirmed.

I telegraphed to the Secretary of State pointing out that co-ordination was essential with armies of three different nations, and that I personally could not undertake any measure of co-ordination in the forthcoming operations as I was already actively engaged on my Eastern and Southern fronts and also threatened on my Lines of Communication.

Nevertheless, I saw General Blanchard and proposed to him that to implement our part of the Weygand plan, we should stage an attack southwards with two British divisions, one French division and the French Cavalry Corps. So far as we were concerned the attack could not take place till the 26th at the earliest owing to the reliefs which were in progress, and the need to assemble 5th and 50th Divisions. I also asked General Blanchard to enquire from G.Q.G. how such an operation could be synchronised with the attack from the line of the Somme which was said to be in process of preparation. These negotiations, as will be seen, were later continued by Sir Ronald Adam on my behalf. I emphasised, both to the Secretary of State and to General Blanchard, that the principal effort must come from the south, and that the operation of the northern forces could be nothing more than a sortie.

I never received any information from any source as to the exact location of our own or enemy forces on the far side of the gap; nor did I receive any details or timings of any proposed attack from that direction.

### *23rd May – Further development of the Canal line.*

39. On 23rd May the organisation was continued of "stops" behind the Canal line.

At Hazebrouck, where the organisation of defences had been begun on 21st May by the staff of the Major-General R.A. at G.H.Q. the garrison was now about 300 strong and included eighteen French light tanks and some Belgian machine gunners.

Cassel was occupied by 13/18th Hussars, less one squadron, and on the same afternoon (23rd) Brigadier Usher's force took over the defence of Bergues.

On the night of 22/23rd May the withdrawal to the frontier defences had been carried out. The French had taken over the sector northwards from Maulde and the right boundary of the B.E.F. was now Bourghelles-Seclin both inclusive to the French. This change of boundary did not however affect the dispositions which the B.E.F. had taken on the Canal line by which the rear of the French positions was protected.

On the left of the B.E.F. the Belgians, who had previously agreed to relieve the 44th Division after withdrawal to the Lys on the night of 23rd/24th May, ordered one of their divisions to occupy the sector Halluin-Courtrai on the night of 22nd/23rd May. 44th Division was concentrated in G.H.Q. reserve on the morning of 23rd May.

On the right, 2nd and 48th Divisions passed through the French on the night of 22nd/23rd May and also concentrated in G.H.Q. reserve.

These moves left only four divisions on the frontier defences and made it possible to withdraw the headquarters and Corps troops of 3rd Corps for employment on the Canal line where they were badly needed. This was done at 4 p.m. on 23rd May, leaving Ist Corps with 42nd and Ist Divisions and 2nd Corps with 3rd and 4th Divisions.

2nd, 44th and 48th Divisions came under 3rd Corps and that night made a march westwards. I had decided to employ 2nd and 44th Divisions on the Canal line facing west, but their move required a further twenty-four hours to complete.

Meanwhile the canal defences required stiffening as much as possible. And accordingly, Polforce temporarily assumed control of the whole front between St. Omer and Raches, and two regiments of 2nd Armoured Reconnaissance Brigade were placed under its command. Polforce also undertook the responsibility for demolitions as far north as Watten including no less than 43 bridges.

The sector eastward from Raches was now handed over to the French, the British demolition parties being left on the bridges at the disposal of French 3rd Corps.

Macforce, now comprising four field batteries, half an anti-tank battery and one battalion, withdrew from the line Carvin-Raches on 23rd May and was moved to a rendezvous in the eastern end of the Forest of Nieppe where it was joined by Headquarters and one regiment of Ist Armoured Reconnaissance Brigade. I39th Infantry Brigade (46th

Division) continued to hold the sector from Carvin to Raches until 26th May.

The situation on the canal line deteriorated during 23rd May and the enemy established bridgeheads at Aire, at St. Omer (which seems to have changed hands twice during the day) and near Watten. His tanks were reported as harbouring in the forest of Clairmarais, and during the day his armoured fighting vehicles came within three miles of Hazebrouck. By the evening, however, these movements had been checked and steps taken to keep the enemy out of the Forest of Nieppe.

The enemy had also been active that day on the canal line at Béthune, where they had been driven off and had then moved towards Carvin. Here the defenders had been reinforced by further artillery under C.R.A. 2nd Division (Brigadier. C.B. Findlay), and the crossings were firmly held.

On 23rd May Calais was finally isolated. Its garrison had been reinforced under the orders of the War Office, by 30th Infantry Brigade (Brigadier C. Nicholson) and 3rd battalion Royal Tank Regiment – a cruiser tank regiment. I had intended to move the latter within the canal line, but it was already too late. After two attempts they were driven back into Calais, with the exception of three tanks which eventually reached Dunkirk by way of Gravelines. The remainder of the gallant defence of Calais was conducted under the orders of the War Office. It was finally concluded on the night of 26/27th May.

Information received at this time indicated that two enemy armoured divisions were converging on Calais and two more, supported by a motorised. S.S. (Schutz-Staffel) division, on St. Omer. A fifth armoured division appeared to be moving on Béthune.

## 24th May. Preparations for counter attack and strengthening of canal defences.

40. During 24th May, I had simultaneously to prepare for a counter-attack southwards on the 26th and also to press forward with the strengthening of the canal line.

To make the detailed arrangements for the counter-attack I appointed the Commander of the 3rd Corps, Lieutenant-General Sir Ronald Adam, who, on my behalf, continued negotiations with General

Blanchard, and with the Commander of the French 5th Corps, General Altmeyer.

The final plan was for a counter attack with three French and two British divisions under the command of General Altmeyer. As a first stage, on the evening of 26th May, bridgeheads were to be established south of the Scarpe, and the main attack was to start the following morning, with the objective Plouvain-Marquion-Cambrai. Sir Ronald Adam with three divisions (two British and one French) was to advance east of the Canal du Nord, and General Altmeyer with two French divisions to the west of the Canal du Nord, his right being covered by the French Cavalry Corps. This attack was never carried out for reasons which will presently appear.[6]

On the same day, I issued orders to dissolve the various improvised forces on the Canal line, and their units were absorbed by the formations in the areas of which they now were. I appointed Major-General Eastwood[7] to take command of the defences on the Canal line, and he assumed command early on 25th May.

The position on the Canal line was considerably strengthened during 24th May. 44th Division began to move into the line between the forest of Clairmarais and Aire, with 2nd Division on its left between Aire and La Bassée, and 46th Division (lately Polforce) from La Bassée to Raches. It was not till the evening however that 2nd and 44th Divisions gained contact with the enemy and for most of the day the defence of the sector still remained under the Commanders of Macforce and Polforce.

Fighting of a somewhat confused character went on for most of the day in and south of the Forest of Nieppe, and the enemy also began heavy bombing and shelling of Cassel. The remainder of Macforce, which included field and anti-tank artillery, was therefore sent to reinforce the I3/I8th Hussars.

48th Division (with under its command part of 23rd Division in the area Gravelines-St.Omer) was ordered to send one infantry brigade to Dunkirk and one to Cassel and Hazebrouck. I45th Infantry Brigade completed its relief of the improvised garrisons of the two latter places on 25th May, but General Thorne found that the French had already made complete dispositions for Dunkirk, and had informed the British Base Commandant. He therefore decided to send I44th Infantry

Brigade to Bergues and Wormhoudt. He established his H.Q. at Bergues, which he rightly regarded as the vital point of defence.

## *The French reinforce Dunkirk.*

4I. The local defences of Dunkirk, in accordance with French practice, were under the Admiral du Nord, Admiral Abrial, whose command included Boulogne, Calais and Dunkirk. Under his authority the command of military forces in these areas was assumed on 24th May by Général de Corps d'Armée Fagalde, commanding the French I6th Corps which up to now had been fighting on the left of the Belgian Army.

The French defences of Dunkirk were based on the peace time organisation of the Secteur Fortifié des Flandres, and extended only as far as the Belgian frontier. They comprised an inner and an outer sector, the inner on the line of the old Mardyck Canal to Spyker, thence by Bergues to the frontier and so to the sea; the outer on the line of the river Aa to St. Omer thence by Cassel and Steenvoorde to the frontier. General Fagalde had at his disposal certain regional troops in numbers equivalent to a weak division, who were located in the outer sector from Gravelines to the Forest of Clairmarais and whose dispositions had been roughly co-ordinated with those of Brigadier Usher. About this time the 68th French Division arrived at Dunkirk from Belgium and took over the inner sector.

On the 24th and 25th May the British posts on the river Aa were taken over by the French, who also began to operate the inundations, which formed part of the defence scheme of Dunkirk and extended each side of Bergues and as far as the Belgian frontier north of the Bergues-Furnes canal.

## *25th May – Attacks on the Canal Line and on the Belgian Army.*

42. On 25th May, enemy activity intensified. Two enemy Corps were reported to be attacking the French in the area Denain-Bouchain; the enemy was also across the canal at St. Venant, and was developing the bridgeheads between that place and Aire and also at St. Omer, whilst further north the situation on the river Aa was still obscure.

At about 7 a.m. on 25th May, news was received that in the late evening of 24th May the enemy had attacked the Belgian 4th Corps on the Lys with a force reported to be of four divisions, supported by tanks. The attack penetrated to a depth of 1½ miles on a front of 13 miles between Menin and Desselghem.

It was fast becoming a matter of vital importance to keep open our line of communication to the coast through a corridor which was hourly narrowing. It was no longer possible to count on using the main road Estaires-Cassel-Dunkirk, while the news which had just been received made it certain that before long, the whole area east of the Yser canal would be in the hands of the enemy, since there was, in fact, no satisfactory defensive position between the Lys and the Yser canal. There seemed, therefore, to be a serious risk of the Belgian right becoming separated from the British left at Menin, and of the Belgian Army being forced to fall back in a northerly, rather than in a westerly direction. I considered it vitally urgent to prolong the British front without delay northwards to Ypres, along the old Ypres-Comines canal, now practically dry, and round Ypres itself to the line of the Yser canal.

As an immediate step, 12th Lancers were sent off early on 25th to watch the left flank of 2nd Corps on the Lys, and gain touch with the right flank of the Belgians.

The remaining infantry brigade of 48th Division (143rd) was later placed under 2nd Corps, and a pioneer battalion sent to begin preparations for the defence of Ypres in case Belgian measures for the purpose should prove inadequate.

The Belgians had at this time one division in reserve between Menin and Ypres, and this was ordered to counter-attack at 2 p.m. However it is doubtful whether it was found possible ever to launch this counter-attack. Orders were also issued for the Belgian 1st Corps to come into line on the right of their 4th Corps between Ghelewe and Ledeghem; this move was carried out on the 26th May.

Sir John Dill (who had now become C.I.G.S.) and whom I had asked to visit me, arrived on the morning of 25th May, and I explained the position to him. He then telegraphed to the Prime Minister and to the Secretary of State, that there could be no disguising the seriousness of the situation. He added that in his opinion the proposed counter-attack to the south could not be an important affair in view of the enemy attacks which had penetrated the Belgian defences.

General Blanchard arrived during Sir John Dill's visit and took part in our discussions.

During the day the Belgians continued to withdraw in a north-westerly direction under enemy pressure. Reports also indicated that a fresh enemy attack would take place next day on the northern end of the Lys position.

## OPERATIONS – THIRD PHASE
### (26th-31st MAY)

*The decision taken, in agreement with the French, to withdraw behind the Lys. H.M. Government authorises withdrawal to the coast. The Dunkirk perimeter organised by Sir Ronald Adam. The Belgians ask for an armistice. General Blanchard at first determines to remain in position but later French 3rd and Cavalry Corps withdraw to Dunkirk. Occupation of perimeter completed. Problems of embarkation of British and French troops. Withdrawal of 2nd and 3rd Corps. G.H.Q. closes and C.-in-C. embarks for England.*

**The decision to Withdraw.**

43. By 6 p.m. that night (25th May) I was convinced that the steps I had taken to secure my left flank would prove insufficient to meet the growing danger in the north. The pattern of the enemy pincer attack was becoming clearer. One movement from the south-west on Dunkirk had already developed and was being held; the counterpart was now developing on the Belgian front.

The gap between the British left and the Belgian right, which had been threatening the whole day, might at any time become impossible to close: were this to happen, my last hope of reaching the coast would be gone. At this time, it will be recalled, I had no reserves beyond a single cavalry regiment, and the two divisions (5th and 50th) already earmarked for the attack southwards.

The French Ist Army, which was not affected in the same way as the B.E.F. by the situation which was developing on the Belgian front, had, it will be remembered, agreed to provide three divisions and the Cavalry Corps for this attack. Therefore, even if no British divisions could be made available, the possibility of carrying out the operation would not be entirely precluded. I did realise however that the French were unlikely to take the offensive unless British support was forthcoming.

Even so, however, the situation on my northern flank was deteriorating so rapidly that I was convinced that there was no alternative but to occupy, as quickly as troops could be made available, the line of the Ypres-Comines canal and the positions covering Ypres. I therefore issued orders to 50th Division to join 2nd Corps at once, and shortly afterwards I ordered 5th Division to follow. 2nd Corps placed 5th Division on its left flank northwards from Halluin along the Ypres-Comines canal with 50th Division on its left around Ypres. At this time also, the greater part of the medium and heavy artillery of Ist and 2nd Corps was grouped under 2nd Corps, and the successful defence of the positions on the Ypres-Comines canal and around Ypres, which was maintained during the next three days; was greatly assisted by these artillery units, which remained in action till they had fired all their ammunition.

The Commander of 3rd Corps, who was no longer required to take part in the attack southwards, was now ordered to take over the command of the front from St. Omer to Raches from Major-General Eastwood, whom he relieved on 26th May.

I immediately communicated my decision to the headquarters of the French First Group of Armies, but I was unable to get into personal touch with General Blanchard that evening as he was visiting the Belgian G.Q.G. at Bruges. However, I went to see General Blanchard at his headquarters at Attiches early next morning (26th May), at a moment when the enemy was attacking at Carvin and had penetrated the front of a North African Division near Bois d'Epinoy. I found that General Blanchard also feared the collapse of the Belgian Army and felt that the time for a counter attack southwards was past. Indeed he had already decided that the situation on both flanks made it necessary to withdraw.

After an hour's discussion, we arrived at a joint plan for the withdrawal of the main bodies behind the line of the Lys. These arrangements were subject to there being no further deterioration in the Belgian situation.

With this decision, there vanished the last opportunity for a sortie. The layout of the B.E.F. was now beginning to take its final shape. Starting from what could be described as a normal situation with Allied troops on the right and left, there had developed an ever lengthening defensive right flank. This had then become a semi-circular line, with both flanks resting on the sea, manned by British, French and Belgians. Later the position became a corridor in shape. The southern end of this corridor was blocked by the French Ist Army; and each side was manned, for the greater part of its length, by British troops. Next to the sea were French troops on the west, and French and Belgian troops on the eastern flank.

The immediate problem was to shorten this perimeter. British and French forces were together holding a front of 128 miles of which 97 miles were held by British troops, though some sectors were held jointly with the French. The virtual closing of Dunkirk as a port of entry was making the supply situation ever more difficult, and the ammunition situation permitted only of very restricted expenditure.

## *The Plan for Withdrawal.*

44. Later, on 26th May, I discussed the plan for withdrawal with the Corps Commanders, and issued orders for the operation in accordance with the agreement reached with General Blanchard that morning. The plan, as agreed with the French First Group of Armies, envisaged the reservation of certain roads for the exclusive use of the B.E.F. In fact, however, French troops and transport continued to use them, and this added very considerably to the difficulties of the withdrawal of British troops. The roads were few and for the most part narrow, and for the next three days they were badly congested with marching troops and horsed transport of French formations, and with refugees.

On the night 26th/27th May, Ist and 2nd Corps, leaving rearguards in the frontier defences, were to swing back to the old divisional reserve position with their right at Fort Sainghin (5 miles south-east of Lille), while the French prolonged this line from Thumeries to the canal at Pont-à-Vendin, linking up there with 2nd Division. The following night (27th/28th May), main bodies were to withdraw behind the Lys, leaving rearguards on the Deule canal up to its junction with the Lys at Deulemont: these rearguards were to stay there until the next night

(28th/29th May). The immediate effect of these dispositions would be to shorten the total perimeter by some 58 miles, but on the other hand I had to face the possibility of having to occupy the front from Ypres to the sea, some 25 miles long, which was still the responsibility of the Belgian Army.

There remained the question of the future. I had not so far discussed with General Blanchard a further withdrawal to the sea. However, the possibility could not have been absent from his mind; nor was it absent from mine, for, although up to now no instructions had been given authorising me to undertake such an operation, I had, as I have said, foreseen the possibility of such a move being forced upon us.

I returned from the conference at General Blanchard's headquarters at about 10.30 a.m. on 26th May to find a telegram from the Secretary of State which read:-

> ... "I have had information all of which goes to show that French offensive from Somme cannot be made in sufficient strength to hold any prospect of functioning with your Allies in the North. Should this prove to be the case you will be faced with a situation in which the safety of the B.E.F. will predominate. In such conditions only course open to you may be to fight your way back to West where all beaches and ports east of Gravelines will be used for embarkation. Navy will provide fleet of ships and small boats and R.A.F. would give full support. As withdrawal may have to begin very early preliminary plans should be urgently prepared ... Prime Minister is seeing M. Reynaud to-morrow afternoon when whole situation will be clarified including attitude of French to the possible move. ...."

I replied that a plan for withdrawal north-westward had been agreed with the French that morning; I added that the news from the Belgian front was disquieting, and concluded by saying:-

> ... "I must not conceal from you that a great part of the B.E.F. and its equipment will inevitably be lost even in best circumstances."

Later in the day, I had a further telegram from the War Office which read as follows:-

">... Prime Minister had conversation M. Reynaud this afternoon. Latter fully explained to him the situation and resources French Army. It is clear that it will not be possible for French to deliver attack on the south in sufficient strength to enable them to effect junction with Northern Armies. In these circumstances no course open to you but to fall back upon coast.... M. Reynaud communicating General Weygand and latter will no doubt issue orders in this sense forthwith. You are now authorised to operate towards coast forthwith in conjunction with French and Belgian Armies."

## *The Situation of the Belgian Army.*

45. The situation on the Belgian front was causing me ever increasing anxiety. At the conference at Ypres on the evening of 2Ist May, His Majesty the King of the Belgians had agreed that, if forced to abandon the positions on the Lys, he would withdraw to the Yser, maintaining touch with the left of the B.E.F. Now, however, signs were not wanting that the Belgian Army were being forced to withdraw northwards and away from the Yser canal. If so, the task of defending the whole line as far as the sea appeared likely to fall on ourselves and the French, as actually did happen.

Admiral of the Fleet Sir Roger Keyes, who had been carrying out liaison duties with H.M. the King of the Belgians since the operations began, came to G.H.Q. on the morning of 26th May, and I expressed to him my earnest hope that the Belgian Army would fall back towards the Yser. Sir Roger Keyes took this message back to the Belgian G.Q.G. at Bruges, where he saw His Majesty. Later he telegraphed to me saying that the Belgians would do their best, but that His Majesty considered that the only method of avoiding immediate and complete disaster was a strong and immediate counter offensive between the Lys and the Escaut. Such an operation was, however, quite out of the question since, now that 5th and 50th Divisions had been committed, my reserves were again reduced to one weak cavalry regiment.

The indication that the Belgian Army would withdraw northwards and not to the Yser, was confirmed in a note, a copy of which I received, sent on 26th May by General Michiels, the Chief of the Staff of the Belgian Army, to General Neissens, head of the Belgian Mission with G.H.Q.

This note contained the following passage:-

... "To-day, 26th May the Belgian Army is being attacked with extreme violence on the front Menin-Nevele,[8] and since the battle is now spreading to the whole of the area of Eecloo, the lack of Belgian reserves makes it impossible to extend our boundaries, which were notified yesterday, further to the right.

We must therefore, with regret, say that we have no longer any forces available to fill the gap in the direction of Ypres.

As regards the withdrawal to the Yser the idea must be ruled out since it would destroy our fighting units more quickly than the battle now in progress, and this without loss to the enemy."

On receipt of this information, on the morning of 26th May, I asked the Secretary of State to bring strong pressure on the Belgian Government to withdraw their Army westwards and to maintain touch with the B.E.F. I also communicated in the same sense to Sir Roger Keyes, but his reply never reached my Headquarters.

### *26th May – The Southern and Western fronts.*

46. On the remainder of the front 26th May was marked by heavy air action everywhere. The enemy attack on the French North African division at Carvin which was in progress when I visited General Blanchard at Attiches, was driven back by the prompt action of two battalions of 50th Division which were deployed behind the French troops. 2nd and 44th Divisions reacted against the enemy and both succeeded in advancing some distance westwards from Merville and Hazebrouck respectively towards the Canal.

Further north, the French had completed the relief of all our troops on the river Aa from St. Momelin northwards but had themselves begun in places to withdraw towards the Mardyck Canal. It therefore became

Field Marshal John Standish Surtees Prendergast Vereker, 6th Viscount Gort, was given command of the British Expeditionary Force in September 1939. John Gort had fought in the First World War, during which he was Mentioned in Despatches eight times, was awarded the DSO with two Bars and received the Victoria Cross for his actions at the Battle of the Canal du Nord in September 1918. In 1939 the BEF had been placed under the orders of the French high command but when Gort saw the rapid collapse of the French forces in the second week of May 1940, he took the bold decision to disregard those orders in order to save the BEF.

A head and shoulders portrait shot of Admiral Sir Bertram Ramsay who, on 24 August 1939, as a Vice-Admiral, was given command of the Dover area of operations in which position he had responsibility for the Dunkirk evacuation. This photograph was taken at his London Headquarters in October 1943.

Lieutenant General Alan Brooke, later Field Marshal Lord Alanbrooke, was in command of the BEF's II Corps and distinguished himself in the handling of his corps during the retreat to Dunkirk. On 29 May he was ordered to return to the UK, being told that he was to be given the task of "reforming new armies". In his diary he described his journey back to the coast: "Congestion on roads indescribable. French army became a rabble and complete loss of discipline. [French] troops dejected and surly and refusing to clear road, panicking every time a Boche plane came over." Understandably Brooke had no confidence in the French and, after consulting with General Gamelin, the French commander, he ordered the withdrawal of all remaining British troops from France.

Troops of the British Expeditionary Force pictured upon their arrival in France. The first deployment was completed by 11 October 1939 at which point 158,000 men had been transported to France. The Secretary of State for War, Leslie Hore-Belisha, said: "158,000 had been transported across the Channel within five weeks of the commencement of the present war. Convoys had averaged three each night and the BEF had been transported intact without a single casualty to any of its personnel." (HMP)

British soldiers from the 51st Highland Division pass over a drawbridge into Fort de Sainghin on the Franco-Belgian Frontier, 3 November 1939. Though this and the other images in the series claim that this shows British troops on the Maginot Line, this is in fact not correct. Built in 1878, Fort de Sainghin was occupied by a garrison and armed with forty-four guns until it was overrun by the Germans in 1914. After the First World War it served as an ammunition depot and did not form part of the Maginot Line. Because of the perceived need for secrecy, the French permitted no photographs of the Maginot Line to be published. In contemporary reports all that was ever allowed were generic drawings. (HMP)

A view looking out from the top of Fort du Hackenberg on the Maginot Line. The positions seen here, and those nearby, dominated the open countryside on the approaches from the German border, which is just out of the shot to the right. This area is part of that which would have been patrolled by troops of the BEF serving on the Maginot Line during the winter of 1939/1940. (HMP)

A soldier from the Cameron Highlanders, part of the 51st Highland Division, looks through a periscope in Fort de Sainghain, 3 November 1939. (HMP)

HM King George VI visits a bunker on the Maginot Line during December 1939. (HMP)

The junction between the main tunnel in Fort du Hackenberg and the branch to the vast underground ammunition stores (on the left). (HMP)

Another anecdote about the British Army's occupation of the Maginot Line concerns the now-disused Army barracks at Veckring (one of the entrances to which is seen here). Veckring is the closest village to Fort du Hackenberg and part of this was used as a British hospital by medical units attached to the BEF troops occupying this part of the front. It is said that a direct telephone link was established between the Officers' Mess in the fort and the hospital. The reason for this is that when the British officers, having sampled too much of the local beverages and were incapable of returning to their billets, a call would be made to the hospital and an ambulance would be sent to pick up the inebriated officers! (Courtesy of Mark Khan)

More than 10,000 men of the 51st (Highland) Division were taken prisoner at Saint-Valéry-en-Caux and surrounding area – the men in this picture forming a small part of that number. The Scots also suffered over 5,000 casualties, including 1,000 killed. (US Library of Congress)

Soldiers of the BEF pictured at their post on the front line in France during the cold winter of 1939-1940. An intelligence report by the German IV Army Corps written in the summer of 1940 included the following comments about the men of the BEF: "The English soldier was in excellent physical condition. He bore his own wounds with stoical calm. The losses of his own troops he discussed with complete equanimity. He did not complain of hardships. In battle he was tough and dogged. His conviction that England would conquer in the end was unshakeable ... Certainly the Territorial divisions are inferior to the Regular troops in training, but where morale is concerned they are their equal." (HMP)

An official announcement in December 1939 reported that "the first British soldier killed in action" during the Second World War had lost his life on 9 December 1939. That man was 27-year-old Corporal Thomas William Priday of the 1st Battalion King's Shropshire Light Infantry – seen here. He was, the press reported, killed in action "while leading a patrol towards the German lines". Roughly four-and-a-half miles from the Franco-German border, it was near the village of Monneren that Corporal Priday's patrol was located when he was killed. (© The Shropshire Regimental Museum)

A wounded French soldier is taken ashore on a stretcher at Dover following his evacuation from Dunkirk. He is one of 338,226 British, French and Belgian troops brought back from the French coast.

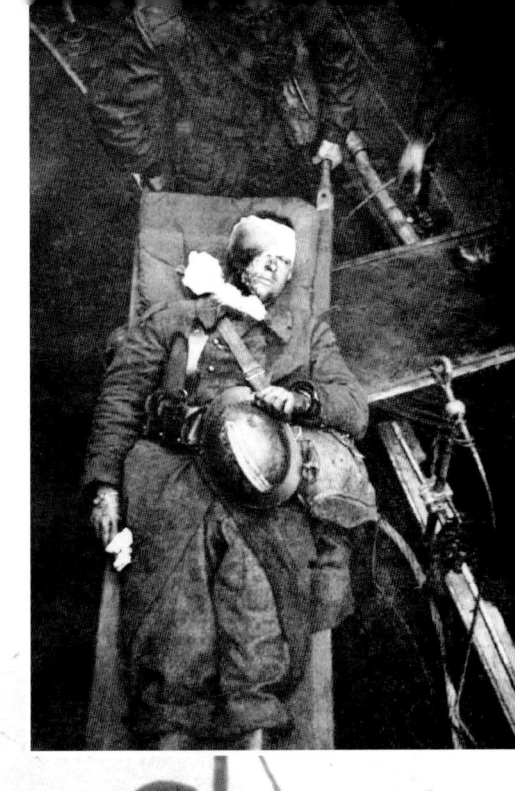

Posted ahead of the Maginot Line the men of the 2nd Battalion Royal Norfolk Regiment were determined that the Germans would not be allowed to rest easy in their positions less than 1,000 yards to the east. During the night of 4/5 January 1940, 'A' Company's Captain Francis Peter Barclay duly led a patrol out from the British line near the village of Waldwisse into No Man's Land. For their actions in the hours that followed, Barclay and another member of the patrol, Lance Corporal H. Davis, would be awarded the BEF's first gallantry medals of the Second World War. Captain Barclay, on the left, can be seen in this staged photograph that was taken on 26 January 1940. (HMP)

This bridge marks the very spot near the Franco-German border where Captain Barclay's patrol clashed with German soldiers on the night of 4/5 January 1940. The British front line was some 1,000 yards beyond the slope at the back of this view. One of the metal stanchions on the bridge, the angled one on the far side of the structure, still displays what appears to be evidence of the fighting when Barclay's patrol clashed with enemy troops – a number of bullet marks and holes. As well as being awarded the BEF's first gallantry medals of the Second World War, the 2nd Battalion Royal Norfolk Regiment achieved another notable "first" during the same night. A second patrol, this time led by Second Lieutenant Patrick Everitt, actually crossed the border into Germany itself. (HMP)

This drawing was created at the request of the Ministry of Information for propaganda purposes during the Second World War. It depicts Captain Harold Ervine-Andrews, The East Lancashire Regiment, during the action for which he was awarded the Victoria Cross. On the night of 31 May/1 June 1940, the company commanded by Captain Ervine-Andrews was heavily outnumbered and under intense German fire near Dunkirk. (HMP)

the more necessary to strengthen further the defences of Bergues, and this was carried out under the orders of 48th Division.

## *Plans for final withdrawal.*

47. On this evening (26th May), I put in hand my plans for a final withdrawal. I was uncertain how far I should be successful in withdrawing the whole of the B.E.F. within the bridgehead at Dunkirk, nor could I judge how much fighting my troops would have to undertake during the withdrawal.

I had, therefore, asked the War Office whether it would be possible to send out an infantry brigade of the Ist Canadian Division so as to provide a nucleus of fresh and well trained troops on the bridgehead position. This request was at once agreed to, and orders were given to despatch the Brigade to Dunkirk on the night 26th/27th May. These orders were, however, cancelled on 28th May.

The contraction of the B.E.F. area and the shortening of its Lines of Communication was now making it possible to dispense with a number of the rearward units. I had already issued orders for the embarkation of a number of key personnel who could be spared so as to ease the supply situation which was becoming acute. I now ordered the withdrawal of all units which were not required to continue the battle. This policy involved leaving most of the fighting troops until the last, but if full use was to be made of the shipping available, and congestion avoided on the beaches, no other course was possible.

The task of organising a bridgehead at Dunkirk and of arranging the details of embarkation was likely to prove an exacting one: work had to begin at once, and my own headquarters were fully occupied with the withdrawal of the forward troops.

I therefore appointed Lieut-General Sir Ronald Adam to undertake this duty, and sent with him my Quarter-Master-General and other staff officers from G.H.Q. He was to take command of the troops already in the area, make arrangements for the troops of Ist, 2nd and 3rd Corps who would be withdrawing into the bridgehead and arrange for the embarkation. He was to act in conformity with the orders of General Fagalde, provided that these did not imperil the safety and welfare of British troops.

Sir Ronald Adam accordingly handed over command of the 3rd

Corps to Major-General S.R. Wason (till then Major-General R.A. at G.H.Q.), and took up his duties on the morning of 27th May.

At 7 a.m. that morning he attended a conference at Cassel as my representative. At this conference there were present Admiral Abrial and General Fagalde from Dunkirk, General Blanchard, General Prioux, now in command of the French Ist Army, and General Koeltz who was representing General Weygand.

Sir Ronald Adam and General Fagalde arrived early, and before the conference began they had the opportunity to reach general agreement on the organisation of the bridgehead position.

The perimeter was to extend from Gravelines south-eastwards to the Canal de la Colme, along the canal to Bergues and thence by Furnes and Nieuport to the Belgian coast. In fact, the French were by now evacuating Gravelines and the western part of the perimeter, and in process of going back to the line of the Mardyck Canal from the sea to Spyker, on the Canal de la Colme. The French were to be responsible for the defence of the western half of the perimeter as far as Bergues inclusive, and the British for the eastern half. By this time, the position of the Belgian Army was so obscure that the possibility of its being included in the bridgehead was not taken into account, though the perimeter could of course have been extended eastwards to include them if necessary.

Sir Ronald Adam then explained to General Fagalde his plan for Corps boundaries, assembly areas and the layout of beaches. He specially stressed the importance of avoiding traffic congestion in the perimeter and said that he had decided to allow no British transport north of the canals except such as was strictly necessary for tactical, supply or medical purposes. He urged General Fagalde to issue similar orders to the French troops under his command. He also suggested that the French troops entering the bridgehead position should all be located in the western part of the perimeter. However, it appeared that these orders did not reach all the French troops, who brought a quantity of transport into the sector.

These matters were later reviewed at the full conference, but the principal business was the issue by General Koeltz of an order of the day by General Weygand.

This enjoined a resolute attitude on the part of every leader, and the counter-offensive wherever possible. General Koeltz then proceeded to urge Generals Blanchard and Fagalde to attempt the recapture of Calais and, though at the time they had nothing available save the 68th Division and the regional troops, they did not demur.

However, so far as I am aware, no action was ever taken in this respect.

## *Description of the Dunkirk Perimeter.*

48. The British sector of the Dunkirk perimeter had its right at Bergues, and thence followed the canals to Furnes and Nieuport. These places were old-fashioned fortified towns, easy to defend but affording good bombing targets. The destruction of the bridges presented no difficulty, and all were in fact blown in time by British or French troops except that at Nieuport which was wide and solid, and could not be demolished before the arrival of the enemy. Two natural switch lines were available: the canal from Bergues to Dunkirk and the Canal des Moeres from Dunkirk south-east towards Hondschoote.

Immediately north of this line came the inundations, extending from Bergues over the district of the Moeres to a width varying from one to three miles. Except in a few places, they did not cover the roads but were designed to leave them clear, while preventing deployment. They did, however, sometimes prevent troops from digging themselves in. On the Belgian side of the frontier the order to begin the inundations was not given by Belgian G.Q.G. till the morning of 26th May and they never became effective.

To the north of the inundations was more low-lying land; then came the Bergues-Furnes Canal, and the main lateral road from Furnes to Dunkirk. Finally there was the narrow strip of dunes giving way to a wide, open beach running the whole length of the position and shelving very slowly to the sea. There were no quays or piers whatever except those at Dunkirk itself. At intervals of about a mile along the shore lay the seaside resorts of Coxyde, La Panne, Bray Dunes and Malo-les-Bains.

## *Layout of the Sector and Problem of Traffic Control.*

49. Sir Ronald Adam, on leaving Cassel, went at once to the

headquarters of the 48th Division at Bergues to find out the latest situation and in particular what troops were immediately available either to hold the perimeter or to control the traffic. He learnt that the enemy were advancing north eastwards from the Forest of Clairmarais: there could therefore be no question of using any of the reserves of 48th Division, and the only troops immediately available were certain engineer units. General Thorne, however, lent his C.R.A. (Brigadier Hon. E.F. Lawson) who was instructed to layout the defence of the perimeter, and to use for the purpose such troops as were on the spot, or were entering the perimeter.

The position was then divided into three Corps areas, each including a collecting area outside the perimeter, a sector of the canal line and a sector of the beach.

Already it was seen that the traffic problem was going to assume formidable proportions. Ever since the l0th May it had been a potential source of trouble, but it had been kept in hand in the early stages by strict adherence to prearranged plans and by the use of infantry for traffic control. Once the withdrawal from the Dyle began, the problem became acute in France as well as in Belgium. Refugees began to leave their homes in northern France before the French Government put into operation the plans they had made. The French organisations were not available and no British troops could be spared to control the traffic. The refugee problem had therefore become increasingly acute, and the tide which at first set westwards from Belgium had now met the enemy again in the Somme area and had begun to turn back on itself. Scenes of misery were everywhere, and the distress of women, children and aged people was pitiable. Fortunately the fine weather and warm nights mitigated their plight to some degree and though the outbreak of famine was expected at any moment it did not actually occur in the area of the B.E.F. Little, unfortunately, could be done to help the refugees, since supplies for the troops were still seriously short. Moreover their presence on the roads was often a grave menace to our movement. It had been necessary to give Corps a free hand in handling them: on occasions it had been necessary to turn vehicles into the fields in order to keep the roads clear.

During the 27th May, troops and their transport began to withdraw into the perimeter on the fronts of all three Corps; and where the troops had received the necessary orders vehicles were disabled and abandoned in the assembly areas. The few troops who could be spared for traffic control did not, however, prove sufficient for the purpose, and consequently a great number of British and French vehicles entered the perimeter and the town of Dunkirk when they should have remained outside. There was inevitably a large number of vehicles which had become detached from their units, and a number of cases also occurred that day in which units became separated from their formations and arrived within the perimeter without sufficiently clear orders. These were sent to reinforce the defence of the perimeter, or embarked, as seemed best to those in control.

Next day (28th May) when Corps started to take charge in their areas, the difficulties with the British traffic were cleared up, only to be replaced by difficulties with the French traffic.

The French 60th Division began to arrive from Belgium and at the same time rearward elements of their light mechanised divisions appeared from the south-east and south. These were soon followed by the transport of the French 3rd Corps, mainly horsed. None of these appeared to have received orders to leave their transport outside the perimeter: seldom did they do so unless compelled by British traffic control posts.

By the 28th, Brigadier Lawson, using the greatest energy, had succeeded in the urgent task of manning the perimeter from Bergues to Nieuport with troops from a number of units, chiefly artillery.

50. The Admiralty had placed the naval arrangements for embarkation in the hands of the Dover Command. A Senior Naval Officer had been sent to Dunkirk to work out detailed plans, and steps had been taken to collect a large number of small ships, and of boats for taking troops from the beach out to the ships.

On 27th May, however, these arrangements had not had time to take effect, nor had it yet been possible to provide sufficient naval ratings to man the beaches. Yet a start was made; beaches were organised at La Panne, Bray Dunes and Malo-les-Bains, one being allotted to each Corps; and military beach parties were improvised on each Corps beach. They carried on without naval assistance for two days, but were hampered by a shortage of small boats and by a lack of experience in their use. The troops were unable to handle boats on a falling tide, and during daylight on the 27th, when only one destroyer and two whalers were available for work on the beaches, not more than two hundred men were embarked.

Dunkirk, which for some days had been heavily bombed, received a particularly severe attack on 27th May; lorry columns had been set on fire in the town and a pall of black smoke from the burning oil tanks hung continuously over the town and docks, impeding the air defence.

Though the outer mole could still be used the inner harbour was now blocked except to small ships.

Dunkirk was therefore cleared of all troops and they were sent to the dunes east of the town to await embarkation. The port itself was kept under the control of G.H.Q. and manned by naval ratings. At one time it seemed likely to go out of use at any moment, but troops were in fact embarked there till the end, in numbers which far exceeded expectations.

Supplies, water and ammunition were despatched from England to the beaches, and on 28th May the first convoy arrived. Unfortunately a high proportion of these stores were destroyed on the way over or sunk when anchored off the shore. Nevertheless considerable quantities were landed at Coxyde and La Panne and served to create a badly needed reserve.

During 27th May, the move of 5th and 50th Divisions was completed and the left flank thus extended as far as Ypres. On the front from Bergues to Hazebrouck enemy pressure steadily increased.

On the same afternoon, G.H.Q. moved from Premesques to Houtkerque (six miles W.N.W. of Poperinghe). Communications were difficult throughout the day since Corps headquarters were all on the move, and it had not yet been possible to re-establish line communications which hitherto had run through Lille.

## *The Belgian Armistice.*

51. During 27th May, I received a further telegram from the Secretary of State which read " . . . want to make it quite clear that sole task now is to evacuate to England maximum of your force possible". It was therefore very necessary to discuss further plans with General Blanchard, for no policy had yet been laid down by G.Q.G. or any other French higher authority for a withdrawal northward of the Lys. I had

no idea what plans either he or Admiral Abrial had in mind.

In the evening, I left my headquarters at Houtkerque with the C.G.S. and the French liaison officer from General Blanchard's headquarters to try and get into touch with General Blanchard. I failed to find him at La Panne, so I went on to Bastion No. 32 at Dunkirk to visit Admiral Abrial, only to find that both he and General Fagalde were equally unaware of his whereabouts.

While at the Bastion, General Koeltz asked me, shortly after II p.m. whether I had yet heard that H.M. the King of the Belgians had asked for an armistice from midnight that night. This was the first intimation I had received of this intention, although I had already formed the opinion that the Belgian Army was now incapable of offering serious or prolonged resistance to the enemy. I now found myself suddenly faced with an open gap of 20 miles between Ypres and the sea through which enemy armoured forces might reach the beaches.

Owing to the congestion on the roads, I did not get back to my headquarters at Houtkerque until about 4.30 a.m. on 28th May. There I found that a telegram had been received from the War Office at I.30 a.m. saying that H.M. the King of the Belgians was capitulating at midnight.

### *Withdrawal to the Sea.*

52. Next morning (28th May), General Blanchard arrived at my headquarters at Houtkerque at about II a.m., and I read him the telegram which I had received the previous day from the Secretary of State. It was then clear to me that whereas we had both received similar instructions from our own Government for the establishment of a bridgehead he had, as yet, received no instructions to correspond with those I had received to evacuate my troops. General Blanchard therefore could not see his way to contemplate evacuation.

I then expressed the opinion that now the Belgian Army had ceased to exist, the only alternatives could be evacuation or surrender. The enemy threat to the North-Eastern flank appeared certain to develop during the next forty-eight hours. The long South-Western flank was being subjected to constant and increasing pressure, especially at Cassel and Wormhoudt, and the arrival of the enemy heavy columns could not be long delayed. These considerations could not be lightly dismissed.

While this discussion was taking place, a liaison officer arrived from General Prioux, now in command of the French Ist Army, to say that the latter did not consider his troops were fit to make any further move and that he therefore intended to remain in the area between Bethune and Lille, protected by the quadrangle of canals.

I then begged General Blanchard, for the sake of France, the French Army and the Allied Cause to order General Prioux back. Surely, I said, his troops were not all so tired as to be incapable of moving. The French Government would be able to provide ships at least for some of his troops, and the chance of saving a part of his trained soldiers was preferable to the certainty of losing them all. I could not move him. Finally he asked me formally whether it was my intention to withdraw that night to the line Cassel-Poperinghe-Ypres.

I replied in the affirmative and informed him that I now had formal orders from His Majesty's Government to withdraw the B.E.F. and that if I was to have any hope of carrying them out must continue my move that night. General Blanchard's parting was not unfriendly, and when he left I issued my orders for withdrawal to provide for that change of mind on the part of the French High Command for which I so sincerely hoped and which in fact took place later.

Ist and 2nd Corps were to withdraw on the night of 28th/29th May to a horse-shoe position on the line Proven-Poperinghe-Ypres-Bixschoote, with outposts on the line Ypres-Godevaersvelde. The position of 3rd Corps was more difficult and obscure. 2nd Division, now reduced to less than the strength of an infantry brigade, had fought hard and had sustained a strong enemy tank attack. It was already in process of withdrawing from the line and orders were issued for it to fall back in the direction of Beveren and Proven, prolonging the right flank of Ist Corps. 48th and 44th Divisions were in contact with the enemy on a front of over twenty miles from Bergues through Cassel to Vieux Berquin, in touch with the French Ist Light Mechanised Division, west of the latter place. The French Ist Army had 3rd and 4th Corps in line between Merville and Sailly-sur-la-Lys, but were out of touch with their 5th Corps.

The orders to 48th Division were to stand for a few hours longer. They withdrew that night under pressure from the enemy, with the assistance of the armoured vehicles of the Hopkinson Mission. The garrison of Wormhoudt was extricated together with such portions of the garrison of Cassel as could disengage from the enemy. 44th Division was also ordered to disengage that night, and to move north-eastwards towards the old frontier defences. 46th Division, which had moved on the night 26th/27th May from the Seclin area to Steenvorde, was to move into the Dunkirk perimeter.

Before he received this order, the Commander of 44th Division (Major-General Osborne) had visited headquarters of the French 4th Corps, where he learned of the Belgian armistice; and heard that General Prioux had orders to stand his ground. He, too, had endeavoured to convince General Prioux that the only hope for his army lay in withdrawal.

Later, on 28th May fresh orders were issued by the French Ist Army. They were to the effect that General Prioux himself would remain with the 4th Corps in its present position, and that General de la Laurencie, with his own 3rd Corps and the Cavalry Corps, would withdraw so as to arrive within the Dunkirk perimeter on 30th May. No copy of this order reached General Osborne, who learned of the change of plans when, at 10.30 p.m. that night, he visited the headquarters of the French Ist Army. As General de la Laurencie had decided to begin his move at 11.30 p.m., General Osborne had some difficulty in conforming, but succeeded in doing so. I was genuinely very glad to learn that part, at any rate, of the French Ist Army would now be sharing in the withdrawal, however great the difficulties might be.

## *Occupation of the Perimeter Completed.*

53. Ist and 2nd Corps were now free to proceed with the occupation of their sectors of the Dunkirk perimeter, and both Commanders met Sir Ronald Adam on 28th May. 2nd Corps had, that morning, ordered Headquarters, 2nd Armoured Reconnaissance Brigade, to take over the sector from Furnes exclusive to the sea at Nieuport, and now ordered 4th Division to move from the line of the Ypres-Comines Canal to relieve them. 3rd Division was to follow as soon as possible and take over the sector between the French-Belgian frontier and Furnes.

These two divisions had been in the line at Ypres since 25th May. They had held positions on the historic ground of the Ypres-Comines Canal, Zillebeke and the eastern outskirts of Ypres, and on these positions, the infantry, well supported by the artillery, had stubbornly held their ground in the face of strong and determined attacks by the enemy.

Ist Corps also ordered Ist Division to move into their sector of the perimeter; on the same day Ist Corps was ordered to reinforce the garrison of Bergues with one battalion. This order could not be carried out that day, but next day (29th May) a battalion of 46th Division (9th Foresters) was sent there.

During this time it had been a constant anxiety to G.H.Q. lest those enemy forces released by the Belgian armistice should forestall our occupation of the perimeter. There had been no time to lose. Early on the 28th the leading enemy mobile troops and tanks had reached Nieuport, and they would have arrived there unopposed had it not been for the work of a troop of I2th Lancers. The state of the roads, congested as they were with refugees and Belgian troops, must also have played their part in delaying the enemy. Throughout the day, however, the defensive positions were improved and a number of additional troops from various units, chiefly Royal Artillery, were collected and organised to occupy them.

On 29th May, troops of I2th Infantry Brigade and Corps Artillery began to arrive; that night 4th Division relieved the mixed detachments which up to now had been holding the sector. Throughout the 29th May the enemy had been attempting to cross the canal between the French-Belgian frontier and Nieuport. At the latter place, where the bridge had not been blown, they established a bridgehead in the town. Everywhere else they were driven back. Some attempted to cross in rubber boats; others were disguised as civilians, even as nuns, and attempted to cross with the refugees, horses and cattle. On this day enemy forces advancing near the coast were shelled by H.M. ships.

Thus, once again the enemy had been forestalled just in the nick of time, and the prompt and gallant action of the troops on the spot had gained the few vital hours which were to make it possible, against all expectation, to embark practically the whole force.

54. On the afternoon of 28th May, I moved my headquarters from Houtkerque to La Panne, which was in direct telephonic communication with London. On arrival I heard reports from Sir Ronald Adam and the Quarter-Master-General.

These reports were not optimistic. No ships could be unloaded at the docks at Dunkirk, and few wounded could be evacuated. There was no water in Dunkirk and very little on the beaches. The naval plans were not yet in full operation, and some 20,000 men were waiting to be taken off the beaches, 10,000 having been taken off in the last two days, chiefly from Dunkirk. The area was congested with French and Belgian troops and their transport, as well as with refugees.

They gave it as their opinion that, given a reasonable measure of immunity from air attack, troops could gradually be evacuated and supplies landed. If, however, intensive enemy air attack continued, the beaches might easily become a shambles within the next forty-eight hours.

I communicated the gist of this report to the C.I.G.S. and I asked that H.M. Government should consider the policy to be followed in the event of a crisis arising, as well it might. In reply, I received two telegrams which read:-

". . . . H.M. Government fully approve your withdrawal to extricate your force in order embark maximum number possible of British Expeditionary Force. . . . If you are cut from all communication from us and all evacuation from Dunkirk and beaches had, in your judgment, been finally prevented after every attempt to re-open it had failed you would become sole judge of when it was impossible to inflict further damage to enemy."

I also received a gracious telegram of encouragement and good wishes from His Majesty, the King, which I communicated to all ranks.

General Weygand telegraphed on this day appealing personally to me to ensure that the British Army took a vigorous part in any counter-attacks necessary; the situation, he added, made it essential to hit hard. When he sent this message, he could have had no accurate information of the real position or of the powers of counter-attack remaining to either the French or the British. General Koeltz had not, as yet, had time to return to G.Q.G. with a first-hand report on the situation, and in any case the time for such action in the northern theatre was long past.

## French troops arrive: Problems of embarkation.

55. By 29th May, the naval arrangements were beginning to bear fruit:

however, during the day, the enemy began to shell Dunkirk from the south-west and the port and the beaches were constantly bombed.

Owing to a misunderstanding, the personnel of certain anti-aircraft units had been embarked instead of being retained for the defence of the port of Dunkirk. Therefore, I was the more dependent on the action of fighter aircraft, and I made this clear to the War Office. I realised how heavy was the demand to be made on the Royal Air Force for the remainder of the operation, and how impossible it would be to expect that they could succeed completely in preventing air action on the beaches. Yet they did succeed in intercepting a large part of the enemy attacks, and those which arrived, though at times serious, were never able to impede our embarkation for long.

French troops were now arriving in the perimeter in large numbers, and, unfortunately, brought with them much transport. The congestion created within the perimeter was well-nigh unbearable and for two days the main road' between La Panne and Dunkirk became totally blocked with vehicles three deep. The French were in process of withdrawing all their troops behind the defences on the Belgian frontier, and for the next two days their dispositions were superimposed on those of the British troops in that part of the perimeter between the frontier and Bergues. The French military forces, within the perimeter or now approaching it, consisted of two weak divisions of the I6th Corps (60th and 68th), General Barthélémy's regional troops, General de la Laurencie's 3rd Corps of two divisions (I2th and 32nd), and the Cavalry Corps, together with some artillery.

The arrival of these troops, though welcome from so many points of view, raised the question of embarkation in an acute form. Admiral Abrial had apparently received no orders from his Government that the whole of the British troops were to be embarked, and he professed great surprise when he heard of my intentions. He had, it seems, imagined that only rearward elements were to be withdrawn, and that British troops would stay and defend the perimeter to the last, side by side with the French. I therefore sent Sir Ronald Adam to see the Admiral. He explained the orders to extricate my Force which I had received from His Majesty's Government and which had been confirmed the day before.

Meanwhile, the French troops were expecting to embark along with their British comrades, notwithstanding that no French ships had so far been provided: the beaches were becoming crowded with French soldiers, and difficulties might have occurred at any time. I urged the War Office to obtain a decision as to the French policy for embarkation and asked that the French should take their full share in providing naval facilities. However, to permit embarkation of the French troops to begin at once, I decided to allot two British ships to the French that night, and also to give up the beach at Malo-les-Bains for their sole use.

## *Medical arrangements.*

56. Hospital ships worked continuously till 31st May though continuous bombing made their berthing difficult and they frequently had to put to sea before they were fully loaded. Walking wounded were taken on board personnel ships from Dunkirk or the beaches, but to prevent delay in embarking fit men, orders were issued that the most serious cases should only be embarked on hospital ships. Casualty Clearing Stations had been established at Dunkirk and at the beach at La Panne. Some of the wounded were, however, too ill to move. They had been collected into two Casualty Clearing Stations, one at Crombeke and one at Rosendael, where they were to be cared for till the enemy should arrive.

## *The Evacuation of 3rd and 2nd Corps.*

57. The 3rd Corps Sector included the canal from Dunkirk to Bergues, with the town of Bergues, and a little more than two miles of front west of the town. By the evening of 29th, 3rd Corps had withdrawn 44th and 2nd Divisions from their positions and Corps headquarters were now embarked. 44th and 48th Divisions were ordered to be transferred to Ist Corps, and 2nd, 23rd and 46th Divisions to proceed to Dunkirk for embarkation, Ist Corps was also ordered to embark what remained of 42nd Division, except for 126th Infantry Brigade. Subsequently a change was made, 44th Division being embarked and 46th Division remaining with Ist Corps.

During the 29th and 30th May, 5th and 50th Divisions came into the 2nd Corps area: the former, sadly reduced in numbers, was withdrawn from the line, while the latter occupied a sector between the Belgian frontier and the right of the 3rd Division.

On the evening of 29th May, therefore, the organisation of the perimeter was complete, and Sir Ronald Adam's task was successfully accomplished. He himself embarked that night.

By 30th May, there remained in the area, at an estimate, 80,000 British troops for evacuation and I had now to complete the plans for the final withdrawal of the Force. I had received a telegram from the Secretary of State, which read as follows:-

> "Continue to defend present perimeter to the utmost in order to cover maximum evacuation now proceeding well. . . . If we can still communicate with you we shall send you an order to return to England with such officers as you may choose at the moment when we deem your command so reduced that it can be handed to a Corps Commander. You should now nominate this commander. If communications are broken you are to hand over and return as specified when your effective fighting force does not exceed equivalent of three divisions. This is in accordance with correct military procedure and no personal discretion is left to you in the matter. . . .The Corps Commander chosen by you should be ordered to carry on defence and evacuation with French whether from Dunkirk or beaches. . . ."

The problem was to thin out the troops, while maintaining a proper defence of the perimeter, yet at the same time not to retain a larger number of men than could be embarked in one lift.

I had received orders from home that French and British troops were to embark in equal proportions. Thus it looked at one time as if the British would have to continue holding a perimeter, either the existing one or something smaller, at least another four or five days, to enable all the troops to embark. Yet the enemy pressure was increasing and there was no depth in our position. A line on the dunes could only be held during the hours of darkness to cover the final phase of the withdrawal.

I discussed the situation with the Commanders of Ist and 2nd Corps on 30th May. Embarkation had gone well that day, especially from

Dunkirk, but enemy pressure had increased at Furnes and Bergues and it was plain that the eastern end of the perimeter could not be held much longer. The enemy had begun to shell the beach at La Panne. I was still concerned lest the arrangements for embarking the French should for any reason prove inadequate. I therefore motored to Dunkirk to inform Admiral Abrial of my views and to assure myself that the arrangements for embarking British and French troops in equal proportions were working smoothly.

The Admiral assured me of his agreement about the evacuation of the sector, and we then discussed the problem of embarkation.

I had already agreed with General de la Laurencie to evacuate 5,000 picked men from his 3rd Corps, which had fought alongside us and of the fighting value of which I had a high opinion. However, the Admiral told me that he had had orders from General Weygand that the personnel of the Cavalry Corps were to be embarked in priority to others. The matter was settled in a most friendly atmosphere and I satisfied myself, so far as it was possible, that no trouble was likely to arise in practice over the sharing of the berths at the Dunkirk mole.

I judged that it would be imprudent to continue to maintain our position on the perimeter outside the permanent defences of Dunkirk for more than twenty-four hours longer, and I therefore decided to continue the evacuation by withdrawing 2nd Corps on the night of 31st May/1st June.

Orders were accordingly issued for 2nd Corps to withdraw 3rd, 4th and 5th Divisions to the beaches and Dunkirk. 50th Division was to fall back to the French defences on the Belgian frontier, and come under command of 1st Corps, together with the British Base staff at Dunkirk. These moves began to take place on the morning of 31st May; by this time there had been a general thinning out of the whole force, and I felt that, however the situation might develop, valuable cadres had been withdrawn which would enable the fighting units of the B.E.F. to be quickly reformed at home.

58. The remains of the B.E.F., on being withdrawn inside the area of the French defences, now came under the orders of Admiral Abrial, and the time had therefore arrived for me to hand over my command, in accordance with the instructions I had received, and to embark for England. I invited Generals Blanchard and de la Laurencie to join me

on the journey. To my regret they were both unable to do so, though I was able to arrange for some of the staff of General de la Laurencie's 3rd Corps to sail with that of G.H.Q.

I had selected Major-General Hon. H.R.L.G. Alexander to remain in France in command of Ist Corps, now numbering less than 20,000 men in all. On the afternoon of 31st May I gave him his instructions, which were based on those I had myself received from H.M. Government. He was to operate under the orders of Admiral Abrial, and to assist the French in the defence of Dunkirk. At the same time he was to occupy himself with arrangements for the evacuation of his command, and I stressed the importance of the French sharing equally in the facilities which were provided for evacuation.

I agreed with Major-General Alexander on the night 2nd/3rd June as a provisional date for evacuating his force.

That evening, therefore, at 6 p.m., my headquarters closed, and after handing over command to Major-General Alexander,[9] I embarked in H.M.S. Hebe, and sailed for England about 2 a.m. on Ist June. At this time the withdrawal of 2nd Corps was proceeding according to plan, but under increasing enemy pressure by land and air; the troops were moving to their places on the beaches steadily and in good order. The plans made by the Admiralty to provide small craft were by now in full operation; embarkation was proceeding far more smoothly than it had yet done, and was favoured by a calm sea that night.

In all, 2II,532 fit men and I3,053 casualties were embarked at Dunkirk and the beaches, in addition to II2,546 allied troops.[10]

## SOME LESSONS OF THE CAMPAIGN

*The importance of equipment; the time factor; liaison; defence in depth; the employment of air forces; river crossing and demolitions; signal communications; traffic control; security; supply and transport; the behaviour of the troops.*

59. So ended a campaign of 22 days which has proved that the offensive has once more gained ascendency in modern war when undertaken with an army equipped with greatly superior material power in the shape of air forces and armoured fighting vehicles.

The British Expeditionary Force had advanced sixty-five miles from the frontier to the Dyle: then the same distance back from the Dyle to the frontier: finally a further fifty miles to the sea at Dunkirk. A frontal advance had become a flank defence; a flank defence the defence of a perimeter which at times exceeded one hundred miles, with my force of nine [11] divisions and parts of three semi-trained and partially equipped divisions sent to France for labour duties. Finally had come the withdrawal to the sea and the shrinkage of this wide front to the twenty-four miles of the Dunkirk bridgehead.

The series of situations which the B.E.F. had to face was not brought about by failure on their part to withstand enemy attacks when holding a position of their own choosing: it was caused by the enemy breaking through completely on a front many miles away from that held by the B.E.F. Nevertheless this break through, once it began, was destined to involve in its ill-fated consequences both the French Ist Army and the B.E.F. In the withdrawal which ensued both these armies lost the whole of their artillery and transport.

It would not be appropriate in this Despatch to discuss questions affecting the higher command of the Allied forces: on these matters I received orders from H.M. Government and through the French commanders under whom I was placed.

Nor is this Despatch the place to deal at length with the military lessons of the Campaign; I have already conveyed my detailed views to the proper quarter.

There are, however, certain matters which it may be convenient to mention, in broad outline, in this Despatch since they may serve in some respects to amplify and to explain the narrative of events. They are dealt with in the paragraphs which follow.

## *The paramount importance of equipment.*

60. It was clear from the outset that the ascendency in equipment which the enemy possessed played a great part in the operations. He was able to place in the field and to concentrate no less than ten armoured divisions in the area which he selected and later, to employ at least five of these against the British rearward defences. On the other hand, the British armoured forces in the theatre of war amounted to seven divisional cavalry regiments equipped with light tanks, one regiment

of armoured cars of an obsolete pattern, and two battalions of infantry tanks, the latter, except for twenty-three Mark II tanks, being armed each with one machine-gun only.

Our anti-tank armament was more ample than that of the French, but did not extend further back than the division. No guns were available for the defence of Corps or rearward areas or for the three "Pioneer" divisions, except by with-drawing weapons from the formations to which they had been allotted in War Establishments.

These instances amongst many others which might be quoted serve to indicate the vital necessity for an expeditionary force, if it is to be used in a first-class war, being equipped on a scale commensurate with the task it is to be called upon to fulfil.

The days are past when armies can be hurriedly raised, equipped and placed in the field, for modern war demands the ever increasing use of complicated material. Indeed the scientific side of warfare has been evolving at a very rapid rate even since the end of the war of 1914-18 and is continuing to do so. Modern equipment requires time to design and produce, and once it is produced, further time is required to train troops in its technical and tactical uses. Improvised arrangements, made at short notice, can only lead to the shortage of essential equipment, the production of inferior articles, and the unskilful handling of weapons and vehicles on the battlefield.

## *The Time Factor.*

61. The speed with which the enemy exploited his penetration of the French front, his willingness to accept risks to further his aim, and his exploitation of every success to the uttermost limits emphasised, even more fully than in the campaigns of the past, the advantage which accrues to the commander who knows how best to use time to make time his servant and not his master.

Again, the pace of operations has been so accelerated by the partnership between offensive aircraft and modern mechanised forces that the reserves available for the defence are of little use unless they are fully mobile or already in occupation of some reserve position. For instance, had it not been that eight Troop Carrying Companies, R.A.S.C., were available, the attack south of Arras could never have been mounted, nor indeed could the flank defences on the canal have been organised in time to forestall the enemy.

We had already foreseen, and taught at the Staff College, that the methods of staff duties in the past war would prove too slow for modern requirements. Headquarters of formations were so frequently on the move that conferences, supplemented by Operation Instructions or messages, usually replaced the formal orders which had been the accepted procedure in past campaigns.

Full use was also made of liaison officers of all grades, who had been provided by the War Office on a generous scale. In the period before active operations began, they were of real value in settling matters of detail and in reconciling points of view which did not always at first coincide; during the fighting they were more often than not the actual bearers of Operation Instructions, and performed most valuable service to their commanders in ascertaining the exact state of affairs in forward or flank units. The junior liaison officers, known as Motor Contact Officers, likewise showed determination and resource in carrying out their duties.

The liaison with flanking French formations was carried out by the exchange of bilingual liaison officers. I was particularly fortunate in the French officers who were attached for these duties from neighbouring formations.

I would also like to take this opportunity of recording my thanks to Général de Division Voruz and the staff of his Mission with G.H.Q. for their unfailing helpfulness at all times.

## *Defence in Depth.*

62. Closely allied to the question of the time factor is that of defence in depth. The speed at which armoured units can advance, once they have broken into a position, calls for a more elastic conception of defence than would be necessary were it designed solely to hold up a marching enemy. Consequently, frontages may, in the future, be considerably shorter than those which the French High Command required the B.E.F. to hold in France.

In more rearward areas, schemes must be prepared for the manning, at short notice, of centres of communication and other important defiles. Therefore, all units, even those designed for purely administrative purposes, must be prepared to take their part in the battle, and they must receive the necessary preliminary training.

Anti-tank defence is a science as well as a craft. It is a science in that it is necessary to perfect armour-piercing weapons and anti-tank tactics. It is a craft in that troops must be trained to stalk tanks by day, to keep track of their movements, and to attack them in their harbours at night.

## *The Employment of Air Forces.*

63. It was clear from the reports of the Spanish war, confirmed by those of the Polish campaign, that the enemy would employ his air forces to further the offensive operations of the army by the use of dive bombers and parachute troops. The latter, though effectively employed in Holland, were less used against the B.E.F.; however, the nuisance value of those which were employed, by their interference with railway, telephone and telegraph communications in rearward zones, was altogether out of proportion to their numbers. There were seldom troops available to isolate and search the areas where they landed, usually at dusk, and no French civil organization existed for the purpose.

The enemy bombers, both high level and low flying, were a more serious menace. Their control by the German command was most efficient, capable of bringing the aircraft to their objective by wireless call at short notice.

Attack by dive bombers was a new experience for British troops. Even those who had grown accustomed to heavy shell fire in France during 1914-18 found that this form of attack, when first encountered, placed a strain on morale. As had been anticipated, it was soon realised that those who were properly entrenched and had perfected the drill of taking cover when on the move, suffered relatively little danger.

Ground anti-aircraft defence, both gun and light automatic, improved in accuracy as time went on and it accounted for the destruction of over 500 aircraft in addition to its effect in breaking up formations of enemy aircraft. But being purely defensive, it can never prove the complete antidote to enemy bombers and reconnaissance aircraft, even when available in sufficient strength. A commander must have at his call sufficient fighters to intercept and attack the enemy.

The commander must, likewise, dispose of a sufficient bomber force to be able to engage opportunity targets of vital tactical importance. Such targets were the enemy mechanised columns at Maastricht, Sedan and Boulogne. The machinery for their control must be efficient enough to ensure that aircraft can be despatched in time.

## River Crossing and Demolitions.

64. The skill and speed of the enemy in crossing water obstacles was very apparent as was also the excellence of his equipment for the purpose. On the other hand, the paramount importance of demolitions on such obstacles as a means of imposing even a short delay, was established: during the operations the B.E.F. destroyed over 500 bridges, and there were few failures. From the number of demolitions which it was found necessary to carry out, it is clear that every engineer unit, no matter what its normal role, must receive the necessary training to execute such work.

## Signal Communications.

65. During the operations a very heavy strain was thrown upon the Royal Corps of Signals: not least upon those responsible for the communications of G.H.Q. The problem was two-fold: first to provide the normal communications within the force, secondly to provide the long-distance communications required to enable G.H.Q. to remain in constant touch with French G.Q.G., the War Office and the Royal Air Force. The latter considerations made it necessary to follow the buried cable, and thus dominated the moves of G.H.Q. Communications within the B.E.F. demanded mobility and rapidity of construction combined with the need to deal with a heavy volume of traffic. The frequent moves, and the time lag which occurred when cipher had to be used, resulted in a heavy demand on despatch riders.

## Traffic Control.

66. The vital importance of controlling movement by road was emphasised over and over again during the operations.

The movements of mechanised columns depend for their success on the proper reconnaissance and allotment of roads, the avoidance of traffic blocks and the power to divert the flow of traffic quickly and without interruption whenever an obstacle occurs. The danger of interference by enemy bombing is always present, but it can be minimised by the employment of fighter aircraft, by an adequate layout of anti-aircraft guns, by the provision of facilities for clearing breakdowns and the repair of roads, and by the training of troops in a proper drill when attacked from the air.

The movement of refugees, as has been described above, laid a further burden on the Provost service. Though the greatest efforts were made by all ranks to cope with the task, it was evident that our organisation required considerable expansion. Recommendations for the creation of a road control organisation under the Quarter-Master-General, on the lines of that in use in the French Army, had already been submitted, but unfortunately too late for more than preliminary results to be achieved.

## *Security.*

67. Akin to the foregoing problem is that of security. Until 10th May the work of the Intelligence Service in this respect had been heavy and constant, but when operations began, it assumed almost unmanageable proportions. This was due to the opening of the Belgian frontier, the mass movement of refugees, and the arrival of enemy saboteurs and agents by parachute.

The troops, however, soon became aware of the danger and realised the importance, of security measures and the paramount need for discretion.

## *Supply and Transport.*

68. As has been already indicated in this Despatch, the operations showed clearly how complete reliance cannot be placed on any one channel of movement or maintenance. Enemy action by mobile forces or by air may put important road or railway routes out of action for hours or days at a time, or even completely sever communications with the bases.

The proportion of reserves held forward, and under load, on rail or on lorry, must therefore be high, despite the resultant extravagance in transport. The War Office had provided Lines of Communication Railhead Companies, R.A.S.C., to operate in the event of a railhead being out of action for a time, and these units fully justified their existence.

During the final phases of the operations, the civilian employees of the French and Belgian railways were often not to be found, and the Railway Operating Companies, R.E., had to take over the working of the trains at short notice.

The change of bases made necessary after 20th May was a fine example of quick decision, flexible administration, and the power of the administrative staffs at home and in France to improvise at short notice.

### *The Behaviour of the Troops.*

69. Most important of all, the Campaign has proved beyond doubt that the British Soldier has once again deserved well of his country. The troops under my command, whatever their category, displayed those virtues of steadiness, patience, courage and endurance for which their corps and regiments have long been famous.

In addition to the fighting troops, the rearward units, as well as the three divisions sent to France for pioneer duties, all found themselves, at one time or another, engaged with the enemy although often incompletely trained and short of the proper complement of weapons.

Time and again, the operations proved the vital importance of the good junior leader, who has learned to encourage, by his example, the men whom he leads, and whose first care is the well-being of the troops placed under his command. Firm discipline, physical fitness, efficiency in marching and digging, and skill at arms, old-fashioned virtues though they may be, are as important in modern warfare as ever they were in the past.

# APPRECIATIONS
*The Royal Navy; the Royal Air Force; Commanders and Staffs*

### *The Royal Navy.*

70. I have already referred to the embarkation of the Force from Dunkirk and its transport to England which evoked the wholehearted admiration of the Army. The operation was carried out in accordance with the finest traditions of the Royal Navy. The plan involved the use of hundreds of privately-owned small craft, and was put into execution

at short notice and at a time when Naval resources were severely strained by demands elsewhere. It was carried through regardless of danger and loss by enemy bombing. My deep gratitude is due to all concerned, particularly to Vice-Admiral Sir B.H. Ramsay, Vice-Admiral at Dover, Rear-Admiral W.F. Wake Walker, who superintended the actual embarkation and Captain W.G. Tennant, R.N., the senior naval officer ashore. Nor can the Army forget the sterling work of all those members of the Merchant Navy and the civilian owners of small craft, in many instances volunteers, who unhesitatingly and regardless of dangers gave their services to the British Expeditionary Force.

### *The Royal Air Force.*

71. Successful operations on land depend more than ever before on the closest co-operation between aircraft and troops on the ground, and the B.E.F. owes a deep debt of gratitude to the Royal Air Force for their work throughout the operations. Pilots returned to the air again and again to carry out essential tasks for both French and British Armies, when they were long overdue for rest and sleep.

The embarkation of the Force would have been well-nigh impossible but for the fighter protection afforded. The toll taken[12] of the enemy aircraft on this and earlier occasions has once again established the individual superiority of the British airman in the air.

I wish specially to record my thanks to Air-Marshal A.S. Barratt (now Sir Arthur Barratt), Air Officer Commanding-in-Chief, British Air Forces in France, and to the Air Officer Commanding my Air Component, Air-Vice-Marshal C.H.B. Blount.

### *Commanders and Staffs.*

72. The course of operations in May afforded very unequal opportunities for the several branches of the Staff, Services and departments to show their efficiency, and it would, therefore, perhaps, be invidious to deal with their work in detail to a greater extent than I have already done in this Despatch. Some, however, were required with their Staffs to bear a specially heavy and prolonged strain of responsibility and I wish to refer particularly to the valuable services of my Chief of the General Staff (Lieut.-General H.R. Pownall), my

Quarter-Master-General (Lieut.-General W.G. Lindsell), and my Engineer-in-Chief (Major-General R.P. Pakenham-Walsh), my Signal Officer-in-Chief (Major-General R. Chenevix-Trench), and my Military Secretary (Brigadier Sir Colin Jardine, Bart.).

From the narrative of events, it will be evident how great is the debt I owe to the Commanders of my three Corps. Lieut.-Generals Sir Alan Brooke, M.G.H. Barker and Sir Ronald Adam, Bart. The sudden turn of events on I7th May threw a violent and unexpected strain on the Commander, Lines of Communication Area (the late Major-General P. de Fonblanque), and I wish to record my sincere appreciation of his good and devoted work during the time that he was serving under my command.

Finally, I desire to express my thanks and good wishes to all those officers in the French Army whose duties brought them into contact with the British Expeditionary Force, and whose goodwill, understanding and personal friendship did so much to foster the good relations which existed between the two armies.

## *Honours and Awards.*

73. I am submitting separately the names of officers and other ranks whom I wish to recommend for reward or to bring to your notice for gallant or distinguished service.

I have the honour to be
Sir,
Your Obedient Servant,
GORT,
General,
Commander-in-Chief,
British Expeditionary Force.

# APPENDIX TO SECOND DESPATCH OF C.-IN-C., B.E.F.

## OPERATIONS OF IST CORPS FROM 6 P.M. ON 3IST MAY TO MIDNIGHT 2ND/3RD JUNE, I940

Major-General Hon. H.R.L.G. Alexander, on taking over command of Ist Corps, handed over command of the Ist Division to Brigadier M.B. Beckwith-Smith. He then proceeded to Dunkirk to see Admiral Abrial, who informed him that he intended to hold the perimeter till all the troops were embarked. A French Corps on the right was to hold the sector from Gravelines to Bergues (Gravelines however had not apparently been in French hands for some days) and a mixed French and British Corps under command of Major-General Alexander was to hold a line from Bergues to Les Moeres, and thence to the sea.

Major-General Alexander at once told the Admiral and General Fagalde that in his view this plan did not take account of the true naval and military situation which was serious and deteriorating rapidly. The fighting condition of the troops was now such that prolonged resistance was out of the question and the present front could not in his opinion be maintained after the night Ist/2nd June: furthermore the line to be held was so close to the beach and to Dunkirk that the enemy might soon stop all further evacuation by short range artillery fire. He gave the same opinion to the Secretary of State and received a reply that the British force should be withdrawn as rapidly as possible on a basis of equal numbers of British and French continuing to be embarked from that time onward. This he showed to Admiral Abrial and General Fagalde informing them that he would hold the sector allotted to him till midnight Ist/2nd June and then withdraw under cover of darkness. They agreed that in the circumstances no other plan was feasible.

The naval situation had by now grown worse, and the Channel from Dunkirk was under direct artillery fire. It was therefore evident that the force could not be evacuated completely on the night Ist/2nd June. Major-General Alexander therefore agreed on a modified plan with Admiral Abrial and General Fagalde at 8 a.m. on Ist June. He arranged to hold his present line till midnight Ist/2nd June; thus he would cover Dunkirk and so enable the French to evacuate as many of their troops as possible. He would then withdraw to a bridgehead round Dunkirk with all available anti-aircraft and anti-tank guns and such troops as had not yet embarked.

During the Ist June, heavy enemy attacks developed on the British sector, supported by bombing and artillery fire. The garrison of Bergues (Ist Loyals) were forced to withdraw to the line of the canal north of the town, and to the west, 46th Division, I26th Infantry Brigade of 42nd Division and Ist Division were forced back north of the canal for about I,000 yards. 50th Division had also to meet enemy penetration from the east, but by nightfall on Ist June the enemy advance had been checked on a line Bergues-Uxem-Ghyvelde, thence due east to the frontier and along the frontier defences to the sea.

Embarkation was temporarily stopped at 3 a.m. on 2nd June to prevent casualties in daylight; by that time there remained in the Dunkirk area about 3,000 men of various artillery and infantry units, with seven anti-aircraft guns and twelve anti-tank guns. They held the outskirts of Dunkirk throughout 2nd June with little interference save heavy shelling and bombing of the beaches.

By midnight on 2nd/3rd June, all the remaining British troops had been embarked. Major-General Alexander, with the Senior Naval Officer (Captain W.G. Tennant, R.N.) made a tour of the beaches and harbour in a motor boat and on being satisfied that no British troops were left on shore, they themselves left for England.

**Footnotes:**

1. *One of the three divisions sent to France for pioneer duties.*
2. *This Sub-Area had been formed to deal with units which remained in the old G.H.Q. and Corps areas when the B.E.F. moved into Belgium.*
3. *The Hopkinson Mission, under the Command of Lieut.-Colonel G.F. Hopkinson, had been formed to secure certain information for the R.A.F. and for G.H.Q. immediately on entry into Belgium.*
4. *Major-General Petre's command was known as Petreforce.*
5. *At this time their strength was reduced to approximately 65 Mark I and 18 Mark II tanks. By the end of the withdrawal from Arras there remained 26 Mark I and 2 Mark II tanks.*
6. *See para. 43.*
7. *Major-General T.R. Eastwood had recently arrived in France to take command of a division, and, pending a vacancy, was attached to the Staff of G.H.Q.*
8. *Eight miles west of Ghent.*
9. *An account of events after Major-General Alexander assumed command is given in Appendix I.*
10. *These figures have been obtained from the War Office.*
11. *Excluding 51st Division on the Saar Front.*
12. *On one day, 77 enemy machines were shot down at the loss of only 16 of our own*

# 2

# Operation *Dynamo*: The Evacuation of the Allied Armies from Dunkirk and Neighbouring Beaches

## By Vice Admiral Bertram Ramsay

### THURSDAY, 17 JULY, 1947

The following despatch was submitted to the Lords Commissioners of the Admiralty on the 18th June, 1940, by Vice-Admiral Sir Bertram H. Ramsay, K.C.B., M.V.O., Flag Officer Commanding, Dover.

*Office of The Flag Officer Commanding, Dover.*
*18th June, 1940.*

Be pleased to lay before Their Lordships the following report on Operation "Dynamo", namely the evacuation of the Allied Armies from Dunkirk and neighbouring beaches between 26th May and 4th June, 1940. The report takes the form of this covering letter, together with detailed narrative and appendices.

## 2. THE POLICY AND THE PROGRESS OF THE EVACUATION.

During the course of the operation some 330,000 troops[1] reached safety in England after being evacuated from Dunkirk, and from the beach stretching I0 miles eastward from the entrance to Dunkirk Harbour. To those on the French coast, when in the early stages anything up to 50,000 troops were waiting to embark on a I0 mile sea front, the presence of perhaps 20 small warships off shore, and 200 small boats spread along the length of coast at any given moment, must have appeared as a feeble effort to tackle this great task. Furthermore, it was impossible to adjust the arrival of ships, either at Dunkirk or opposite the beaches, to synchronise with the ebb and flow of the troop concentrations.

Broadly speaking, for the first 5 days of the movement, had more beaching craft been available to ferry from the beach to offshore vessels, it would have been possible to have evacuated a greater number. For the last 3 to 4 days, however, when the main bulk of the B.E.F. had already been evacuated, the rate of lifting was governed by the availability of the troops during the limited hours evacuation was possible.

3. Throughout the operation one of the greatest difficulties was the ever changing situation presented. Within 24 hours of the start, the operation took the shape of a forlorn hope to rescue the maximum number, say up to 45,000 before the whole force was to be overwhelmed by the enemy.

Next, the military situation became more stable, and it appeared that some three to four days would be available to complete evacuation of the B.E.F., estimated at some I75,000. During this stage evacuation by British resources of French troops was introduced, some 25,000 being mentioned.

During the course of the fifth day (30th May) a tentative decision to lift the rearguard of the B.E.F. off the beaches at a definite time, viz. 0I30 on Ist June, was reached. Twenty-four hours later this plan was altered by military considerations, involving an extension of the period of evacuation. At the same time, the Naval authority was definitely committed to provide for the evacuation of French forces, then mentioned as about 40,000/50,000.

Later, the French number rose and 150,000 or more was quoted. Finally no agreement could be reached with the French as to any termination of the operation which threatened to drag on painfully and finally to lose momentum and expire through the exhaustion of Naval personnel and the liquidation of shipping.

It will be seen, therefore, that the initial problem called for a maximum effort over a limited period regardless of the future, and accordingly all resources in the way of small boats were thrown on the beaches, before adequate provision had been made for their maintenance off the coast in such matters as relief of the personnel and the provision of large beach parties.

It was only due to the foresight of the Admiralty in making arrangements for a continued flow in ever increasing numbers of small power boats and beach craft, which became available on the fifth day onwards, that the continued evacuation from the beaches remained a reasonable proposition after the initial crisis had passed.

4. A perusal of the signals that passed between Dover and the French coast reveals the many occasions on which the responsible officers stationed on the coast considered so little had been achieved from the beaches that they advocated restriction of evacuation to Dunkirk Harbour. Many complaints of "no boats," "no ships," might lead a detached observer to the conclusion that the great effort that was being made was proving abortive.

At Dover, where the whole operation could be viewed in truer perspective, the number and origin of the troops being landed in England being always to hand, it was clear that the evacuation from the beaches required by the military situation, was, in fact, achieving a considerable success, as the following figures will show. Of the 248,000 troops landed in the United Kingdom, between May 28th and June Ist inclusive – the period during which both Dunkirk and the beaches eastward were available day and night except for enemy interference – no fewer than 100,000 were lifted from the beaches.

## 5. WEATHER CONDITIONS.

The operation was favoured by extremely good weather. It was found, however, that any northerly wind caused a considerable surf, which greatly reduced the rate of lifting from the beaches. It must be fully realised that a wind of any strength in the northern sector between South West and North East would have made beach evacuation impossible. At no time did this happen.

### 6. DISPOSAL OF TROOPS AFTER REACHING ENGLAND.

On arrival in England the despatch of troops from the points of disembarkation proceeded with great smoothness under the War Office movement control organisation.

### 7. ENEMY EFFORTS TO FRUSTRATE OPERATION.

Attempts by the enemy to frustrate the operation consisted of the following:-

   (*a*) Minelaying by aircraft.

   (*b*) Intensive air attack.

   (*c*) Action by Motor Torpedo Boats.

   (*d*) Gunfire by coast artillery.

   (*e*) Submarine operations.

(a) *Minelaying by aircraft.* Minelaying during the dark hours probably commenced during the night 28th-29th and was maintained with great intensity during the following two nights. Not only were the Dunkirk Roads mined, including the Zuydecoote Pass, but also Route X and the area round the Kwinte Buoy. Folkestone and Dover Harbour entrances were also mined. Considering the number of mines laid, it is interesting to note that only two British ships are known for certain to have been mined, the personnel vessel MONA'S QUEEN and the F.A.A. Yacht GRIEVE. One Hospital Carrier was damaged at anchor off Dover when a mine was blown up by a LL. Trawler sweeping close at hand. Two A/S trawlers on patrol to the northward of the operational area were blown up by what was at first thought to be a M.T.B., but later evidence suggests they were victims of moored mines. The impunity with which degaussed ships were able to operate in this heavily mined area alone made the operation possible and one reaches the conclusion that if the enemy on this occasion had had at hand the means of laying moored contact mines by aircraft, instead of magnetic mines, the results would have been very different.

(b) *Air Attack.* On the evening of the 29th, the first occasion on which a massed target of ships was presented in Dunkirk Harbour, the enemy seized the opportunity for air attack in great strength, and it was only by good fortune that the vital Dunkirk Harbour channel was not blocked by sinking ships at this early date. From then onwards the scale and vigour of the air attack increased, and during the Ist June all ships in Dunkirk, off the beaches, or in the approach channels, were subjected every two hours to an unprecedented scale of air attack by aircraft in such numbers, that the R.A.F. were unable to deal with the situation. The scale of enemy air attack on June Ist, and the fact that the Germans could by now command the newly-swept central route at its exits into the Dunkirk Roads with gunfire from the shore, were responsible for the suspension of daylight evacuation on June 2nd.

(c) *Attack by M.T.B.s.* These caused 4 casualties, namely two destroyers and two trawlers, while the north Route $Y^2$ was in use. When the middle Route $X^2$, some 26 miles further to the South Westward, was brought into use the enemy M.T.B. units failed to follow up, though the continuous stream of unescorted traffic during the dark hours and the ships lying in Dunkirk Roads provided a tempting target to any enterprising Commander.

(d) *Shore Artillery.* At the commencement of the operation, the southern Route $Z^2$ was found to be under gunfire from batteries near Calais, and consequently could only be used by night. The northern Route Y was usable only by night when later the batteries near Nieuport brought fire to bear on the Zuydecoote Pass, which was too narrow to permit a reasonable chance of ships running the gauntlet of fire. By this time, however, Route X was available, and was free of gunfire until German batteries near Gravelines brought its exit into the Dunkirk Roads under gunfire. This occurred in the afternoon on Saturday, Ist June, and in conjunction with the result of enemy air attack, led to the suspension of daylight traffic altogether.

(e) *Submarines.* U-Boats do not appear to have caused any casualties. It is unlikely that the one thought to be present penetrated further than the northern Route Y. It may well be that this U-Boat laid moored mines, which are thought to have caused the loss of two A/S trawlers.

## 8. AIR CO-OPERATION[3]

It is unnecessary to stress the vital necessity for effective air co-operation in an operation of this nature. Not only did German air effort interrupt and reduce seaborne traffic, but it also prevented embarkation by suspending troop movement. To both Naval and Military observers on the coast, the situation at times was extremely disheartening. Rightly or wrongly, full air protection was expected, but instead, for hours on end the ships off shore were subjected to a murderous hail of bombs and machine gun bullets.

Required by their duty to remain offshore waiting for the troops, who themselves were unable to move down to the water for the same reason, it required the greatest determination and sense of duty, amounting in fact to heroism, on the part of the ships' and boats' crews, to enable them to complete their mission.

In their reports, the Commanding Officers of many ships, while giving credit to the R.A.F. personnel for gallantry in such combats as were observed from the ships, at the same time express their sense of disappointment and surprise at the seemingly puny efforts made to provide air protection during the height of this operation, though the gallantry of our out-numbered airmen was the admiration of all.

## 9. No. II GROUP FIGHTER PATROLS – DUNKIRK AREA HISTORY

| Date | Patrols | Total flying hours daily | Enemy aircraft assessed as destroyed |
| --- | --- | --- | --- |
| 26th May. | 22 | 480 | 20 |
| 27th May. | 23 | 536 | 38 |
| 28th May. | 11 | 576 | 23 |
| 29th May. | 9 | 674 | 65 |
| 30th May. | 9 | 704 | - |
| 31st May. | 8 | 490 | 38 |
| 1st June. | 8 | 558 | 43 |
| 2nd June. | 4 | 231 | 35 |
| 3rd June. | 4 | 339 | - |
| 4th June. | 3 | 234 | - |
| Totals | 101 | 4,822 | 262 |

*Notes:*

*(1) It will be observed that the number of patrols decreased from 27th May onwards, whilst there was an increase in the daily flying hours. This is due to the fact that the fighters were employed in increasingly bigger patrols as the enemy air opposition increased.*

*(2) Operation "Dynamo" suffered most from enemy air effort on 29th May and on 1st June, after which latter date the combination of enemy air attack and shore artillery fire led to the suspension of the operation by day.*

10. The position of enemy batteries had been located by air reconnaissance by nightfall on 31st May, and additional batteries in the Gravelines area on the 1st June. Air Bombardment of these batteries during the 1st and 2nd June undoubtedly reduced their fire during dusk and dawn on each of the nights 2nd/3rd June and 3rd/4th June, when seaborne traffic was passing within range of the enemy batteries commanding the south end of X Route, the Dunkirk Roads and Dunkirk Harbour. This was a valuable contribution by the R.A.F to the successful outcome of the operation. A similar beneficial result was obtained by the bombing of the batteries which had Dunkirk Pier and roadstead under fire.

## II. CONTROL OF ALLIED TROOPS.

In the earlier stages the large number of British troops located in the dunes off the beach were of rear formations with few officers. There was little control over these mixed units, aggravated no doubt by the fact that Army Officers' uniform is indistinguishable from that of other ranks which makes the presence of an Army Officer difficult to recognise by troops other than those under their own Commands. The appearance of Naval Officers, in their unmistakable uniforms, helped to restore order and the troops responded to commands in a disciplined manner. In the early stages, in the absence of any Army embarkation staff or organisation a strong naval party was required to form up and embark the troops. Later, no difficulty was experienced when troops of fighting formations were encountered. Difficulty was experienced in controlling some French troops, whilst others were so rigidly bound by discipline and tradition that they would not embark except by complete formation under their own unit officers. In either case the rate of embarkation was much slower than with British troops.

## I2. INITIATIVE SHOWN BY COMMANDING OFFICERS AND SUBORDINATE PERSONNEL.

A most satisfactory feature of the operation was the high degree of initiative shown by Commanding and Subordinate Officers of units operating off the coast, ranging from H.M.

Destroyers to commandeered motor boats. The majority of officers and ratings in command were in situations requiring independent action in extremely difficult conditions. Often the easiest course was to be satisfied with work already achieved and to return to the United Kingdom with a final load of troops. The reverse action was invariably executed, namely, continued operation off the coast as long as there were both troops ashore to be evacuated and vessels offshore to receive them. If the craft in use was damaged or sunk the crew invariably seized some other boat to continue their efforts.

Unaware of the military situation ashore and often forced to move westward by bombardment from German artillery or even by rifle fire from advancing German forces, the majority of these boats, commanded often by stokers or "hostility only" seamen, had only one object in view, to lift from the beach any, and all troops, British or Allied, within sight of the water's edge.

On their return to the United Kingdom when asked to report their proceedings it was only in answer to direct enquiry that it would transpire that these young men had been subjected in many cases, to an unparalleled bombardment from the air. They appeared to consider that this was part of the day's work requiring no comment.

## I3. LOSSES OF TROOPS AFTER EMBARKATION.

It is a distressing fact that many ships were sunk or damaged on the return voyage when laden with troops. But it is fortunate that in most of such cases the majority of troops were saved owing to the large volume of traffic that was coming and going between Dunkirk and the United Kingdom. Exceptions to this were due to the rapidity with which certain ships sank after having been bombed or torpedoed. Such cases are as follows:-

WAKEFUL. Torpedoed. Ship broke in half and only those on the upper deck were saved. About 600 troops were below.

CRESTED EAGLE. Was bombed and then beached in a burning condition. Only about 300 saved out of 600 on board.

SKIPJACK. 250-300 troops on board, most of whom, unfortunately, went down with the ship when she sank.

WAVERLEY. 600 troops were on board before ship was abandoned in sinking condition, but only 200-300 were picked up.

In all it is regretted that about 2,000 troops must have been lost through these and similar disasters on the return voyages to England.

## 14. CO-OPERATION OF THE FRENCH NAVY.

French warships and other vessels were employed evacuating French troops from Dunkirk Harbour, and on the last three nights from the beach 1½ miles eastward from Dunkirk. Details are given in Appendix IV.

## 15. BASE ORGANISATION.

An operation of this magnitude involving the maintenance and movements of close on 900 vessels and boats could not have been conducted without the wholehearted and unceasing efforts of the base establishments at Dover and Ramsgate, as well as those at Sheerness and Harwich in the Nore Command. At all these places officers and men, Naval and civilian, laboured unceasingly throughout the Operation.

In particular I wish to acknowledge the great assistance received from the Commander-in-Chief, Nore, Admiral the Hon. Sir Reginald A.R. Plunkett-Ernle-Erle-Drax, K.C.B., D.S.O., who in many cases anticipated my requests for assistance through his constant watch on the progress of the Operation.

The prompt and unfailing assistance afforded by the Chatham Depot in providing personnel for the numerous small craft, working parties and beach parties, was a feature essential to the successful outcome of the Operation.

The Naval Officer-in-Charge, Ramsgate, Captain W.R. Phillimore, R.N., by taking over the servicing and control of the great majority of the small craft of the inshore flotillas relieved Dover of an immense volume of work which it would otherwise have been impossible to handle.

It was also brought to my notice that at Harwich an exceptional Naval and Military system was in being for assisting those ships which called there to make a quick turn round, relieving the tired ships' companies of the work of cleaning and clearing their vessels.

## 16. SERVICES OF STAFF, INCLUDING OFFICERS TEMPORARILY APPOINTED.

I was fortunate in having the services of Rear Admiral W.F. Wake-Walker, C.B., O.B.E., as Flag Officer afloat off Dunkirk, and Captain W.G. Tennant, C.B., M.V.O., as Senior Naval Officer, Dunkirk on shore. Admiral Wake-Walker was responsible for supervising the embarkation afloat and Captain Tennant for organising embarkation from the shore, keeping touch with the French Naval Authorities and the staff of the British Commander-in-Chief.

I cannot conclude this despatch without reference to the splendid work of my staff under the guidance of my Chief Staff Officer, Captain L.V. Morgan, C.B.E., M.V.O., D.S.C. Augmented by additional officers, including both Army and Royal Air Force, especially appointed for the occasion, their task of organising and operating the large and varied collection of H.M. Ships continued without a pause day and night throughout the 10 days that the Operation lasted, and I can never testify adequately to the excellence of their work, upon the efficiency of which successful results depended.

Finally I would like to pay tribute to the valuable support and assistance which I received throughout the whole course of the evacuation from Vice Admiral Sir James Somerville, K.C.B., D.S.O., who was appointed to H.M.S. LYNX for special service in connection with the evacuation. The attributes of this officer for initiative and resource are well known throughout the Service, but I venture to express the opinion that never in the course of his long and distinguished career have they been put to better use than during the operations for the evacuation of the Allied Armies from Dunkirk.

## I7. RECOMMENDATIONS OF PERSONNEL.

I have already transmitted a brief list of those recommended for immediate award or decoration (which His Majesty has been pleased to accept) and I will forward a further list at a later date when time has permitted a full examination of all the reports.

(Sgd.) B.H. RAMSAY,<br>*Vice Admiral.*

# OPERATION "DYNAMO" NARRATIVE OF EVENTS

## INTRODUCTION

As far as the Dover Command is concerned, the genesis of this operation took place at a War Office meeting on Sunday the 19th May, 1940, at which the Vice Admiral, Dover, was represented. This meeting discussed (I) Temporary maintenance of the B.E.F. through Dunkirk, Calais and Boulogne, and (2) Evacuation of personnel through Dunkirk, Calais and Boulogne. Under this last item was included, amongst other items, the problem of "the hazardous evacuation of very large Forces". This was considered "to be unlikely". (This problem ultimately became that of Operation "Dynamo").

2. The main decision of this meeting was that the control must be delegated to the Vice Admiral, Dover, and available shipping placed at his disposal.

3. Further meetings were held at Dover on the 20th May, and at the War Office on the 2Ist May, to consider the "emergency evacuation across the Channel of very large Forces" These meetings determined the number of personnel vessels and small craft available, and confirmed that the control of all sea movements rested with the Vice Admiral, Dover, a liaison officer from the War Office Movement Control and from the Ministry of Shipping being attached to the Vice Admiral.

4. The need for air protection of sailings, including the period of embarkation and disembarkation was recognised, and was to be arranged by the Vice Admiral, Dover, direct with the Fighter Command.

5. The reception arrangements at the points of disembarkation were provided for. At the Dover meeting it was pointed out that in the event

of evacuation it would be necessary to make provision for lifting troops from beaches, and that owing to the very gradual shoaling of the beaches it would be necessary to have a large number of small boats to carry troops from the beaches to the off-shore ships. Further, it was thought extremely doubtful if the whole of the troops to be evacuated could be lifted from the beaches, and that, if at all possible, the ports must be used as well.

6. Subsequent to the Dover meeting of the 20th May, continual telephone conversations took place between Dover, the Admiralty, Ministry of Shipping and the Commander-in-Chief, Nore, as to the provision of small craft for the final evacuation, and the provision of Naval personnel for manning the small boats required for ferrying and skoots and other small vessels taken up for transport purposes.

7. A meeting was held at the Admiralty on Sunday, the 26th May, to consider the same subject and to examine the number of craft available. The notes of this meeting were subsequently supplied to the Vice Admiral, Dover, who was not represented at the Admiralty.

8. Meantime, on the 23rd May, evacuation of Boulogne was started and completed on the 24th. The position was more complicated at Calais where evacuation was limited to non-fighting personnel; the fighting personnel having to hold on in order to assist the main B.E.F. Further, a supply ship with stores and transport had to be unloaded at Calais for this Force.

9. It was then apparent from all these events that if the B.E.F. was to be evacuated the only port available would be Dunkirk.

10. *P.M. Sunday, the 26th*: The military situation was thought to have deteriorated so rapidly that the Vice Admiral was informed by the Admiralty that it was imperative for "Dynamo" to be implemented with the greatest vigour, with a view to lifting up to 45,000 of the B.E.F. within two days, at the end of which it was probable that evacuation would be terminated by enemy action.

# OPERATION "DYNAMO". NARRATIVE OF EVENTS.

*Sunday, 26th May, 1940.*

Admiralty ordered Operation "Dynamo" to commence at 1857. Prior to the receipt of this order, the despatch of Personnel Vessels[4] to Dunkirk had already commenced at 1500. At this time a flow of two vessels every four hours had been agreed to by the B.E.F., the first of these reached Dover on the return trip at 2230 and 1,312 personnel were landed.

2. On this day the only Inshore Craft available to Vice-Admiral, Dover, were four Belgian Passenger Launches and the Naval Small Craft of the Dover Command such as Drifters, and Motor Boats from the Contraband Control Base at Ramsgate. The only ones capable of lifting personnel direct from a beach being the boats from Ramsgate. The Admiralty had been asked for the supply of small boats, especially whalers and cutters,[5] but there was always the difficulty of arranging for the personnel to man them. When matters became urgent, the Admiralty made a signal to the various Home Ports asking them to report how many cutters and whalers could be made available for immediate service under Vice-Admiral, Dover.

*Monday, 27th May.*

3. The Vice-Admiral, Dover, was informed by the Admiralty of the various steps taken to supply coasting vessels, skoots,[6] motor boats and other small craft including rowing boats for inshore work off the

beaches. Very few of such inshore craft could be available during the day and the main effort was concentrated on maintaining the flow of Personnel Vessels to Dunkirk at the rate of 2 every 3½ hours. After a good start during the night 26th/27th the effect of enemy action against these transports was felt. Between sailings timed 0300/27 and 1500/27, no less than 5 transports were shelled and returned to United Kingdom without making the trip. In addition MONA ISLE was damaged by shell fire and QUEEN OF THE CHANNEL was bombed and sank during the early hours of the 28th. As a result the Vice-Admiral, Dover, reported to the Admiralty that the normal channel, Dover to Dunkirk, was impracticable in daylight owing to fire from shore batteries extending from Les Hemmes to Gravelines. Zuydecoote Pass had to be used instead and consequently the distance run for the round trip increased from 80 miles to 172 resulting in a general slowing up of traffic. This route had to be used before it could be swept. Work was also commenced to sweep a channel from the North Goodwin to the Ruytingen Pass and thence into the Dunkirk Roads, thus shortening the round trip from 172 miles to 108.

4. The S.N.O. Dunkirk, with naval beach and pier party of 12 officers and 160 ratings, plus communication staff, left Dover in WOLFHOUND at 1345, and were attacked by dive bombers at half-hour intervals between 1600 and 1800, on the voyage to Dunkirk.

5. During the day preparations were advanced for embarkation from beaches in the La Panne-Dunkirk area, as such matters as crews, fuel and general organisation were taken in hand. Five Personnel Vessels routed to start in daylight completed the round trip during the 27th and lifted a total of 3,952. In addition 17 drifters of the Dover Command sailed from Dover for the Malo Beach, and during the night lifted 2,000 troops from the beach by ships' dinghies. During the day destroyer patrols had been established to the Northward to cover the passage of merchant ships between Dunkirk and the Downs, and the Admiralty asked Western Approaches to reinforce the Dover destroyers.

6. Commander-in-Chief, Nore, sailed 6 small skoots for the South Downs to co-operate in Dunkirk, and sailed 4 skoots loaded with Army stores direct to Dunkirk. In the evening Naval Officer-in-Charge, Ramsgate, was asked to take over the fuelling and despatching of all small power boats with the attendant pulling boats forming the inshore

flotilla. Some unnecessary delays occurred at this stage as the majority of Naval Authorities were directing the small craft for Dunkirk to be routed to Dover, although the Vice Admiral, Dover, had asked for the Downs to be their destination. Once despatched by the Authorities no communication with these vessels was possible until they arrived at their destination, and so the requirements of assembling these craft at the Downs or Ramsgate were in many cases delayed by as much as 24 hours or more since during the night misfortune befell many tows that came adrift due to moderate weather or collisions and the business of rounding them up could not be effected until daylight.

7. The Vice Admiral had intended to maintain a destroyer at Dunkirk as a W/T link, but the S.N.O., on arrival, decided that conditions at Dunkirk made this impossible.

8. At 2025 the Vice Admiral, Dover, received a Most Immediate message from the S.N.O., Dunkirk, who had just reached his station, as follows: "Port consistently bombed all day, and on fire. Embarkation possible only from beaches East of harbour A.B.C.D. Send all ships and passenger ships there to anchor. Am ordering WOLFHOUND to load there and sail. T.O.O.[7] 2005/27." Meanwhile Vice-Admiral, Dover, had asked the Commander-in-Chief, Nore, to send every available shallow draught power boat, capable of ferrying from beaches to ships lying off the beaches Eastward of Dunkirk, stocked with fuel and provisions for two days; this move being made with a view to saving time by cutting out the passage to, and subsequent reorganisation, at Ramsgate, prior to proceeding to the French Coast. It should be noted at this time (2000/27) there were no pulling boats, cutters or whalers immediately available for attendance on Power Boats. A further signal: "Please send every available craft to beaches East of Dunkirk immediately. Evacuation tomorrow night is problematical. T.O.O. 1958/27" was received from S.N.O. Dunkirk.

Later that evening a report was received from 2 Military Officers from G.H.Q. which suggested that the situation of the B.E.F. was precarious and it was possible that the enemy might succeed in cutting off this force from Dunkirk. This report appeared to confirm the results of air reconnaissance, which indicated that German armoured units were operating to the south of Dunkirk. Since it appeared that evacuation might well be strictly limited, both in regard to numbers and time available for the operation, it was decided to concentrate every effort in sending over as many craft as possible to the beaches without delay. Had the situation appeared to be less critical, an organised flow of large and small craft working in reliefs would have been arranged.

9. On receipt of these signals from S.N.O. Dunkirk, all available forces were diverted to the beaches, the Personnel Ships to the beach, code letters A.B.C. and D., the destroyers on patrol being diverted to La Panne. Destroyers that were working off Dunkirk were ordered to divert the Personnel Ships going into Dunkirk to lay off the beaches and the smaller craft such as drifters and motor boats were ordered to be used for ferrying troops from the beach to the larger ships. Two important strings of boats being towed by a tug were lost in the night through the tows being run down and cut in half, the boats being scattered.

10. As a result of the above action there were assembling off the beaches 2 transports, 9 destroyers, 4 minesweepers, CALCUTTA, 17 drifters and a few skoots, and all the ships were ordered to use their own boats for ferrying as none of the inshore flotilla had arrived. From signals received it appeared that the situation was desperate, that little could be lifted direct from the Port of Dunkirk and that the maximum effort must be made from the beaches. Commander-in-Chief, Nore, at this stage provided additional reinforcements of minesweepers and paddlers. During the night, Vice Admiral, Dover, was informed of continuous bombing and machine gunning of troops in the beach areas, and directed Senior Officers present on the beach to use their discretion in ordering withdrawal of the Naval forces, observing that a strong fighter protection should be expected after dawn; this having been arranged after a special visit by the Liaison Officer to Hawkinge to procure the maximum effort.

11. Limiting factors were thought most likely to be restrictions due to enemy action at Dunkirk and on the beaches, and the difficulties of concentrating the ships and troops at a common point or points. The general evacuation plan had been conveyed to the G.O.C. by the S.N.O. on his way to Dunkirk, and the Vice Admiral, Dover, hoped to receive in return some outline of the Military's operational plan upon which the rate of evacuation in the various areas under the scheme must depend. Subject to the development of beach evacuation and the

continuation of fine weather, it appeared to the Vice Admiral that adequate shipping for his plans was either in, or on its way to the Dover area, except for a chronic shortage of beaching boats.

*Tuesday, 28th May.*

12. By 0100/28 a large number of craft was approaching the Belgian-French coast, while two Personnel Carriers were crossing to Dover with 1,400 troops. Two other carriers, whose entry into Dunkirk had been stopped as a result of S.N.O., Dunkirk's signals 2005/27 and 1958/27, were unable to make the beaches and one, the MAID OF ORLEANS was damaged by enemy bombing and another, the QUEEN OF THE CHANNEL was sunk. During the preceding afternoon the Hospital Carrier[8] ISLE OF THANET was shelled and damaged by the Calais Battery. All available destroyers were working off the La Panne-Malo beaches using their own boats, since the supply of beaching boats from the United Kingdom had not yet reached across the Channel. A moderate surf on the beaches reduced the rate of embarkation, exhausted the boats' crews, the majority of whom were "hostility only" ratings, rendering the whole operation slow and difficult.

13. In view of the heavy casualties experienced during the last 24 hours to personnel carriers caused by the development of German air threat over Dunkirk and the increasing artillery fire on the sea approaches to Dunkirk, it was decided that until the situation was restored, these personnel vessels could not be used on the French Coast during full daylight, and consequently for the moment evacuation from Dunkirk by day must be confined to warships and other small vessels. Furthermore, since evacuation from the beaches by day with the troops exposed to bombing and machine gunning was likely to be ineffective with the small number of beaching craft at the Vice Admiral's disposal, the plan provided for evacuation from both Dunkirk and the whole length of beaches by night. (At that time – 1100/28 – information was being received of the loss of a great number of the small beaching craft during the preceding night and of the considerable amount of organisation still manned almost wholly by members of the Merchant

Navy and Fishing Fleets required to bring the surviving boats effectively to bear on the beaches.)

I4. During the forenoon it became more evident that the greatest effort must be made the following night and the Admiralty instructed Commander-in-Chief, Western Approaches, and Commander-in-Chief, Portsmouth, to sail every available destroyer to Dover. In addition the 7th and 8th M/S Flotillas were ordered to Harwich under the orders of the Vice Admiral. Commander-in-Chief, Nore, arranged a patrol of all available M.T.B.s and A/S Trawlers to cover the North-east flank of the evacuation area against attack by enemy surface craft from the North between 2030/28 and 0600/29.

I5. At this time great concern was felt over the lack of water which had been reported on the beaches and joint Naval and Military measures were set on foot to provide for the supply of water in receptacles and in tanks to the beaches apart from the arrangements for evacuation. Ships off the beaches were also instructed to do what they could with their own resources to help in this matter.

I6. Evacuation plan for the night was communicated to S.N.O. Dunkirk by signal – timed I555/28 – and provided for the use of 3 Hospital Carriers, 7 personnel steamers and 2 destroyers at the East Pier, Dunkirk, while some 20 destroyers, I9 paddle and fleet sweepers, I7 drifters, 20 to 40 skoots, 5 coasters, I2 motor boats, 2 tugs, 28 pulling cutters and life-boats were to be distributed between La Panne and point I½ miles East of Dunkirk, on the beaches; the destroyers running continuous round trips.

It was estimated that the personnel vessels and hospital carriers would be clear of the danger area by 0630. As regards the beaching and other small craft which had not yet reached the Dover Straits, arrangements were made with other authorities to route all small craft, which had not already been despatched, direct to the beaches East of Dunkirk, provided they had charts, food, fuel, etc.

At this time some difficulty was experienced in having at hand the large number of charts required for these additional vessels.

I7. Owing to the suspension of daylight work by personnel vessels it was necessary to increase the number handled in Dunkirk during the dark hours as the attempt to use the surplus personnel vessels off the beaches by night seemed unlikely to bear fruit. Accordingly, S.N.O.

Dunkirk, was asked whether personnel vessels could be berthed inside Dunkirk Harbour, the only information in Vice Admiral's possession having indicated that the East Pier of the harbour entrance was the only suitable berth for such ships to which British troops could have access. To increase the off-shore forces, Commander-in-Chief, Nore, was asked to sail CALCUTTA to be opposite La Panne at 2200 to embark troops using own boats.

Orders were issued that all ships proceeding to Dunkirk from Dover were to use the Southern Route Z provided that the passage from No. 6 Calais Buoy to Dunkirk could be made in darkness.

18. At 1830 GRAFTON reported that several thousand troops remained on beaches at Bray and that more were arriving. At that time there were off Bray, one tow of pulling boats, number uncertain, 2 power boats, at least 2 skoots, CALCUTTA, GALLANT, WAKEFUL, VERITY, and GRAFTON, using what survived of their own whalers and motor boats. This force was reinforced by 2 minesweepers at 2115. Later reports of concentrations of troops on the beaches were received, particularly at La Panne and Bray. Craft approaching the coast were directed accordingly. Naval Officer-in-Charge, Ramsgate, was requested to maintain a continuous evacuation service by skoots between Margate and Ramsgate and the beach, and take over responsibility for servicing those vessels. Meantime CALCUTTA, who was off La Panne, reported that conditions for embarkation there were very bad owing to heavy surf, but that they might improve with the rising tide.

Shortly after midnight CALCUTTA was informed that the Third Corps of the B.E.F. and the Commander-in-Chief were all now at La Panne. She was directed to make every endeavour to concentrate all destroyers and light craft at that end of the beach with the object of embarking that force as soon as possible.

19. As regards enemy activity, this day the Germans contented themselves with bombing the town and port of Dunkirk, but on a small scale compared with that to be experienced later, probably because of increasing R.A.F. air cover and also due to the fact that a heavy pall of smoke from the burning town covered the operation most of the day.

*Wednesday, 29th May.*

20. The Northern Route Y having been swept, it was arranged to sail personnel ships to Dunkirk at daylight and to continue to sail throughout the day; this route would take ships clear of the artillery fire on shore. Personnel ships accordingly started at 0230.

2I. Much consideration had been given to the practicability of building piers on the beaches using lines of barges. Reports from ships that worked off the beaches showed, however, that owing to the very gradual shoaling of the water at all states of the tide such a barge pier to be effective, would have to be of very great length, beyond the resources available.

22. Information was received that the personnel vessels with their Mercantile Marine crews were having difficulty in making the entrance to Dunkirk Harbour in the face of the navigational difficulties caused by a heavy smoke pall over the entrance and in face of bombing and shelling encountered en route and whilst alongside. Nevertheless it subsequently transpired that at Dunkirk there had been a good number of ships throughout the night, at times exceeding the influx of troops.

23. S.N.O. Dunkirk, and other Senior Officers on the Coast reported during the early hours that surf on the beaches was retarding boat work. S.N.O. Dunkirk, at 0709, asked for all ships to go to Dunkirk. The Vice-Admiral could not accept this as it was essential to maintain lifts off the beaches as well as from Dunkirk Harbour, both from the aspect of the military situation and from the fact that Dunkirk was limited by a bottleneck, formed by the narrow gangway along the East Pier to the points of embarkation. Furthermore, there was every prospect of the weather improving and the surf reducing as the tide rose. Nevertheless, an increased number of H.M. Ships was ordered to Dunkirk to augment the personnel vessels, though it was feared that an accumulation of ships alongside the East Pier at Dunkirk by day might well invite intensive air attacks.

Subsequently, this fear was fully to be justified.

24. Meantime, considerable anxiety was felt as to the fate of the personnel vessels which had been despatched in a steady stream to Dunkirk commencing the previous evening. The first of these was due back at Dover about 0300, but by 0900 nothing had been sighted or

reported. But at 0700, S.N.O. Dunkirk had reported that the embarkation there was going on at the rate of 2,000 an hour, so it was presumed that the transports had failed to enter the harbour during darkness, had waited outside, and had commenced to enter in succession at dawn. The necessity for continuous fighter protection in view of the exposure of these unarmed ships while at Dunkirk and during the daylight passage through coastal waters, was obvious. Constant touch was maintained with the R.A.F. Commands to obtain continuous fighter protection during the hours when the Vice-Admiral, Dover, estimated the largest concentration of vessels would be present, it being realised that the R.A.F. resources were not sufficient to provide continuous air cover, and to dispense with full cover at less important periods.

25. At 0930 the belated return of the personnel vessels from Dunkirk commenced, and proceeded steadily through the day. In addition to the personnel vessels using Dunkirk the Admiralty were informed of the necessity for X-lighters and other self-propelled lighters to increase the facilities for beach evacuation. A Medical Party was shipped in VERITY for use on the beaches, and a Naval Medical Party was sent to Dunkirk.

26. The considerable alarm as to the immediate safety of the B.E.F. felt during the evening and early night of the 28th, which caused all available resources to be immediately concentrated on the French Coast, eased during the 29th. But emergency measures taken late on the 28th had an adverse effect on the orderly organisation for evacuation so necessary if effective measures were to be devised and put in force.

27. Meantime, in the early hours of the 29th, an unfortunate disaster occurred involving the loss of H.M. Destroyers WAKEFUL and GRAFTON, and the danlayer COMFORT. WAKEFUL, after embarking troops at Bray, sailed for Dover at 2300/28 by the Zuydecoote Pass and North Channel. Approaching the Kwinte Whistle Buoy the speed of the ships was 20 knots, and a zigzag of 40 degrees every four minutes was started. At 0045 two torpedo tracks were observed, one torpedo missed, the other hit amidships. WAKEFUL broke in half and the two portions sank in I5 seconds, each remaining standing with the midship end on the bottom. All the troops on board

went down with the ship; certain of the crew floated clear. After about half-an-hour motor drifters NAUTILUS and COMFORT arrived and started to pick up survivors, later joined by GOSSAMER. Captain of WAKEFUL was in the COMFORT. GRAFTON and LYDD were close and Captain of WAKEFUL warned GRAFTON she was in danger of being torpedoed. At that moment, 0250, GRAFTON was torpedoed, COMFORT was lifted in the air, and Captain of WAKEFUL washed overboard. COMFORT was going full speed and as she came round in a circle LYDD and GRAFTON opened fire on her, evidently thinking she was an enemy ship. It is believed that COMFORT crew, except one, and WAKEFUL survivors, except four, were killed. LYDD then bore down on COMFORT, rammed and sank her.

Previously GRAFTON, who was proceeding to Dover with troops, had observed a ship torpedoed, and lowered her boats to pick up survivors, subsequently ascertained by signal to LYDD to be WAKEFUL. A small darkened vessel, thought to be a drifter, was signalled and told to pick up survivors. Within a few seconds of this, GRAFTON was torpedoed. The bridge was also hit, either by a shell or grenade, and the Captain killed instantly. LYDD then tried to come alongside but after hitting starboard side sheered off, and appeared to ram a vessel on port quarter. This was COMFORT. GRAFTON opened fire under the impression

LYDD had rammed the M.T.B. Target was then shifted to another vessel further away on port quarter, and vessel was observed to blow up with a bright flash. This may well have been the enemy M.T.B.

28. During the forenoon JAGUAR, GALLANT and GRENADE were dispatched via the new Middle Route X to test the opposition by shore batteries prior to introducing this route as an alternative to the long Northern route. GRENADE arrived Dunkirk, reported no fire from shore batteries, but that she had experienced heavy bombing. These three destroyers were attacked by dive bombers when approaching Dunkirk at about noon, and GALLANT was damaged. At least six attacks were carried out, one enemy aircraft was brought down by gunfire and others by fighters. An hour later MALCOLM reported Dunkirk heavily bombed with a large number of aircraft and during the afternoon this bombing extended up the coast to ships off Bray. During the afternoon the Middle Route X was brought into use for destroyers,

but small ships were still routed round the Northern route to Zuydecoote Pass. LOCUST and MOSQUITO joined Dover Command and were dispatched to work on the beaches during the afternoon. Shortly after noon enemy shore batteries near Nieuport began to bring Zuydecoote Pass under spasmodic gunfire and the state was being reached whereby the new Middle Route would become the only practicable daylight approach to Dunkirk and the beaches. At noon, CALCUTTA, who was able to get across to La Panne beach to receive troops by small boats, embarked 1,200 troops from the minesweepers and then sailed for Sheerness, the minesweepers remaining to load up again. At 1606, the New Route X having been fully swept, all ships were ordered by the Vice Admiral to use Route X, exercising navigational caution, and those from Dover were instructed to proceed by Route Z, the South route, provided the passage between Calais Bell Buoy and Dunkirk be made in darkness.

Route X passed some 26 miles to the South-Westward of the extreme N.E. point of the Northern Route Y, the locality in which enemy M.T.B. attack threatened, and was shielded by the French minefields in the Ruytingen and Dyck channels. It appears that the enemy M.T.B. command failed to appreciate the withdrawal of traffic to the S.W. and did not follow up.

In the evening it was reported that there was no congestion anywhere on the coast, except at La Panne. The force at La Panne was accordingly reinforced as ships became available.

29. An additional beach party of seven officers and a number of ratings under Captain J. Howson was sailed in SABRE at 1600 for Dunkirk, and Captain E. Bush, who had already visited Dunkirk and was aware of the general conditions, was sent to HEBE as S.N.O. afloat off the beaches. An M.T.B. was placed at the disposal of the S.N.O. on the coast.

30. At about 1600 a heavy air attack commenced on the East Mole Pier, Dunkirk harbour, mainly by dive bombing, which lasted continuously for more than two hours. At the same time, other air attacks took place on ships lying off Bray. Attacks were renewed from time to time up till after 2000, not only on Dunkirk, but on ships off Bray, in the Zuydecoote Pass and those in the Southern end of X Route. These attacks were to have a disastrous result on the evacuation

arrangements at Dunkirk. There were present alongside the inner side of the Eastern Arm two destroyers GRENADE and JAGUAR, three trawlers ahead of the GRENADE and JAGUAR, three more trawlers ahead of them with CANTERBURY in the next berth, and a French destroyer ahead of the CANTERBURY. Outside the harbour on the outside of the Eastern Arm the Transport FENELLA was berthed opposite the GRENADE and JAGUAR and the CRESTED EAGLE opposite the six trawlers. In addition, the MALCOLM and VERITY were also in the harbour but further inside. This presented a very good target and the ships were soon hit and embarkation of troops ceased for the time being. CANTERBURY, accompanied by JAGUAR, succeeded in leaving harbour, but both were hit by bombs and damaged. Both succeeded in reaching Dover, though JAGUAR had to be towed part of the way and was subjected to many attacks on passage. CANTERBURY reached harbour at 2115 and disembarked 1,950 troops but was sufficiently damaged to prevent her being used again in these operations. To return to Dunkirk, FENELLA was lying alongside on the outside of the pier, and was hit and sunk. GRENADE and one of the trawlers on the East side were hit and the trawler sank in the fairway. GRENADE sinking and on fire had to be abandoned and appeared to be about to sink in the fairway. A trawler was detailed to tow her clear. VERITY, who witnessed this occurrence, was continuously straddled by bombs for 35 minutes. Passage all along the pier having ceased, she cast off, and skirting the burning GRENADE and trawler, proceeded out of harbour, grounding slightly on a sunk drifter in the entrance. At about 1800 KING ORRY arrived to find the harbour occupied only by burning and sinking ships, with no sign of any one on the pier nor any boat moving in the harbour. She was immediately subjected to heavy bombing attacks, having previously had her steering gear put out of action by a dive bombing attack when about half mile outside of the entrance. She remained in sole occupation of the harbour until shortly after midnight 29th/30th, when her Captain rightly decided to take the ship out of harbour before she also was sunk, thus freeing the berth and safeguarding the channel from being blocked.

Little information of these disasters filtered through to Dover, except that it was known that Dunkirk was under heavy air bombardment and that the destroyers there were being hit soon after 1600.

31. At 1906 the Vice Admiral promulgated the plan for the night by signal as follows: "Evacuation of British troops to continue at maximum speed during the night. If adequate supply of personnel vessels cannot be maintained to Dunkirk East Pier, destroyers will be sent there as well. All other craft except hospital carriers to embark from beach which is extended from one mile East of Dunkirk to one mile East of La Panne. Whole length is divided into three equal parts referred to as La Panne, Bray, Malo, from East to West with a mile gap between each part. La Panne and Bray have troop concentration points each end and in middle, Malo at each end. These points should be tended by inshore craft. Pass the message by V/S to ships not equipped W/T as opportunity offers."

32. About 1900 a telephone message was received from La Panne Military Headquarters through the War Office and the Admiralty to the effect that Dunkirk Harbour was blocked by damaged ships, and that all evacuation must therefore be effected from the beaches.

About the same time a corrupt message from S.N.O. Dunkirk, was received stating continuous bombing, one destroyer sinking, one transport with troops on board damaged and impossible at present to embark more troops, though pier undamaged.

33. In this confused situation the Vice Admiral, Dover, at 2128, ordered all ships approaching Dunkirk not to close the harbour, but instead to remain off the Eastern beach to collect troops from the shore, and the drifters and minesweepers which were about to be despatched to Dunkirk Harbour were also diverted to the beaches.

It appeared, therefore, at this time that the use of Dunkirk Harbour would be denied to us except possibly to the small ships.

Signals addressed to S.N.O. Dunkirk, HEBE, VERITY, who were known to be in the vicinity of Dunkirk, were sent requiring information as to the accessibility of the Eastern pier for personnel vessels. Admiral Nord was also informed that Dover was out of touch with Captain Tennant, and asked whether it was still possible for transports to enter the harbour and berth alongside.

No reply to these enquiries could be expected until after midnight.

34. In the event only four trawlers and a yacht entered Dunkirk during the hours of darkness, and as enemy activity was much reduced only two bombing attacks being made, it subsequently transpired that

a good opportunity had been missed. It is probable that ships to lift some 8,000 to 10,000 troops could have been made available for Dunkirk during the night at little loss to embarkation from the beaches.

35. Rear Admiral Wake-Walker proceeded from Dover in ESK at about 1900 for passage to HEBE off the coast where he was to carry out the duties of S.N.O. Dunkirk in charge of all embarkation arrangements, taking over from Captain Bush who had been working in HEBE under the orders of S.N.O. Dunkirk. He expected to arrive at Dunkirk at 2330.

36. As a result of the heavy casualties and losses amongst the destroyer force, particularly the misfortunes which befell those of the larger and more modern types, a consultation was held between the Admiralty and the Vice Admiral which led to a decision to withdraw destroyers of the "H", "I" and "J" Classes from "Dynamo". All destroyers of the "G" Class were already out of action.

There remained available for "Dynamo"
15 destroyers:-

| ESK | WORCESTER |
| EXPRESS | WINDSOR |
| ANTHONY | VERITY |
| KEITH | VANQUISHER |
| CODRINGTON | SABRE |
| MALCOLM | SCIMITAR |
| WHITEHALL | SHIKARI |
| WINCHELSEA | |

Excluding any casualties, this number of destroyers might be expected to maintain a flow of one destroyer per hour to the coast and would lift 17,000 troops in 24 hours.

37. The day closed with a formidable list of ships lost or damaged, a marked reduction in the number of destroyers available and with failure to achieve the high rate of evacuation hoped for. Some 38,000 were landed in England during the 24 hours, but the effect of the day's occurrences was to be more marked next day when instead of some 50,000 to 60,000 which had been calculated as the probable achievement only 48,000 odd were in fact transported.

*Thursday, 30th May.*

38. As an example of the difficulty of any one man appreciating the situation at Dunkirk and the beaches during the night, at 0300/30 the S.N.O. on the French Coast reported that he had no destroyers. In fact, at that time, all available destroyers, namely 10, in the Dover Command, were either on, or on passage to or from, the coast, and the remaining five were at Dover discharging troops, embarking ammunition, fuelling, etc. and were to sail within the next four hours.

Simultaneously the V.C.I.G.S. reported that the beaches were well organised, the troops in good heart, and there had been no bombing since dark, but that there was still a great shortage of small craft, urgently required. This last fact was well known to the Vice Admiral, Dover.

39. Commander-in-Chief, Nore, was requested to send as much towing hawser as possible to Ramsgate, as quickly as possible, for supplying the skoots, to haul boats off the beaches, thus speeding up the boat work to compensate for the shortage of boats, which would continue for at least another 24 hours.

40. At 0500 the seven modern destroyers remaining with Vice Admiral, Dover – ICARUS, IMPULSIVE, INTREPID, IVANHOE, HARVESTER, HAVANT and JAVELIN – sailed to Sheerness in accordance with Admiralty instructions. The MONTROSE and MACKAY sailed for repairs.

41. Meantime the Vice Admiral, Dover, had been much exercised regarding the possibility of the continued use of Dunkirk Harbour for personnel vessels and was anxiously awaiting the report from VANQUISHER, who had been sent to investigate the reported obstruction. VANQUISHER'S report was received at 0610 stating entrance was practicable but that obstruction exists towards outer inside end of the Eastern Arm. Pending amplifying reports, the sailing of personnel vessels to Dunkirk was resumed, although at this time there were still 4 personnel vessels presumed to be in the vicinity of Dunkirk Harbour, whose movements and whereabouts throughout the night still remained obscure.

The Vice Admiral asked R.A. Dover, who was in HEBE, whether personnel ships could, in fact, still use Dunkirk. In the meantime a series of signals from Rear Admiral, Dover, and destroyers off the coast, were received, stating that the beaches were filling up rapidly and more ships and boats were urgently required there. Although it was known that the destroyers could use Dunkirk, it appeared at this time that the best division of transport was to send the great majority of destroyers to the beaches, where urgent demands could not be ignored, and the personnel vessels to Dunkirk Harbour, only an occasional destroyer being sent to Dunkirk from the reduced number now available for the operation.

42. At Dunkirk there were no air attacks in the early morning and all was quiet. Later, when ships began to arrive in quantity, in view of the massive target presented by a number of ships alongside the East Pier at a time, the S.N.O. Dunkirk ordered destroyers alongside only one at a time. At about 0800 a store ship arrived at Dunkirk with provisions but no water. This caused so much congestion on the pier that unloading was abandoned when half complete, and the store ship filled with troops. A certain amount of water was obtained from destroyers.

43. During the forenoon the Military constructed a long pier of lorries with deck planking, into the sea off Bray. This was an excellent piece of work, but was insufficiently stable for use by such craft as paddle steamers, nor even smaller power craft in a lop. It was invaluable later for embarking troops into small boats. As regards general embarkation off the beaches, it was later learnt that it was a common occurrence for processions of small boats loaded with troops to be cast adrift when empty and allowed to float away to seaward, owing to the lack of sufficient naval ratings as boat-keepers. For the same reason many of the smaller pulling boats were swamped and sunk due to overloading by uncontrolled "rush" of soldiers. Both these faults were remedied later.

44. Matters proceeded smoothly throughout the day owing to the mist and there being a big smoke cloud over Dunkirk which prevented the enemy bombers attacking the ships in large numbers.

In order to increase the rate of embarkation through the bottleneck of the East Pier gangway, the troops were urged to quicken their pace and eventually thousands of troops, tired and without food and water for days, broke into the double and kept it up the whole length of the pier for more than two hours.

45. The attempt to maintain an adequate rate of lift using only the older destroyers was by now shown to be impracticable. The destroyers were lifting about 17,000, personnel vessels about 9,500 in the 24 hours. Remaining vessels were estimated to be worth about 15,000 per day. This gave a total lift of about 43,000 per day. The situation called for a lift of at least 55,000 per day. Verbal representations being made to the 1st Sea Lord, authority was received for the return to the Dover Command of the modern destroyers released the night before.

Accordingly Commander-in-Chief, Nore, at 1531 gave orders to HARVESTER, HAVANT, IVANHOE, IMPULSIVE, ICARUS and INTREPID to proceed at once to Dunkirk. Subsequently some of these destroyers were diverted to the beaches.

46. *Arrangements for the final evacuation of the Rearguard of the B.E.F.* During the forenoon representatives of the Commander-in-Chief of the B.E.F. and staff attended a conference with the Vice Admiral.

The Military officers explained the Commander-in-Chief's plan and gave daylight on Saturday, 1st June, as the latest reasonable date up to which the B.E.F. might be expected to hold the eastern perimeter, the size of the corresponding force being about 4,000.

By that date and time the Vice Admiral knew that he should be in possession of ocean-going tugs, ships' lifeboats and ships' power lifeboats which he could specially reserve for the climax of this critical operation. Accordingly, agreement was reached on the following:-

(*a*) That evacuation should proceed with the utmost vigour to ensure that by 0130 on 1st June, the British Forces ashore should have been reduced to the rear guard of 4,000.

(*b*) That special boats and tugs should be accumulated and held aside to ensure them being available in the early hours of 1st June.

(*c*) That the plan should provide for lifting a rear guard of 4,000, plus R.N. beach parties, in one or more flights between 0130 and 0300 on the 1st June.

(*d*) Final decision based on the progress of the evacuation of the main body to be made by the Vice Admiral at 1400 on Friday, 31st May, as to the possibility of adhering to the plan.

Other technical details were settled at the meeting and the Military staff were given the assurance that the ever increasing rate of lifting showed every promise of enabling an affirmative decision to be given at the critical hour of 1400/31st May. After the conference the Military officers communicated the plan both to the War Office and the Commander-in-Chief, B.E.F.

47. *Remarks.* The organisation of traffic to and from the beaches was recovering from the setback it had received when all resources had to be thrown upon the beaches and Dunkirk Harbour when the outflanking and forcing back of the B.E.F. was thought to be imminent consequent upon the surrender of the Belgian forces. Furthermore, a number of organised, and freelance groups of small power boats, were commencing to arrive off the coast, who, by seizing the abandoned and drifting pulling boats, were able to do much to increase the rate of lifting from the beaches.

*Friday, 31st May.*

48. The Admiralty informed the Vice Admiral that the policy of H.M. Government was that both British and French troops be given an equal opportunity of being evacuated in British ships and boats.

49. Personnel ships had been sailed the previous evening and throughout the night of the 30th/31st to provide for a continuous flow into Dunkirk harbour. But at 0320 the S.N.O. reported that once again the majority of these personnel ships had failed to enter the harbour during the dark hours. MALCOLM, however, left Dunkirk with 1,200 troops at 0300, during heavy shelling, on relief by IVANHOE. S.N.O. Dunkirk, however, continued to call for more ships. No more destroyers were available and there were no means of accelerating the arrival of the vessels despatched there. By 0700 the Vice Admiral had no news of the fate of the personnel ships that had sailed the previous evening and during the night. None of these ships had reached the U.K. to unload, and it appeared probable that these ships may have concentrated in the narrow waters close to Dunkirk, inviting a repetition of the heavy air attacks with consequent damage and loss to transports which had occurred on the two previous occasions when personnel

vessels, together with other ships, had been concentrated in large numbers in the approaches to Dunkirk.

At this time there were no less than nine personnel vessels and three hospital carriers known to be on the round trip U.K. – Dunkirk and back and one other personnel vessel had been ordered to sail during the night, but her whereabouts was unknown. In addition, three other personnel vessels were under orders to sail between 0900 and 1030. Pending the return of the ships en passage, and while the coal-burners were being rebunkered, the further sailing of personnel vessels was in suspense.

> *Note:* – Owing to the casualties to personnel vessels at this stage, coal burning cross channel steamers had to be used for some of the trips and short endurance necessitated coaling between trips which could not be done in the vicinity of Dover, thus preventing a quick turn round.

50. During the night a considerable amount of enemy minelaying activity by air was reported. Shelling was heavy during the evening and night, and operations were greatly hampered. Nevertheless, with the cessation of shelling at about 0300, very good progress was made and by full dawn the beaches were very nearly clear of troops. At 0530 attacks on Dunkirk Harbour and the beach from Dunkirk to Bray developed more strength and the bombardment of Dunkirk continued. Nevertheless, the S.N.O. reported that the embarkation there was proceeding satisfactorily but stressed the need for more ships and constant fighter protection. At this time French troops began to appear at Dunkirk Pier and on the beaches, and were embarked with the British troops.

51. At 0600 VIMY sighted submarine off the N.W. Goodwins and commenced to hunt.

52. The arrivals at the home ports indicated that in spite of the frequent requests for more ships and more boats received from the various authorities on the French coast, the rate of evacuation was steadily increasing and would permit, all being well, of implementing the final evacuation plan during the night of 31/5-1/6. Accordingly, instructions were issued for the special tows to leave Ramsgate at 1300/31 for Dunkirk via Route X, and the Commander-in-Chief, Nore

and Flag Officer in Charge, Harwich, were requested to provide all available M.T.B.s to escort this convoy for as much of the outward passage as possible, which was timed to commence from Ramsgate at 1300/3I. Speed of advance – 5 knots. A party of Naval officers had been assembled at Dover to embark in these tows and had been given detailed instructions on the plan. Two M.A/S. boats and two M.T.B.s in the Dover Command were ordered to accompany the boat convoy and subsequently embark the Commander-in-Chief, B.E.F. and Staff off the beaches.

53. Shortly after sunrise an on-shore wind arose and boat work became difficult, many whalers capsizing and the prospects of completing the evacuation to plan began to be less favourable. The following extract from the report of Captain Howson, S.N.O. on the beaches illustrates conditions at Bray at this time:

"At 0400 there was a very considerable number of destroyers, paddlers, trawlers, skoots, etc., off Bray, and embarkation was proceeding satisfactorily, but a lop had already started. There were about 10 motor yachts which had arrived from England. These craft drew 6-7 feet and were unable to get close in to any of the beaches. During the forenoon, considerable towing of empty craft towards the beach was carried out, and only about two boats were allowed to get adrift and ultimately ground. With the falling tide, however, a number of boats were seen to ground and remain ashore until the tide rose in the afternoon. These included an A.L.C.[9] motor boat and a lifeboat. Other power boats broke down. Nevertheless, the embarkation, much hindered by the lop, proceeded satisfactorily. As further destroyers and sloops arrived, they were directed to lower their motor boats and whalers as this had not already been done; these boats were quite invaluable. About noon, the lop began to subside and with the rising tide conditions for embarkation very greatly improved, more boats were sent in and more boats floated off and matters were proceeding very well, when the gun at La Panne started to shell the beaches and foreshore with great accuracy. A certain number of light craft were sunk. The A.L.C. broke down and was towed away by a steamer. MOSQUITO, destroyers and sloops proceeded westward clear of the firing."

54. Rear-Admiral Wake-Walker was able to make a survey of the

general conditions of the beaches, and at 1130 the Vice-Admiral received a signal from him stating that the majority of the pulling boats were broached to and without crews, conditions on the beaches being very bad owing to a freshening shore wind, only small numbers being embarked. Under present conditions any large-scale embarkation from beach impracticable. Motor boats could not get close in. He considered only hope of embarking any number was at Dunkirk, and further stated he would attempt to beach ship to form a lee to try to improve conditions.

Simultaneously with this bad news the Vice-Admiral received a signal from S.N.O. Dunkirk to the effect that Dunkirk was being continuously and heavily bombarded and that the enemy artillery were gradually finding the range of the loading berth. He stated he wished only to enter ships which were necessary for the flow of troops.

This latter signal fortified the Vice-Admiral in his decision to suspend the sailing of personnel vessels to Dunkirk until the accumulation of those en route had been evened out.

55. One group of minesweepers who, up to this time had been working continuous round trips between Sheerness and La Panne, were diverted to round trips between Dunkirk beach and Margate to compensate for the gradual drift of troops westward along the Coast, and to compensate for the reduced flow of troops off Dunkirk Pier consequent on the artillery bombardment. At the same time, by using Margate the duration of the round trip was reduced. The Rear-Admiral, Dover, from off the coast was instructed to run a paddle minesweeper bows ashore on rising tide to be used as a bridge, deeper draught ships coming to her stern, if conditions were suitable. It was not thought, however, that this would be an effective measure of bridging the gap between waterline and off shore ships, as the length of a paddle minesweeper was so small compared with the length of the shallow water to be traversed.

56. During the forenoon beaches at La Panne were subjected to heavy artillery fire. Action was taken with the R.A.F. Commands to locate batteries shelling the beaches and Dunkirk pier and include air bombardment of these positions in the R.A.F. protective measures undertaken during the operation.

57. During the afternoon additional beach parties were sent out, and

barges with provisions, ammunition and water arrived at the beaches during the day, and were grounded. Two further drifters were despatched with petrol, diesel oil and lubricants to the beach area to refuel the inshore craft.

58. Arrangements were made to be ready to embark Lord Gort and Staff from La Panne 1800 or later, by M.T.B. After 1700 weather conditions off the beaches improved, particularly as the tide rose and it appeared once more possible to take effective quantities direct from the beaches, and to use the special tows, ships lifeboats, power lifeboats and tugs, which were on passage from Ramsgate and which had been earmarked for lifting the final covering force.

In the afternoon, however, it was learned that the Military plan had been changed, and that it was no longer possible for the original covering position, as planned, to be held by 4,000 troops who were then to withdraw to the beaches for embarkation by boat. Instead, it was learned that the Eastern-most Division was to be withdrawn Westward from the La Panne area, and that the special flight of boats was to be used to lift this force from the beaches. At the same time, the troops in the Bray and Malo sectors were being thinned out by movements Westward towards Dunkirk itself. This change of plan involved concentrating the special tows and the minesweepers – to which they were to transfer the troops – into the stretch opposite the beach between Bray and one mile East of La Panne and also advancing the commencement of the operation by one hour. The risk of this change of plan was obvious as the boat tows were not in communication with the Vice Admiral, and reliance had to be placed on the Minesweepers to inform and see that the escorting M.A.S.B.s would shepherd the tows to the new positions. The minesweepers had anchored so as to serve as guiding marks, as had been explained to the Naval Officers in each tow.

Apart from the special tow, a very large number of small power boats despatched, in most cases direct, from the South East ports, Newhaven to Sheerness, were arriving off the beaches, and compensated in a large measure for the heavy losses that had occurred amongst the original towing boats, whalers, cutters, lifeboats and ships' boats, which had occured on the beaches during the preceding three days.

On the La Panne beaches after 1600 very good progress was made.

The piers of pontoons built by the Military the previous day were extremely useful, and were largely responsible for the rapid evacuation of troops. All the troops that could be found were embarked by midnight and ferried off to the ships. The local Beachmaster (Captain R. Pim, R.N.V.R.) searched the adjacent beaches for stragglers at midnight, and was informed by a Staff Officer that no more troops would embark from the La Panne beaches, but would march to Dunkirk, as it was anticipated that these beaches would be shelled and probably be in German hands the following day. This, as it turned out, was a correct forecast. The Beachmaster estimates that 5,000 men were lifted from the La Panne beaches during the evening and up to midnight.

59. At 1920 all ships in the fleets were informed by the Vice Admiral that the final evacuation of the B.E.F. was expected on the night 1st/2nd June, and that the evacuation of the French from Dunkirk and Malo beach would continue from 1st June by both British and French ships.

60. General Lloyd informed the D.M.O. of the new plan, stating that General Alexander had been placed in command of the final phase of the evacuation. Composition of force not known. Further, that it was impossible now to say how long the French evacuation would take but that the Alexander force would remain till the last. No firm information could be obtained from the French as regards:-

(i) The number of French troops to be evacuated.

(ii) The nature and extent of French seaborne transport.

(iii) The French military plan for the defence of the perimeter and the final withdrawal of French troops.

61. *General Remarks:* The main features of the day were:-

(*a*) The increased enemy artillery activity on Dunkirk and La Panne beach, and on the approach channels.

(*b*) The set-back to evacuation from the beaches that occurred during the choppy weather of the forenoon, followed by an excellent recovery in the afternoon and evening when large numbers were lifted from the beaches.

(*c*) The change in the military plan as regards the locality and time of lifting the final contingents of the B.E.F.

It should be noted that in spite of (*b*) the rate of embarkation had, in fact, come up to expectations, and if other circumstances had permitted it would have been possible to adhere to the original plan of lifting the final 4,000 B.E.F. off the beaches between 0I30 and 0300 Ist June.

*Saturday, Ist June.*

62. Two Hospital Carriers which had sailed the previous evening returned shortly after dawn. Only one had succeeded in entering Dunkirk Harbour, the other had laid off four hours under heavy fire and returned to Dover. Four personnel vessels failed to enter Dunkirk during the night, but succeeded in the early hours of the morning. One of these, the PRAGUE, was bombed and severely damaged half-way across on the return journey, but succeeded in making the Downs with the assistance of tugs, where troops transferred to other ships particularly A/S trawlers LADY PHILOMENA and OLVINA. The supply of personnel vessels was maintained throughout the day, not without a series of setbacks caused by 3 ships failing to sail and by 2 being turned back when on passage by French Destroyers owing to heavy bombing and shelling of the approaches to Dunkirk. Of those that operated during the 24 hours, I was sunk, 2 damaged by bombs and shell-fire and I by collision.

63. During the middle watch it transpired that no further troops were attempting to evacuate from La Panne off which were stationed one paddle minesweeper, a fleet sweeper and two destroyers, probably due to the heavy shelling from German guns eastward, and later information was received that the troops were marching from La Panne through Bray towards Dunkirk. Accordingly, during the night the Rear Admiral, Dover, instructed all small craft to move west, with boats in tow, towards Dunkirk, and the Vice Admiral directed all ships under orders for La Panne to other positions further west, concentrating the main effort on the beach immediately east of Dunkirk.

To a request from Dunkirk for Hospital Ships, the Vice Admiral replied at 07I5 that the large ship berths alongside at Dunkirk must be occupied by personnel ships and the wounded that could conveniently be embarked should go with personnel. This direction was in accordance with the Government policy previously communicated to the Vice Admiral.

64. Soon after dawn enemy aircraft were active and heavy bombing and machine gun attacks developed at 0500 over the whole area from Dunkirk to La Panne. A second series of attacks commenced at 0830 and lasted until 0900, during which time nearly every ship off the coast was subjected to intensive bombing and machine gunning, formations of 30 and 40 machines being noted. During this attack BASILISK was put out of action off La Panne and later sank while struggling home. KEITH, SALAMANDER and SKIPJACK, who were moving westward along the coast as the Bray and La Panne beaches had been emptied, were heavily bombed, the former was hit and set on fire and the latter sank. KEITH was abandoned and finally sank. Nearly all troops on board KEITH and the crews of both vessels were rescued by other ships. A third attack started over Dunkirk, extending well out along Route X, and occurred between I000 and I040, to be again resumed at noon. After that there was a lull until I550, when another attack was delivered on Dunkirk Harbour and all shipping therein for over half an hour. At I800 the Vice Admiral received the following signal from Dunkirk: "Things are getting very hot for ships; over I00 bombers on ships here since 0530, many casualties. Have directed that no ships sail during daylight. Evacuation by transports therefore ceases at 0300. If perimeter holds will complete evacuation to-morrow, Sunday night, including most French. General concurs." The sense of this message was passed on to Rear Admiral, Dover, off the coast.

65. In addition to the heavy scale of air attack during the afternoon the sea traffic was very seriously interrupted by artillery fire brought to bear on Route X near No. 5 buoy. The fire appeared to be accurate and it is believed some French ships were sunk. Two French destroyers in the vicinity stopped British ships approaching from England on X Route short of this point, and it became evident that a very serious threat to daylight evacuation was in being. Meantime, the toll of casualties of ships during the day was mounting, particularly amongst the destroyers and shortly after midday the Commander-in-Chief, Nore, called the attention of the Admiralty to this, suggesting the

discontinuation of the use of destroyers by day off the French coast. The summarisation of all these incidents led to the Admiralty directing the Vice Admiral, Dover, to suspend evacuation from Dunkirk at 0700, Sunday 2nd June, and for it to be resumed the following night or from I730/2, depending upon the circumstances. From the above it will be seen that there were to be no ships proceeding to Dunkirk between 0700/2 and I730/2. The above Admiralty directions crossed a message from the Vice Admiral stating that all ships had been ordered to withdraw from Dunkirk before daylight the following day, owing to the heavy casualties to shipping.

66. In spite of enemy action more than 60,000 troops were landed in the United Kingdom during the 24 hours, thanks to the unremitting determination of Naval vessels who all executed a succession of round trips, interrupted only by necessary refuelling and who accounted for 70 per cent. of this total. The majority of the surviving vessels had been operating ceaselessly for at least five days, and officers and men were approaching a condition of complete exhaustion.

67. As for personnel ships, steps were taken to place on board each a Naval Lieutenant Commander or Commander to advise the Master, and ten seamen to assist in handling the wires in going alongside under fire. By this means it was hoped not only to ensure the timely sailing of these essential ships, but also to eliminate the occasions when these vessels had remained outside Dunkirk Harbour to await a quiet opportunity to enter.

68. Early in the forenoon a number of Senior Officers were despatched from Dover in fast motor boats to round up all stray motor boats in the Downs and along the routes, and direct them back in the evening to the beach stretching I½ miles eastward of Dunkirk, and a second large flight of tugs with lifeboats was prepared at Ramsgate to send over for what was hoped to be a final effort off the beach. In addition a number of flotillas under Commodore A.H. Taylor and Captain the Hon. G. Frazer were reorganised for the night's effort.

69. General Alexander was informed at 095I that on the likely assumption that complete evacuation would be ordered that night, the problem of transport made it essential to use the beach adjacent to Dunkirk as well as the harbour facilities and that the Vice Admiral was planning evacuation to start at 2200.

70. At 1841 the following signal was received from C.I.G.S. for the Senior Military Commander: "We do not order any fixed moment for evacuation. You are to hold on as long as possible in order that the maximum number of French and British may be evacuated. Impossible from here to judge local situation. In close co-operation with Admiral Abrial. You must act in this matter on your own judgment."

71. S.N.O. Dunkirk, was informed that drifters and other small craft would be sent into the inner harbour at Dunkirk to take troops from the Felix Faure Quay, North Quay, in the shipyard, and the quay in the new outer harbour.

72. The plan for the night provided for all minesweepers including paddlers, skoots and all small craft, except certain special flotillas especially organised, to go to the beach stretching eastward 1½ miles from Dunkirk. Dunkirk Harbour was to be served by up to seven personnel ships, eight destroyers, and the inner harbour nine drifters and special power boats organised from Ramsgate. The French vessels were to serve the Quay in the new outer harbour and private small boats, the Quay Felix Faure, and in addition about 100 French small beach fishing craft and drifters for the beach immediately east of Dunkirk. It was estimated that the British vessels could lift about 17,000 between 2100/1 and 0300/2, probably in the proportion 50 per cent. British and 50 per cent. French. The plan was set in motion without incident until 2200, when it was reported that a number of towing craft and small boats were returning empty from the coast. All ships were warned to look out for these and to send them back to their duty on the coast.

Subsequent investigation gives reason to believe that this defection was due to false information being passed between ships on the coast and believed to originate from a non-identified skoot.

73. Commander G.O. Maund proceeded to the mouth of the harbour in a motor boat commanded by a Dutch Naval Officer with a Dutch naval crew and led all ships into harbour to their berths. The Rear Admiral, Dover, was also afloat in a M.T.B. supervising traffic control.

By 2300 the night was very dark, sometimes as many as 6 or 7 vessels were entering the port of Dunkirk at once whilst yet others were leaving. All were without lights and displayed the highest degree of seamanship in these difficult and fateful circumstances.

74. At 2315 the S.N.O. Dunkirk signalled "Withdrawal now proceeding according to plan. Shall have certain reserves here tomorrow to assist French. Intend to complete evacuation tomorrow by midnight."

**Remarks.**

75. The outstanding feature of the day was the series of events leading to the abandonment of daylight evacuation. Increasing enemy air attack, which the R.A.F. were unable to smother with the means at their disposal, caused serious loss of ships, and continual interruption of embarkation on the beaches and in Dunkirk. Further, the sole remaining cross channel route was now under fairly heavy and accurate shore artillery fire.

In these circumstances, it was apparent that continuation of the operation by day must cause losses of ships and personnel out of all proportion to the number of troops evacuated, and if persisted in, the momentum of evacuation would automatically and rapidly decrease.

*Sunday, 2nd June.*

76. The arrangements to set in motion the night's evacuation had proceeded smoothly as far as could be ascertained at Dover. During the early hours, reports of sailings from Dunkirk indicated that destroyers at least were doing well.

At about 0200, however, a signal was received from LYDD, who was off the Dunkirk beach, as follows:

"Brigadier tells me that C.-in-C. says it is essential that rearguard B.E.F. embarks from the beaches east of Mole on account of French congestion on Mole. Considerable number British troops still on Mole. Military are expecting further arrivals there. Rearguard expects to arrive at beach by 0230."

The Vice Admiral accordingly ordered all ships known to be outside Dunkirk Harbour to endeavour to embark the rearguard from the beach, remaining after 0300 if necessary. Owing to the time in transit and coding it was feared that this signal would reach few ships still on the coast, unless they had remained on their own initiative after 0300, the previously ordered time of withdrawal.

At 0200, authority was received from the Admiralty to continue evacuation by destroyers from Dunkirk Harbour until 0700, transports to leave Dunkirk at 0300.

77. During the early hours there was considerable haze and smoke off Dunkirk Harbour, Dunkirk East Beach, Dunkirk Roads and the entrance therefrom to X Route. For this reason some of the smaller vessels, including minesweepers, failed to make either Dunkirk Harbour or Dunkirk East Beach, but on the whole it appears that evacuation, both from the beach and from the harbour had proceeded satisfactorily with the resources available.

Between 0200 and 0900, 6 personnel vessels reached United Kingdom from Dunkirk Harbour with about 5,500 troops. Two others had been turned back before reaching Dunkirk by two unknown destroyers, and one had been in collision before reaching Dunkirk and had to return.

78. Considerable doubt existed during the forenoon as to the numbers remaining to be evacuated in Dunkirk. It was thought that 2,000, plus the 4,000 rearguard British troops, might well be found in Dunkirk. The number of French troops remaining was increasing from the 25,000 quoted the previous evening to figures in the region of 50,000 to 60,000.

79. The Rear Admiral, Dover, arrived back from the coast in a M.T.B. and during the forenoon a joint Naval and Military conference was held to devise a plan for the forthcoming night's evacuation. The fact that evacuation traffic was suspended in daylight hours enabled all transport resources to accumulate during the day and to be held available for a massed descent upon Dunkirk Harbour during the night. By making provision for increased pier and berthing parties and traffic controlled by motor boat in the harbour channels, it was hoped to berth all craft that were available between the hours of 2100/2 and 0300/3.

The times of sailing of all vessels were adjusted so as to space them out over the evacuation period at Dunkirk, and allowance was made for a proportion failing to make the passage.

The French agreed to make their own arrangements for embarkation from the Dunkirk East Beach and the West Pier on the new outer harbour.

At 1530 two R.A.F. Motor Boats, 243 and 270, left in company for Dunkirk carrying Commander J.C. Clouston and an augmented pier party. When off Gravelines attacks were made on the boats by eight Junkers 87 with machine guns and small bombs. No. 243 had a near miss which damaged her. For ten minutes No. 270 carried on trying to avoid attacks. She then returned to No. 243 but Commander Clouston who was in the water instructed 270 to proceed. Destroyers were instructed to look for survivors. Two were picked up only. One stated that he saw Commander Clouston dead in the water.

80. At 1030 an urgent request transmitted "en clair" was received from Dunkirk for Hospital Ships as follows:-

"Wounded situation acute and Hospital Ships should enter during day. Geneva Convention will be honourably observed it is felt and that the enemy will refrain from attacking."

As this appeared to be the only way of evacuating the wounded, observing that the whole facilities of the port during the night evacuation hours would be required for fighting troops, it was decided to send two Hospital Ships. The WORTHING sailed at 1300 and the PARIS at 1700. At 1440, the A/S patrol was overheard on R/T reporting that the WORTHING was being bombed at a point about two-thirds of the way across the Channel. She returned to United Kingdom reporting that she had been attacked by 12 Junkers. The attack caused no casualties, but plates were started and there was some superficial damage. She had to return to harbour to refuel before commencing another trip to Dunkirk.

At 1915 PARIS reported that she was bombed and badly damaged with engines useless, at the point where the WORTHING had been attacked, and at 1947 she sent out an S.O.S. Tugs were sent to her assistance.

Thus the last attempt to evacuate the wounded by Hospital Carrier from Dunkirk was brought to nought.

The PARIS subsequently sank shortly after midnight at W. Buoy 10 miles off the French coast.

81. At 1700 movement towards Dunkirk commenced. The Armada

consisted of 13 personnel vessels, 2 large store carriers, 11 destroyers, 5 paddle minesweepers, 9 fleet sweepers, 1 special service vessel, 9 drifters, 6 skoots, 2 armed yachts, 1 gunboat, a large number of tugs, lifeboats, etc. formed either in organised tows or free lance. The composition of the French contingent was unknown, it was thought to consist of 6 small destroyers, 4 avisos and about 120 fishing craft.

82. At 1538 the S.N.O. Dunkirk made the following situation report:-

"French still maintain front line except for area east of Bergues where the Germans have penetrated two miles on a two-mile front. Counter attack being made at 1500. In port no movement. Present situation hopeful."

83. At 2145 it was learned that the ROYAL DAFFODIL, the first of the personnel vessels, had been bombed near the North Goodwin Light Vessel on the outward passage whence she returned to Ramsgate. At 2200 it was learned that loaded vessels were leaving Dunkirk.

84. At 2330 S.N.O. Dunkirk reported "B.E.F. evacuated."

*Monday, 3rd June.*

85. The hopes that a large number of French troops would be lifted following the completion of B.E.F. embarkation, was shaken when at 0030 Rear Admiral, Dover, reported from Dunkirk that four ships were now alongside, that there were no French troops. Reported again at 0115, "Plenty of ships cannot get troops."

At 0312, Dunkirk reported that all ships were leaving and that the block ships had entered.

When the ships returned to United Kingdom, it was learnt that the flow of French troops had dwindled away shortly after midnight. One ship waited 2½ hours to embark her load instead of the normal half hour. A possible explanation was thought to be that a French counter attack, which had been arranged for the afternoon of the 2nd, had had to be postponed to the evening, no doubt deranging despatch of troops to the rear for evacuation. The result was that between midnight and 0300/3 a lifting capacity of about 10,000 was left empty.

86. The night's embarkation at Dunkirk had been carried out without disturbance by enemy action. During the forenoon a conference was held at Dover to improve the arrangements for the night 3/6-4/6 as a result of experience gained. The general plan remained unaltered except that provision was made for the use by British ships of the west pier in the New Outer Port, since it appeared that the French had insufficient ships at their disposal to make full use of this valuable berth. Similarly a number of power boats which had been working off the Malo Beach were, on this occasion, to be sent in to Quay Felix Faure. No assurance could be obtained that this coming night would terminate the operation and considerable anxiety was felt regarding the effect of the gradual exhaustion of officers and men of the ships taking part in the "Dynamo." This exhaustion was particularly marked in the Destroyer force the remnants of which had been executing a series of round trips without intermission for several days under navigation conditions of extreme difficulty and in the face of unparalleled air attack.

The Vice Admiral accordingly represented to the Admiralty that the continuance of the demands made by evacuation would subject a number of officers and men to a test which might be beyond the limit of human endurance, and requesting that fresh forces should be used if evacuation had to be continued after the coming night, with the acceptance of any consequent delay.

87. The evacuation plan was communicated to Units taking part at I440 and was briefly as follows:-

Commence 2230/3, withdraw 0230/4. From East Pier evacuation by Personnel Vessels, Destroyers and Paddle Minesweepers. From West Pier, new outer port, by other Minesweepers, Corvettes, Skoots and French vessels. Drifters and smaller craft into the inner harbour, LOCUST remaining outside entrance receiving loads ferried out by small boats. Tugs available outside entrance to assist ships in berthing and in leaving.

88. In the evening the Vice Admiral was informed by the B.N.L.O. Marceau that it was estimated 30,000 French remained and that the French Admiralty agree that evacuation should be terminated that night if possible. Force used was to consist of nine Personnel Vessels with one in reserve, nine Destroyers (maximum, number available), four Paddle Minesweepers, seven Fleet Minesweepers, nine Drifters,

LOCUST, two Corvettes, four French Destroyers and a number of organised motorboat flotillas including lifeboats from Ramsgate and Dover, together with a large number of French and Belgian fishing vessels. The lifting capacity of this force, if used to the full, was more than 30,000 but it was certain that the facilities within Dunkirk could not permit more than about 25,000 to be embarked in the time available, and this number only if the French troops moved with the greatest rapidity at all points of embarkation. This point was impressed upon the French Liaison Officers and a number of French officers and ratings added to the augmented pier parties which were despatched to Dunkirk at 2200 in advance of the evacuation force.

89. The movements commenced according to plan. The weather conditions at Dunkirk, although favourable as regards tide were adverse with a north easterly wind tending to blow Personnel Vessels and Destroyers off the vital East Pier making berthing difficult. The MANXMAN, the seventh Personnel Ship due to sail failed to sail, and her place was taken by the ROYAL SOVEREIGN.

*Tuesday, 4th June.*

90. At midnight when the earlier vessels had commenced the return voyage fog was reported in mid-channel and off the Thanet coast and a number of ships had to anchor before entering harbour. The EXPRESS and SHIKARI were the last ships to leave Dunkirk at 0318 and 0340 and carried approximately 1,000 troops and the British pier parties. Except for an air attack on SHIKARI this final passage was made without interruption by the enemy and though the fog made navigation extremely difficult it undoubtedly served to shield the Armada from enemy aircraft.

91. When the count was taken later in the day it was ascertained that 27,000 troops had been evacuated as a result of the night's operation and Admiral Nord agreed that the operation should be considered as completed, observing that all ammunition at Dunkirk had been expended and that the numbers left behind were small consisting principally of non-combatant troops. This decision was agreed to by

the French Admiralty at 1100, and the operation "Dynamo" terminated by Admiralty Message 1423/4.

92. It was realised that in all probability there might be a number of open boats, barges, etc., drifting about in the Channel with troops on board. It was accordingly decided to have an air reconnaissance over the Channel.

It was reported that a Transport was lying on its side between Dunkirk and Gravelines and also a barge east of the Goodwins with survivors on board.

C. in C. Nore despatched 2 M.T.B.s to find the transport with no avail. On the 5th the R.A.F. speedboat did a sweep south of a line Goodwin/Boulogne and recovered 33 French troops and two Naval ratings. In addition French troops were picked up by patrols and brought in to Dover, Margate and Ramsgate. Troops also arrived in French and Belgian Trawlers totalling in all some additional 1,100.

Air reconnaissance was also carried out on the morning of the 5th but nothing was reported.

## REMARKS ON THE INSHORE FLOTILLAS AND NAVAL SHORE PARTIES.

93. About 400 small craft, ranging from Dutch Skoots to 30 ft. Motor boats, set out at various times to the Flanders Coast. In addition scores of pulling boats, merchant ship lifeboats, Naval cutters and whalers, were sent off in tow. Only a proportion – particularly of the pulling boats – succeeded in reaching the coast and taking active part in the evacuation. Fewer still were able to remain off the coast for more than one period. Nevertheless, these small craft, in conjunction with the pulling and power boats of H.M. Ships off the coast, were responsible for lifting more than 100,000 Allied troops direct off a stretch of open beach in shoal waters between 1600/27/5 and 0400/2/6. Further, a large number of the power boats operated within Dunkirk Harbour on the last three nights, working principally in the inner harbour, which was continually under artillery fire, ferrying a further large uncounted number out to the comparative safety of ships lying off.

94. Throughout the period all these craft of the inshore flotillas were

subjected at one time or another to intense attack from the air, both by bombing and machine gun, and a large proportion also to sporadic bombardment by German artillery. Under this fire no case occurred of boats ceasing work as long as troops were in sight on shore, and movements of boats westward away from the fire zone only occurred as dictated by the military situation ashore.

95. The initial despatch of requisitioned and volunteer small craft was controlled from:-

| | |
|---|---|
| Naval Control Service, | London, |
| Westminster Pier, | Ramsgate, |
| Gravesend, | Dover, |
| Southend, | Newhaven, |
| Sheerness, | Portsmouth, |

preliminary action in most cases having originated in the Admiralty Small Vessels Pool. As the operation proceeded, Ramsgate was used as the main base for such craft, as being nearest to Dunkirk, but a small number of motor boats and skoots continued to work from Dover.

96. The work of servicing this multitude of small craft entailed an enormous amount of work by the base organisation at Ramsgate, and to a lesser extent at Dover. Items typical of the work of the Ramsgate organisation are as follows:-

(*a*) Approximately 1,000 charts were issued by the Naval Control Service, Ramsgate, to the various vessels taking part, some 600 of which had the routes laid off on them for those Commanding Officers who had neither parallel rules nor dividers, together with approximately 500 sets of routeing instructions.

(*b*) During the period 26th May to 4th June the number of vessels dealt with for defects of all kinds, included power, engine and electrical, at Ramsgate, was 170. Included in this number were Dutch Skoots, Tugs, Drifters, Trawlers, Motor Lighters, Ferry Floats and Motor Boats of every conceivable type.

(*c*) All the small craft were initially without armament.

Seventy-five of the larger Motor Boats, Skoots and Tugs were armed with A.A. Lewis guns at Ramsgate, this armament being transferred from vessel to vessel as requisite during the operation. Twenty-three Lewis gunners arrived from London and 2 officers with 12 R.A.S.C. cadets were also accepted for this service at Ramsgate. When British fighting troops were being evacuated in the later stages, the soldiers invariably mounted and fought their Bren guns as A.A. armament for the ship they were in.

97. A large number of boats were quite unsuitable for work off an open beach. For example, a convoy of 6 Thames Bawley boats were shepherded over from Southend and arrived off Dunkirk beach at 1930/3I but owing to ground swell and the many offshore obstacles, such as semi-submerged lorries, it was considered impracticable to beach these craft. Bawley boats accordingly went along the outside of the East Pier of Dunkirk Harbour and started ferrying service to the Skoots lying empty outside the harbour entrance. The swell alongside made embarkation duties from outside the jetty too difficult, so Bawley boats proceeded inside Dunkirk Harbour working mainly from the inner harbour which was under heavy shell fire. All Bawley boats were loaded up and left harbour about 0300/I. On reaching Ramsgate at 0930/I the boats were so much damaged as not to be fit for further service.

The conduct of the crews of these cockle boats was exemplary. They were all volunteers who were rushed over to Dunkirk in one day, probably none of them had been under gun fire before and certainly none of them had ever been under Naval discipline. These boats were Thames Estuary fishing boats which never left the estuary and only one of their crews had been further afield than Ramsgate before. In spite of this fact perfect formation was maintained throughout the day and night under the control of a Sub-Lieutenant, R.N.V.R., in command of the Unit and all orders were carried out with great diligence even under actual shellfire and aircraft attack.

98. The difficulties of passage from the United Kingdom to the Flanders coast were great. With compasses of doubtful accuracy and no navigational instruments other than a lead pencil, once a boat lost

contact with a main convoy the chances of making a correct landfall in the strong currents of the straits were slight. Many of the small craft had not even a compass, yet all who left the Flanders coast in safety managed to reach the English coast to refuel and the majority set off again to repeat the adventure. Cases occurred, however, of boats attempting to enter Calais instead of Dunkirk, where they received a rousing reception from the Boche, and yet another case where the landfall was made between Gravelines and Calais and the Sub-Lieutenant in command landed, finding it necessary to shoot two German soldiers before leaving for his proper destination of Dunkirk.

Open boats of all kinds, from the naval cutters and whalers to seaside dinghies, were towed over from England by the motor boats themselves or in special tows by tugs. Some of these pulling boats were manned by odd naval ratings as boat keepers, and others by soldiers off the beach. One of the principal difficulties was to avoid fouling the motor boats' screws with painters and lines attached to all these pulling boats. Carley floats and inflated motor inner tubes also played their part in carrying men from the beach to the motorboats.

99. Having reached the coast the business of ferrying from the water line to the offshore craft was by no means easy. Apart from the surf, which was usually experienced for some hours every day, derelict lorries, which had been abandoned below the high tide mark, proved a serious danger to boats. Another source of much trouble close inshore was the large amount of floating grass rope which various craft had used and lost in their rescue work, and numerous articles of military equipment such as great coats jettisoned during the evacuation. A great number of small power boats were put temporarily out of action by such ropes and garments fouling the screws, usually resulting in broaching to and being swamped while they were thus unmanageable.

The number of soldiers taken off the beaches by motor boats cannot be estimated. One 35 ft. motor launch, however, ferried off 600 men to transports and carried 420 direct to England.

100. Of the pulling boats used, the main difficulty was insufficient provision made for Naval boat keepers to take charge of the outgoing boats and bring them back to the disembarkation points. As a result the soldiers detailed to act as boat keepers for an outward trip, failed to return the boat on the inward trip and it was necessary for the Naval

boat keepers to swim or to wade out to the drifting boats which, had been cast away by the soldiers on disembarkation.

I0I. By the night of the 30/3Ist a considerable number of collapsible boats and pontoons had been received from the Royal Engineers of the B.E.F. These were of great assistance and paddled off about I0 men in each trip, but again, in spite of all efforts, in the vast majority of cases the soldiers left these craft when they arrived at the offshore ship.

I02. Much of the most meritorious work of lifting off the beaches was done by the offshore warships' own boats, who were tireless in their efforts. All small pulling boats and small power boats were lowered and were lent from ship to ship when their own parent ship left the coast to unload at a United Kingdom port. In addition, H.M. Ships seized drifting and abandoned boats as opportunity offered and manned them up with boat keepers. Owing to the physical exhaustion of these boats' crews after hours of work, relief crews of stokers were frequently provided from amongst the many volunteers that came forth.

I03. A typical example of dogged work by a ship's boat was afforded by the action of JAVELIN'S and JAGUAR'S boats off Bray beach in the afternoon of 28/5. When their two motor cutters and two whalers first grounded offshore they were rushed and swamped by soldiers. Order being restored the boats had to be baled out and the wet engines restarted, following which 700 troops were embarked by these few boats in a short time during continuous bombing attacks.

I04. Of the power boats available by far the most useful and suitable were the A.L.C.s, M.L.C.s[10] and the small type of R.N.L.I. lifeboat. The high speed service motor boats such as DOLPHIN'S and EXCELLENT'S boats and the R.A.F. Seaplane tenders proved unsuitable for work in shallow waters on a lee shore owing to the vulnerability of their propellers and rudders and their poor manoeuvring powers at low speeds.

I05. Of the civilian manned craft one of the best performances was that of the London Fire Brigade fire float MASSEY SHAW. All the volunteer crew were members of the London Fire Brigade or Auxiliary Fire Service and succeeded in doing 4 round trips to the beaches in their well-found craft. Reference should also be made to the Royal National Lifeboat Institution crews of the Ramsgate and Margate lifeboats who took their boats over to Dunkirk.

106. Locally, at both Ramsgate and Dover a number of civilian volunteers came forward to man the boats and to drive their engines. These men did good work.

107. At both Ramsgate and Dover when the business of manning these civilian power boats was set about the same difficulties were experienced:-

(i) of obtaining drivers with knowledge of the very varied types of internal combustion engines;

(ii) of making the engines of these boats run, most of them having been laid up since the previous summer.

Throughout the operation all engines continued to give trouble. Many engines were old and almost all were of different types. Several boats could not be used as they had diesel engines and no stokers or civilians trained in these were available. Each engine, especially the older ones, required careful nursing, and signs of distress from the engines were not understood. These difficulties were partly overcome by obtaining engine drivers from Chatham and by the provision of cadet ratings, and Sub-Lieutenants, R.N.V.R. from KING ALFRED who claimed knowledge of I.C. engines, but many engines were of types unknown even to these.

108. Fresh water for the motor boats was difficult to supply in sufficient quantity, owing to lack of water tanks in most boats, especially those of the open type. Large supplies were required as the troops were reported to be suffering severely from thirst. Both at Ramsgate and Dover the Base Staff provided as many galvanised iron cylinders and tanks as could be found and made serviceable, and these proved most satisfactory.

109. On two occasions skoots and small boats approaching the coast were turned back through false information. On the first occasion on the afternoon of 28th May, at least 6 skoots, who were without definite orders where to proceed, encountered a returning skoot when about 10 miles off the coast. This skoot stated that Dunkirk had already fallen into German hands and that the evacuation had ceased. As a result of this ill-judged comment, the arrival of at least 6 skoots was delayed at over 24 hours, until this situation had been cleared up.

The second occasion occurred during the night of 1st June, and has been referred to in paragraph 72 of the narrative. On this occasion although the services of a number of small craft were lost to the coast, it transpired that sufficient were already there to cope with the troops available.

110. An important flotilla was formed by 40 Dutch motor coasters, referred to in this report as skoots, 21 of whom were commissioned at Tilbury and Sheerness, and 19 at Poole. All these vessels ultimately made the Flanders coast and operated with a varying degree of success, usually governed by the reliability of their strange engines when handled by Naval stoker ratings. Too large to be used as beaching craft except under the best conditions, they were mainly used as intermediaries between the small boats and the offshore warships to reduce the distance the pulling boats had to traverse and periodically returned to U.K. themselves fully loaded when beach work ceased, or the supply of reception warships temporarily decreased.

Some of these skoots handled more than 1,000 troops during the course of the operation.

111. It is of interest to note that on the final night after the last two destroyers had left at 0340 a number of the larger power boats continued to work in Dunkirk Harbour and only left when they came under small arms fire from German troops who had penetrated into Dunkirk at certain points.

112. About 30 Naval Officers and 320 ratings were employed for varying periods in pier parties and at shore signal stations in Dunkirk and as beach parties. A great number worked unceasingly without relief or rest, exposed to incessant air attacks, for seven days. The work of these officers and men was of the greatest value and contributed largely to the success of the undertaking.

113. As regards the bearing and behaviour of the troops, British and French, prior to and during the embarkation, it must be recorded that the earlier parties were embarked off the beaches in a condition of complete disorganisation. There appeared to be no Military officers in charge of the troops, and this impression was undoubtedly enhanced by the difficulty in distinguishing between the uniforms of such officers as were present and those of other ranks. It was soon realised that it was vitally necessary to despatch Naval Officers in their unmistakable uniform with armed Naval beach parties to take charge of the soldiers

on shore immediately prior to embarkation. Great credit is due to the Naval officers and Naval ratings for the restoration of some semblance of order. Later on when troops of fighting formations reached the beaches these difficulties disappeared.

Dover,
18.6.40.

# APPENDIX I TO F.O. DOVER'S DESPATCH

*List of H.M. Ships, Personnel Ships and Hospital Carriers taking part, showing those lost or damaged*

(by bomb, gunfire, mine or collision)

*A.A. Cruiser:*
CALCUTTA

*Destroyers*

BASILISK (sunk 29th May)
GRAFTON (sunk 29th May)
GRENADE (sunk 29th May)

HAVANT (sunk Ist June)
KEITH (sunk Ist June)
WAKEFUL (sunk Ist June)

ANTHONY (damaged 30th May)
EXPRESS (damaged 31st May)
GALLANT (damaged 29th May)
GREYHOUND (damaged 29th May)
HARVESTER (damaged 31st May)
ICARUS (damaged 31st May)
IMPULSIVE (damaged 31st May)
INTREPID (damaged 29th May)
IVANHOE (damaged Ist June)
JAGUAR (damaged 29th May)
MALCOLM (damaged 3Ist May and 2nd June)
MONTROSE (damaged 29th May)

SABRE (damaged 30th May and 2nd June)
SALADIN (damaged 29th May)
SCIMITAR (damaged 3Ist May)
VENOMOUS (damaged Ist June)
VIMY (damaged Ist June)
VIVACIOUS (damaged Ist June)
WHITEHALL (damaged Ist June)
WINDSOR (damaged 28th May)
WOLFHOUND (damaged 29th May)
WOLSEY (damaged 3Ist May)
WORCESTER (damaged 30th May)

BLYSKAWICA (Polish)   MACKAY            WHITSHED
CODRINGTON            SHIKARI           WILD SWAN
ESK                   VANQUISHER        WINCHELSEA
JAVELIN               VERITY

Total 4I, of which 6 were sunk and 23 damaged.

## Sloops and Gunboats

BIDEFORD (damaged Ist June)      MOSQUITO (sunk Ist June)
LOCUST

## Corvettes

KINGFISHER (damaged Ist June)    GUILLEMOT

## Guardships and Armed Boarding Vessels

KING ORRY (damaged 27th May and sunk 30th May)    LLANTHONY
MONA ISLE (27th May and Ist June)                 LORMONT

## Minesweepers

BRIGHTON BELLE (sunk 28th May)   SKIPJACK (sunk Ist June)
DEVONIA (3Ist)                   WAVERLEY (29th May)
GRACIE FIELDS (28th)             HEBE (damaged 3Ist May)
PANGBOURNE (damaged 29th May)    KELLETT (29th)
WESTWARD HO (3Ist)

ALBURY              HALCYON              QUEEN OF THANET
BRIGHTON QUEEN      LEDA                 ROSS
DUNDALK             LYDD                 SALAMANDER
DUCHESS OF FIFE     MARMION              SALTASH
EMPEROR OF INDIA    MEDWAY QUEEN         SANDOWN
FITZROY             NIGER                SNAEFELL
GLEN AVON           ORIOLE               SPEEDWELL
GLEN GOWER          PLINLIMMON           SUTTON
GOSSAMER            PRINCESS ELIZABETH   SHARPSHOOT

*Total* 36, of which 5 were sunk and 4 damaged.

## Trawlers
### (Minesweeping, Anti-Submarine and "LL" sweep)

ARGYLLSHIRE (sunk Ist June)  
BLACKBURN ROVERS (2nd June)  
CALIR (29th May)  
COMFORT (29th May)  
NAUTILUS (29th May)  

POLLY JOHNSON (sunk 29th May)  
STELLA DORADO (Ist June)  
THOMAS BARTLETT (28th May)  
THURINGIA (29th)  
WESTELLA (2nd June)  

---

KINGSTON ALALITE (damaged 2nd June)

SPURS (damaged 2nd June)

---

ARLEY  
BOTANIC  
BIOCK  
CAYTON WYKE  
CHICO  
CORRIDAW  
FLYDEA  

GRIMSBY TOWN  
GULZAR  
INVERFORTH  
JOHN CATLING  
KINGSTON ANDALUSITE  
KINGSTON OLIVINE  
LADY PHILOMENA  

LORD INCHCAPE  
MARETTA  
OLVINA  
OUR BAINS  
SAON  
SARGASSO  
WOLVES  

*Total* 33, of which 10 were sunk and 2 damaged.

---

### Special Service Vessels

AMULREE (sunk Ist June)  
GRIEVE (Ist)  

CRESTED EAGLE (sunk 29th May)

---

GOLDEN EAGLE

ROYAL EAGLE

*Total* 5, of which 3 were sunk.

---

### Drifters (Mine Recovery and Flare Burning).

BOY ROY (sunk 28th May)  
GIRL PAMELA (29th)  

LORD CAVAN (sunk Ist June)  
PATON (28th May)  

---

EILEEN EMMA  
FIDGET  
FISHER BOY  
FORECAST  
GERVAIS RENTOUL  
GIRL GLADYS  
GOLDEN GIFT  

GOLDEN SUNBEAM  
JACKETA  
LORD HOWARD  
LORD HOWE  
MIDAS  
NETSUKIS  
SHIPMATES  

SILVER DAWN  
THE BOYS  
TORBAY II  
UT PROSIM  
YORKSHIRE LASS  
YOUNG MUN  

*Total* 24, of which 4 were sunk.

*M.T.Bs.* 16, 67, 68, 100, 102 and 107.
*M.A.S.Bs.* 6, 7 and 10.

## Personnel Ships

FERRELLA (sunk 29th May)  NORMANIA (sunk 29th May)
LORINA ( ·· ·· ·· )  QUEEN OF THE (28th )
CHANNEL
MONA'S QUEEN ( ·· ·· ·· )  SCOTIA (Ist June)

BEN MY CHREE (damaged 2nd June)  PRAGUE (damaged Ist June)
BIARRITZ ( ·· 27th May)  PRINCESS MAUD ( ·· 30th May)
CANTERBURY ( ·· 29th ·· )  ROYAL DAFFODIL ( ·· 2nd June)
MAID OF ORLEANS ( ·· Ist June)  ST. SEIROL ( ·· 29th May)

| ARCHANGEL | LADY OF MAN | NEWHAVEN |
| AUTOCARRIER | LOCH GARRY | ROUEN |
| COTE D'ARGENT | MALINES | ROYAL SOVEREIGN |
| KILLARNEY | MANX MAID | ST. HELIER |
| KING GEORGE V | MANX MAN | TYNWALD |

*Total* 29, of which 6 were sunk and 8 damaged.

## Hospital Carriers

**PARIS (sunk 2nd June)**

ISLE OF GUERNSEY (damaged 29th May)  ST. JULIAN (damaged 30th May)
ISLE OF THANET (27th)  WORTHING (2nd June)
ST. DAVID (Ist June)

DINARD  ST. ANDREW

*Total* 8, of which I was sunk and 5 damaged.

**Note**.

1. In addition some 23 of H.M. Trawlers, Drifters and Yachts of the Nore Command assisted by taking one or more tows of boats to the French coast.
2. A large number of skoots, launches, motor boats, ships' lifeboats, Naval cutters and whalers were wrecked or foundered during the operations.

# APPENDIX II
## TO F.O. DOVER'S DESPATCH

*Daily List of Disembarkation in U.K. Ports, classified by types of ships*

### Date

| | May 26 | 27 | 28 | 29 | 30 | 31 | June 1 | 2 | 3 | 4 | Total |
|---|---|---|---|---|---|---|---|---|---|---|---|
| Destroyers | - | - | 11,327 | 15,972 | 18,554 | 25,722 | 14,440 | 5,649 | 6,432 | 5,303 | 103,399 |
| Personnel Ships | 2,287 | 3,168 | 2,161 | 17,525 | 2,981 | 12,477 | 11,314 | 4,977 | 7,477 | 10,013 | 74,380 |
| Mine sweepers | - | - | 420 | 4,307 | 7,671 | 4,714 | 7,594 | 1,842 | 2,552 | 1,940 | 31,040 |
| Paddle Minesweepers | - | - | 1,336 | 1,454 | 1,477 | 2,682 | 9,148 | 2,075 | 1,777 | 1,079 | 21,028 |
| Trawlers | - | - | 100 | 3,894 | 7,405 | 3,976 | 2,762 | 900 | 50 | 1,200 | 20,287 |
| Skoots | - | - | - | 90 | 1,116 | 1,797 | 647 | 1,975 | 418 | 418 | 6,461 |
| Drifters | 24 | - | 3,138 | 3,158 | 2,931 | 2,938 | 1,797 | 2,632 | 2,526 | 2,023 | 20,167 |
| Hospital Carriers | - | - | - | 818 | 780 | 907 | 130 | - | - | - | 2,635 |
| Miscellaneous | 1,936 | 2,550 | 45 | 3,133 | 5,293 | 4,596 | 10,803 | 2,649 | 3,018 | 2,637 | 36,660 |
| French Destroyers | - | - | - | - | 2,620 | 2,026 | 651 | - | 750 | 1,116 | 7,623 |
| Other Vessels | - | - | - | 520 | 2,399 | 2,306 | 2,271 | 905 | 4,641 | 1,960 | 15,002 |
| Total | 4,247 | 5,718 | 18,527 | 50,331 | 53,227 | 64,141 | 61,557 | 23,604 | 29,641 | 27,689 | 338,682 |

**Notes.**

1. This list is not complete as a number of vessels did not record their totals.
2. Evacuation after 1st June was by night only.

# APPENDIX III
## TO F.O. DOVER'S DESPATCH

*Summary of Aircraft Data concerning R.N.*

Naval Aircraft Employed

> Squadron No. 801} "Skuas"
> No. 806}
>
> Squadron No. 815} "Swordfish"
> No. 825}
>
> Squadron No. 826 "Albacore"

These aircraft were the only available British "dive bombers," the R.A.F. possessing none at the time.

These squadrons operated under the orders of Coastal Command and carried out attacks on tanks, transport, batteries, gun emplacements and enemy positions in the Calais and Dunkirk areas as well as attacks on E-Boats.

In spite of their relative inadequacy for the purpose the "Skuas" were also detailed for fighter-escort of ships.

*Enemy Aircraft Destroyed by Ships' fire off Dunkirk*
(between 0300/27th May and 2000/1st June)

| | |
|---|---|
| 27th May | 4 |
| 28th | |
| 29th | 4 |
| 30th | Nil[II] |
| 31st | 11 |
| 1st June | 13 |
| TOTAL | 35 |

In addition over the same period 21 others were heavily damaged by ships' fire and seen in distress but not seen to crash definitely.

# APPENDIX IV
## TO OPERATION "DYNAMO" – NARRATIVE OF EVENTS

*Co-operation of the French Navy*

(*a*) *The following French warships and other vessels wearing the French flag were employed evacuating French troops from Dunkirk harbour, and on the last three nights, from the beach 1½ miles eastward from Dunkirk:-*

| *Destroyers* (9) | BRANLEBAS | INCOMPRISE | SIROCCO |
|---|---|---|---|
| | BOUCLIER | BOURRASQUE | CYCLONE |
| | FLORE | FOUDROYANT | MISTRAL |

| *Avisos* (4) | AMIENS | BELFORT | ARRAS | AMIRAL MOUCHEZ |

| *Fast Motor Boats* | 3 |
|---|---|
| *Sub Chasers* | 3 |
| *Auxiliary Minesweepers* | 6 |
| *Small Cargo Vessels* | 3 or 4 carrying munitions to Dunkirk returning with troops. |
| *Trawlers, Drifters and other small craft.* | 167 concentrated from the French coast between Boulogne and Cherbourg, and employed mainly off the beach. In addition the French mail packets COTE D'ARGENT, COTE D'AZUR, NEWHAVEN and ROUEN were transferred to the orders of the Vice-Admiral, Dover, and were employed as required side by side with the British personnel vessels. |

(*b*) The French losses included:-

| *Destroyers:* | BOURRASQUE and FOUDROYANT sunk by bomb, and SIROCCO by torpedo. |
|---|---|
| | CYCLONE badly damaged by torpedo, and MISTRAL by bomb. |

| Trawlers, etc.: | EMILE DESCHAMPS and DUPERRE, the drifter PIERRE MARIE and 15 other small craft were sunk, including the Dutch yacht DEMOG I under French orders. |
| French packet: | COTE D'AZUR sunk by bombs before her first trip. |

(*c*) Covering patrols, mainly in the Dyck, were provided by the two small cruisers LEOPARD and EPERVIER, and when not employed evacuating troops, the four avisos acted as escorts along "X" Route.

(*d*) Of the troops landed in U.K. during "Dynamo," the following French troops were carried in the above French vessels.

| Date of disembarkation in UK | French troops disembarked in U.K. ||
|---|---|---|
| | Carried by French Vessels | Total by French and British Vessels |
| 27th May | Nil | Nil |
| 28th May | Nil | Nil |
| 29th May | 655 | 655 |
| 30th May | 5,444 | 8,616 |
| 31st May | 4,032 | 14,874 |
| 1st June | 2,765 | 35,013 |
| 2nd June | 905 | 16,049 |
| 3rd June | 4,235 | 19,803 |
| 4th June | 2,349 | 26,989 |
| 5th June | 140 | 1,096 |
| TOTALS | 20,525 | 123,095 |

Besides the above 20,525 troops landed in U.K., an unknown number was transported direct to French ports in French vessels.

**Admiralty footnotes:**

*About one-quarter of these troops were carried in ships manned by the Merchant Navy. Admiralty footnote*

1. *For Routes X, Y and Z see Diagram. [not published]. Admiralty footnote*
2. *It was not to be expected that all air action would be visible from points on the coast; many enemy raids were in fact intercepted and enemy aircraft destroyed. Moreover, fighter patrols formed only one part of the air operations in connection with Dunkirk, as a considerable reconnaissance and bombing effort directly connected with the operation was also being made.*

*Air protection could not be complete for the following reasons:-*

*(a) the enemy air force had the initiative and could choose the times of their attacks.*

*(b) the operations were outside the range of controlled interception provided by radar stations in the United Kingdom. In consequence, all that could be done was to put up patrols and to trust that these would intercept or generally discourage enemy air attacks.*

*(c) the demand for continuous fighter cover, with the limited size of our fighter force, meant that patrols were necessarily weak in numbers of aircraft, and our fighters were thus placed on disadvantageous terms with the enemy. When evacuation was eventually limited to the dusk and dawn hours it was possible to concentrate our fighters in much greater strength for these periods, with a corresponding improvement in the cover provided.*

*Only in conditions of complete air supremacy could the Dunkirk evacuation have been completed without interference from the enemy. Such air supremacy could only have been attained by prolonged previous air operations or by the local concentration of a far greater force of fighters than the R.A.F. then had. Air Ministry footnote*

3. *The cutters and whalers are rowing boats carried by H.M. Ships. Admiralty footnote*
4. *A skoot is a Dutch type of coasting vessel. Admiralty footnote*
5. *The Personnel Vessels were manned almost wholly by members of the Merchant Navy and Fishing Fleets. Admiralty footnote*
6. *T.O.O. = Time of origin. Admiralty footnote*
7. *Hospital Carriers were manned almost wholly by members of the Merchant Navy and Fishing Fleets.*
8. *A.L.C. = Assault Landing Craft. Admiralty footnote*
9. *M.L.C. = Mechanised Vehicle Landing Craft. Admiralty footnote*
10. *On 30th May flying conditions were bad and few enemy aircraft operated. After 1st June evacuation proceeded only between evening dusk and dawn. Admiralty footnote*

# 3

# Despatches on Operations of the British Expeditionary Force, France from 12th - 19th June, 1940

## By Lieutenant-General Sir Alan Brooke

WEDNESDAY, 22 MAY, 1946

*The War Office,*
*May, 1946.*

*The following Despatch was submitted to the Secretary of State for War on 22nd June, 1940, by Lieutenant-General Sir ALAN BROOKE, K.C.B., D.S.O. Commanding II Corps, British Expeditionary Force, France.*

I have the honour to report that, in accordance with the Instructions of 10th June, 1940, received by me from the Secretary of State for War, I duly left Southampton by ship at 1400 hours on 12th June, and reached Cherbourg at 2130 hours the same evening.

For reasons connected with local French orders, it was not possible to disembark until 0030 hours on 13th June, when Brigadier G. Thorpe

(Base Commandant) came out to the ship in a tug and took me ashore with my staff.

2. At 0800 hours 13th June I left Cherbourg by car, and reached Le Mans at 1400 hours after a journey much hampered by the crowds of refugees on the roads. There I was met by Lieutenant-General Sir Henry Karslake, Major-General P. de Fonblanque, G.O.C., Lines of Communication Troops, and Brigadier J.G. des R. Swayne. I at once took command of all British troops in France from General Karslake. I instructed him to return to England, which he did by plane that afternoon.

3. At 1500 hours I left Le Mans with Brigadier Swayne for an interview with General Weygand and, after a journey of some 170 miles, reached the Headquarters of No. 1 Mission[1] (Major-General Sir Richard Howard-Vyse) at 2000 hours that evening.

General Weygand was away at a Cabinet meeting, but, on his return, he sent a message to say that he would see me at 0830 hours on 14th June.

4. I had left my staff at Le Mans to get in touch with the situation as it was known by General Karslake and Major-General de Fonblanque The general inference of the enemy's intention seemed to be that, after crossing the Seine south of Rouen, the bulk of the troops engaged would move South in order to encircle Paris.

The situation on the front that evening, so far as it was known, was that the Tenth French Army, which included the 157th Infantry Brigade of the 52nd Division, Armoured Division (less one Brigade) and Beauman Force[2], was holding a line from the sea West of the Seine to Neubourg and thence to Conches. Between the Southern flank of the 157th Infantry Brigade and Damville, there was a gap of some 8 miles, which was only lightly held by elements of the 3rd D.L.M. South of this area the Army of Paris was supposed to be holding a line from Dreux to Bonnecourt on the Seine, but there was no confirmation that this Army was actually in position.

*14th June.*

5. At 0830 hours I saw General Weygand. He spoke most frankly and

explained the situation to me. He said that the French Army was no longer capable of organised resistance, that it had now broken up into four groups – one of which was the Tenth Army (General Altmayer), with which the B.E.F. was operating – and that considerable gaps existed between the groups.

The Armies, he explained, would continue to fight under the orders of their own Commanders, but co-ordinated action of the force as a whole would no longer be possible. Reserves were exhausted and many formations worn out.

He then informed me that, in accordance with a decision taken by the Allied Governments, Brittany was to be defended by holding a line across the peninsula in the vicinity of Rennes. He suggested that we should proceed to General Georges' Headquarters to discuss with him the details of this project.

We then went to General Georges' Headquarters, at Briare, where we continued the discussion. I pointed out that the length of the proposed line was some 150 kilometres which would require at least fifteen Divisions. I gathered from both General Weygand and General Georges[3] that they did not consider the Brittany project to be a feasible proposition with the forces that now remained available in the Tenth French Army including the B.E.F. General Weygand referred to the project as "romantic," and said that it had been adopted without military advice. General Weygand stated, however, that, since the Allied Governments had issued instructions for the defence of Brittany he must carry out their orders. Consequently, in consultation with General Georges, he had drawn up instructions for the participation of the B.E.F. in the scheme. Being under the impression that H.M. Government had approved this plan, I signed the document which prescribed the rôle of B.E.F. in it. (Copy attached at Appendix 'A').

6. In view of the gravity of the situation which General Weygand had described to me, I immediately sent a telegram to inform the C.I.G.S. I also requested Major-General Sir Richard Howard-Vyse to proceed to the War Office as soon as possible to report more fully to the C.I.G.S., and to take to the C.I.G.S. a copy of the document reproduced in Appendix "A".

7. I then returned to my Headquarters at Le Mans, arriving at 1615 hours. I spoke to the C.I.G.S. by telephone at 1630 hours and explained

the situation. I asked whether the Brittany scheme had H.M. Government's approval and told him that both Generals Weygand and Georges appeared to consider it impracticable with the force available. The C.I.G.S. informed me that he knew nothing of the Brittany scheme, but said he would refer the matter to the Prime Minister.

I told the C.I.G.S. that, in view of the general state of disintegration which was beginning to spread in the French Army, I considered that all further movement of troops and material to France should be stopped, and that arrangements should be started for the evacuation of the B.E.F. from available ports. The C.I.G.S. informed me that orders had already been issued to stop the dispatch of further troops and material to France.

8. An hour later (1715 hours) the C.I.G.S. telephoned to say that the Prime Minister knew nothing of the Brittany plan, and that all arrangements were to start for the evacuation of those elements of the B.E.F. which were at that time not under the orders of the Tenth French Army.

As H.M. Government had not been consulted with regard to the Brittany scheme, and the withdrawal of the B.E.F. had been approved, I considered that I was no longer in a position to carry out the dispositions settled with Generals Weygand and Georges. I therefore requested the C.I.G.S. to inform General Weygand, and I understood this was to be done. The instructions which I received later (see paragraph 10 below), stating that I was no longer under General Weygand's orders, confirmed this opinion.

Orders outlining the arrangements for the evacuation were at once issued, and an officer was dispatched to Lieutenant-General J.H. Marshall-Cornwall requesting him to come to my Headquarters.

9. The C.I.G.S. telephoned again at 2015 hours and said that it was most important that everything should be done to ensure good relations between ourselves and the French, and to avoid, in every possible way, giving the impression that the B.E.F. was deserting them. I replied that I would most certainly see that this was done, that I was moving no troops engaged with the Tenth Army, but that I was arranging to move back all other troops and material towards the ports.

At this stage the Prime Minister himself spoke and asked about the employment of those elements of the 52nd Division which were not under the orders of the Tenth French Army. I assured him that I considered that no useful purpose could be served by adding them to the forces already with that Army. They could not possibly restore the situation on that front, nor could they close the gap of some 30 miles which now existed between the Tenth French Army and the Army of Paris.

The Prime Minister then agreed to my proposal that the troops under orders of the Tenth French Army should remain fighting with that army for the present, whilst the withdrawal of the remainder of the B.E.F. should proceed.

Moves to ports of embarkation were therefore continued, Canadian forces moving on Brest, corps troops on St. Malo, 52nd Division (less elements with Tenth French Army) on Cherbourg, L. of C. troops and material on St. Malo, Brest, St. Nazaire, Nantes and La Pallice. Finally those elements with Tenth French Army were to embark at Cherbourg when the situation admitted of their withdrawal from that Army.

10. At 2235 hours I spoke to the C.I.G.S. and told him of the Prime Minister's approval for evacuation. The C.I.G.S. informed me that I was no longer under the orders of General Weygand, and that the B.E.F. was to act as an independent force. I was, however, to continue to co-operate in every way possible with the Tenth French Army.

11. During the night of 14th/15th June, my staff and myself were busily engaged in perfecting the arrangements for the embarkation and evacuation of approximately 150,000 personnel, with large stocks of vehicles and material which had been accumulated since September, 1939. Major Macartney of the Quartermaster General's Movement Staff arrived from the War Office that night. He brought with him a list showing the order of priority for shipment of stores, etc., and a suggested outline plan for evacuation. A Senior Naval Officer also arrived early next morning.

*15th June.*

12. At 0315 hours Lieutenant-General J.H. Marshall-Cornwall reported to me, and we discussed the situation. I placed all British troops with the Tenth French Army under his command, and gave him orders to

co-operate with that Army until an opportunity arose to disengage his troops and withdraw them to Cherbourg for embarkation to the United Kingdom.

The subsequent operations of Lieutenant-General J.H. Marshall-Cornwall's troops (Norman Force[4]) are described in that officer's report which is attached at Appendix "B".

13. The withdrawal of B.E.F. started in the early hours of 15th June. The flights of the Canadian Division which had arrived in the Concentration Area were sent back to Brest for embarkation, corps troops were re-embarked at St. Malo, and various L. of C. troops in the Le Mans area were moved nearer the port areas.

14. Information as to the position of the enemy on the front of the Tenth French Army and southwards was very meagre as bad visibility prevented air reconnaissance, and there were no ground troops to reconnoitre between Alençon and Tours.

The general inference, however, was that there was little enemy activity west of Rouen, but hostile infantry were engaging the 157th Infantry Brigade in the area of Conches.

A British pilot of a Bomber aircraft, who had made a forced landing, reported that he had run into heavy anti-aircraft fire about Evreux and that he had seen a column of all arms moving south in that area. This report seemed to confirm previous information that the Fourth German Army was moving South with its left on Chartres.

15. At 0810 hours I considered that my position at Le Mans was too exposed, since there was no known body of troops covering that area. I therefore moved my Headquarters back to Vitre, just west of Laval. I took with me the G.O.C. L. of C. Area, a part of whose staff I had amalgamated with my own since I was entirely dependent on L. of C. Signals for my communications. My own staff consisted only of four officers and two clerks, the remainder having been stopped at St. Malo and sent back to England.

16. At 1230 hours the C.I.G.S. telephoned to say that the Prime Minister was anxious about the withdrawal of the 52nd Division (less the detachment with Tenth French Army). The Prime Minister wished the embarkation to be cancelled, as he feared the effect of such a withdrawal on the morale of the French.

I pointed out that my plans had already received approval, that orders had been issued for the move, and that any alterations now would complicate the embarkation at Cherbourg and might well endanger it. The C.I.G.S., however, said that the Prime Minister did not wish the division to be embarked without the approval of His Majesty's Government.

17. At this time the complete absence of any information of the whereabouts of the enemy on the Le Mans front caused me some anxiety, as any penetration of enemy troops towards Laval and Rennes would have seriously endangered the safety of the B.E.F.

18. I spoke again to the C.I.G.S. at 2150 hours. I explained to him the situation as I knew it, and I once more impressed on him the need to evacuate 52nd Division (less the detachment with Tenth French Army). The necessary shipping was available at Cherbourg and was being kept idle. The air situation was also at that time favourable.

An hour and a half later the C.I.G.S. gave permission to embark one field regiment, one field company and other details of 52nd Division which were not needed to support the infantry of the Division. Orders implementing these instructions were at once issued.

19. Later that night another battalion and a troop of anti-tank guns from 52nd Division were put under General Marshall-Cornwall's orders for the protection of the Cherbourg peninsula at St. Sauveur.

No information of the enemy's movements could be obtained, but he did not appear at the moment to have exploited the gap at Le Mans.

20. During the preceding 24 hours just over 12,000 troops were reported to have been evacuated from the different ports.

*16th June.*

21. At 0700 hours the C.I.G.S. rang me up and said that all arrangements could be made for the evacuation of 52nd Division (less the detachment with Tenth French Army), but that no actual movement was yet to take place. At 0830 hours, however, he rang up again and confirmed that 52nd Division (less the detachment with Tenth French Army) could now begin to embark: Norman Force itself was to continue to cooperate with the Tenth French Army. I then asked the C.I.G.S. what the policy should be with regard to troops of the French Army who might

wish to embark at Cherbourg. He informed me that they would be allowed to do so. Orders for the embarkation of 52nd Division (less the detachment with the Tenth French Army) were issued.

I issued orders to G.O.C. L. of C. to the effect that work of re-embarkation of personnel, stores, and vehicles, was to continue at all ports as long as the tactical situation permitted.

22. Owing, once more, to poor visibility no air reconnaissance was possible, but reports from Motor Contact Officers and from Norman Force showed that the enemy was in contact with the Tenth French Army along its front but that he was attacking seriously only against I57th Infantry Brigade. Further to the South enemy movement seemed to be directed on Chartres.

Information was received later from captured orders which showed that the Fourth German Army was to attack that day with the ultimate object of gaining Cherbourg and Brest.

23. The C.I.G.S. telephoned at I325 hours to confirm that 52nd Division (less the detachment with Tenth French Army) could now embark. He said that he was still unable to give orders as to the future of Norman Force, which was to continue in the meantime to co-operate with the Tenth French Army. I pointed out that that Army was carrying out the Brittany plan and had been ordered to withdraw on Laval and Rennes. I therefore asked that Norman Force should be allowed to disengage and withdraw on Cherbourg.

The C.I.G.S., however, was not prepared to give the decision, and asked that I should ring him up again on my arrival at my new Headquarters.

24. At I430 hours, I moved my Headquarters S.W. from Vitre to Redon, which lies about 30 miles N. of St. Nazaire, and reached Redon soon after I6I5 hours. I then rang up the C.I.G.S. who said that it had been decided that Norman Force was to stay with the Tenth French Army until that Army started to disintegrate, when General Marshall-Cornwall could withdraw his force for embarkation either to Cherbourg or the nearest available port.

25. I had previously arranged that 90,000 rations, as well as ammunition, should be sent up to Cherbourg, as this was the port on which Norman Force would be based. Any alterations to this plan at this stage would have caused a breakdown in the supply arrangements

which were very difficult because the roads were congested and the railways working spasmodically.

26. During that evening I was in touch with Major-General J.S. Drew commanding the 52nd Division. He informed me that he had embarked one of his brigades and expected to get the other away the next day. I gave him orders to proceed to the United Kingdom with his second brigade.

27. Brigadier J.G. des R. Swayne, Head of No. 2 Mission[5], reported to me on this way to the United Kingdom.

I also dispatched Brigadier N.M. Ritchie, B.G.S., 2nd Corps, to the United Kingdom that night, as there was no longer need for his services in France on account of the reduction of the number of troops.

28. Throughout the day the Germans maintained their pressure on the Tenth French Army. In the evening a message was received from General Marshall-Cornwall in which he gave it as his opinion that the Tenth French Army would disintegrate if it were seriously attacked. This opinion was confirmed by his G.S.O. I (Lieutenant-Colonel R. Briggs, R.T.R.) who called at my Headquarters about 2300 hours that night. On the rest of the front the German advance continued, and the gap between the Tenth French Army and the Army of Paris was well over 50 miles wide. What German forces were in this gap it was impossible to say, as no Allied fighting troops were in the area and air reconnaissance was much hampered by low cloud and thunderstorms.

29. During the previous 24 hours about 47,000 troops and 250 vehicles of all kinds were reported to have been embarked.

*17th June.*

30. Early that morning I received a message from General Marshall-Cornwall to the effect that the Tenth French Army was in full retreat on Laval and Rennes, and that he was withdrawing his troops to Cherbourg. His own Headquarters were moving to Avranches and would go next to Cherbourg. At 1015 hours I spoke to the C.I.G.S. and explained the situation to him.

On receiving General Marshall-Cornwall's report, I ordered Air Commodore Cole-Hamilton – Commanding the Air Component – to

*174  The BEF In France 1939-1940*

move with two fighter squadrons and his one flight of reconnaissance aircraft to the Channel Islands whence he was to co-operate with Norman Force by carrying out reconnaissance tasks and by protecting the embarkation of that Force at Cherbourg. As soon as he had completed these tasks he was to proceed to the United Kingdom. The remaining Fighter Squadron was to operate from Brest to give close protection to that port during the embarkation of the B.E.F.

31. At 1130 hours, I spoke to Air Marshal Barratt, and explained my plan to him. I also discussed with him the arrangements for the withdrawal from La Rochelle of his party, which was defending Nantes and St. Nazaire during the evacuation. He expressed himself as satisfied with the arrangements that were being made.

32. At 1300 hours the C.I.G.S. telephoned and informed me that the B.B.C. had reported that the Petain Government had asked the Germans for an Armistice (this was subsequently confirmed by Capitaine Meric of the French Mission). He agreed that, in view of this, all efforts should now be directed to getting personnel away and afterwards, if the situation allowed it, as much material as possible. He further agreed that I should leave with my staff for the United Kingdom that evening. I said that I would ring up again about 3 p.m. to see if there were any final orders and that, if I should be unable to communicate owing to the cable being cut, I would embark as arranged.

I then saw General de Fonblanque and the Senior Naval Officer (Captain Allen, R.N.), explained the situation and ordered them to make every effort to get all personnel away, and also as many guns and vehicles as possible.

33. At 1445 hours I rang up the C.I.G.S. as arranged, but he had not returned to the War Office. At 1530 hours I rang up again, but was informed by Signals that all communications with London had been cut at Rennes, and that it was also impossible to get in touch with any port except Nantes. I, therefore, decided to leave Redon – which I did at 1615 hours – and proceeded with my staff and the G.O.C. L. of C. Area and the Senior Naval Officer to a point about 4 miles outside St. Nazaire. There I remained until 2045 hours.

34. At 2130 hours I left St. Nazaire in the armed trawler H.M.S. "Cambridgeshire." The destroyer which had been sent for my use by the Commander-in-Chief Western Approaches was not available as she

was being used to assist in carrying survivors from the "Lancastria," which had been sunk by enemy aircraft that afternoon. The "Cambridgeshire" remained in the harbour during the night. During that time, three enemy air raids took place, but no damage was done, although a few bombs were dropped ashore.

*18th June.*

0300 hours. The "Cambridgeshire" sailed as escort to a slow convoy.

*19th June.*

1800 hours. The "Cambridgeshire" reached Plymouth. I went up to the Commander-in-Chief's house where I rang up the C.I.G.S. and reported my arrival in the United Kingdom.

That evening, with my staff, I caught the midnight train to London and reported to the C.I.G.S. at 0900 hours on 20th June.

# APPENDIX A.

*Commandement en Chef*
*Du Front Nord-Est.*
*Au Q.G. Nord-Est 14 Juin, 1940.*
*10h. 30.*
*NOTE.*
*Etat-Major*
*3° Bureau*
*Secret.*
*No. 2063 3/Op.*

Le Général Brooke Cdt. le Corps Expéditionnaire Britannique a pris contact le 14 Juin matin avec le Général Weygand Cdt. l'ensemble des Théâtres d'Opérations et le Général Georges Cdt. le Front N.E. pour prendre des directives en ce qui concerne l'emploi des troupes britanniques en France.

Dans le cadre de la décision prise par les gouvernements britannique et francais, d'organiser un réduit en Bretagne, il a été décidé:

1°). Que les troupes britanniques en cours de debarquement (E.O.C.A.[6] Brooke, fin de la 52° division et D.I. canadiénne) seront concentrées à Rennes.

2°). Que les troupes britanniques engagées à la X° Armée (D.I. Evans, D.I. Bauman et 52° D.I. non compris ses éléments non encore débarqués) continueront leur mission, actuelle sous les ordres du Général Cdt. la X° Armée.

Leur emploi dans la manoeuvre d'ensemble de cette Armée devra les amener autant que possible à agir dans la région du Mans pour faciliter leur regroupement ultérieur avec les forces du Général Brooke.

Signé BROOKE.
WEYGAND et GEORGES.

Pour copie conforme:
Pour le Général Cdt. en Chef.
sur le front Nord-Est.
Le Général Chief d'Etat Major.

# APPENDIX B

## SUMMARY OF OPERATIONS OF B.E.F. IN FRANCE FROM IST TO 18TH JUNE, 1940.

I. After the evacuation of the main British Expeditionary Force from Flanders in the first week of June the only British troops remaining in France were the 51st Division, which had been holding a sector of the Sarre Front, and the incomplete 1st Armoured Division, which had begun its disembarkation on 20th May and had been rushed up piecemeal in a desperate effort to relieve the sorely tried right flank of the B.E.F. By the 1st June this attenuated Division, which was incomplete when disembarked and had lost heavily in its first engagement on the Somme, could only muster roughly one-third of its quota of tanks.

2. These two formations, the 51st Division and the 1st Armoured Division, the only British fighting formations remaining in France, were placed under the orders of General Altmayer, commanding Tenth French Army, which held the left sector of the Somme front from Amiens to the sea. The handling of the British troops, which had been delegated to General Altmayer by General Weygand, was co-ordinated and supervised by a British Military Mission at Tenth Army Headquarters.

3. The frontage allotted to the 51st Division on the Somme sector was sixteen miles in extent, an excessive amount, but probably not much greater than that which many French divisions were holding at the time owing to their depleted resources. The Division had already been in action on the Sarre front, and had had a long and arduous journey from the Eastern frontier to its new sector. On 4th June the 51st Division Commander was ordered to carry out an attack on the Abbeville bridgehead, for which operation the newly arrived French

31st Division was placed under his orders, as well as 160 French tanks and a considerable reinforcement of French artillery. The attack, however, was not a success, mainly owing to the difficulty of arranging effective co-operation between British and French infantry, guns and tanks at such short notice, and the 51st Division suffered fairly heavy casualties.

4. On the following day (5th June) the Germans launched a powerful offensive against the whole front held by the Seventh and Tenth French Armies, from St. Quentin to the sea. The 51st Division was by this time in an exhausted condition, after 12 days of continual movement and battle, and was holding too wide a front to be able to resist effectively. The Tenth Army Commander, when asked to relieve the Division from the front, replied that he had no reserves available. The Division fought bravely, but was forced back by German infiltration between its widely scattered posts. Owing to the extent of its frontage the division had no depth in its defences, and had no time to organize rearward defences, nor any reserves with which to counter-attack. It was forced back to the line of the river Bresle, the next natural obstacle, 15 miles in rear.

5. Meanwhile the 1st Armoured Division was re-fitting south of the Seine. Its tanks were in poor mechanical condition, owing not only to battle casualties, but also to the long road distances they had been forced to cover and to the lack of opportunity for adequate maintenance. It was in fact in no condition for offensive operations.

6. On the 7th June the Germans put in a smashing attack with their 5th and 7th Armoured Divisions on the point of junction between the two Corps of the Tenth French Army. This drive was directed from west of Amiens on Rouen and the lower Seine, with the object of splitting the Tenth Army and cutting off its IX Corps between the Seine Estuary and Dieppe. The IX French Corps then comprised the British 51st Division on the extreme left, and then further east the 31st and 40th French Divisions and the 2nd and 5th Light Cavalry Divisions. The whole of this force was completely sundered from the X Corps on its right by the penetration of the German tanks.

7. Meanwhile, owing to the threat developing to the British base at Rouen, General Sir Henry Karslake, G.O.C. the Lines of Communication, had scraped together an improvised force for its local defence. This force comprised nine infantry battalions of a sort; they

consisted partly of second line Territorial units sent out to France for pioneer duties and partly of composite units made up from miscellaneous reinforcements at the base. They had no war equipment except rifles and a few odd Bren guns and anti-tank weapons, which they had never fired before. They were without artillery, means of transport and signal equipment. They were placed under the command of Brigadier Beauman, in charge of the North District, Lines of Communication. Very unfortunately this heterogeneous collection of untrained and ill-equipped units was given the title of a Division. The French were thus misled into thinking that it was a fighting formation, complete with artillery and ancillary services. Beauman's so called Division had been given the task of holding a back line along the rivers Bethune and Andelle covering Rouen, and had done good work in organizing the defence of this position.

8. While the German armoured attack was at its height on the afternoon of the 7th June, General Weygand personally visited Tenth Army Headquarters east of Rouen and impressed on General Altmayer, and on General Evans commanding the British Armoured Division, the necessity for holding the German attack on the Seine at all costs as this was "the decisive battle of the war."

It was now becoming obvious that to enable the IX Corps to fall back in good order to the line of the Lower Seine, a cover position would have to be held along the river Andelle, some 12 miles east of Rouen. General Evans, therefore, at once ordered his 3rd Armoured Brigade (in fact reduced to some four weak squadrons of 30 tanks in all) to stiffen up the right flank of Beauman's defensive line.

9. On the 8th June the German armoured drive continued on the axis Amiens-Rouen, and succeeded in penetrating the weak British defences on the watershed between the rivers Andelle and Bethune, west of Forges-Les-Eaux. Beauman's ill-equipped units, with the British tanks supporting them, fell back to the line of the Seine. That night German armoured units penetrated into Rouen, and the French Tenth Army lost all touch from then onward with its IX Corps in the Rouen-Dieppe cul-de-sac.

10. The 51st Division was thus completely cut off from its proper line of retirement via Rouen. This was mainly due to the failure or inability of the French High Command to withdraw their left wing while there

was still time and space for this manoeuvre. Throughout all these operations it was becoming clear that the French High Command was issuing "die in the last ditch" orders, which their troops had no intention of carrying out. From this time onwards, until the final evacuation of the B.E.F. on the 18th, it was obvious that the spirit of the French Army was crushed and that it had little intention of offering serious resistance. This spirit was also shared by the higher commanders; beginning on the 8th June, the Tenth French Army Headquarters literally ceased to function for 48 hours; it had lost all touch, and its X Corps was broken and in full retreat.

11. The Germans had on the 9th June reached the line of the Seine and had established bridgeheads at several points. The 3rd Armoured Brigade and Beauman's fragmentary units were withdrawn to reorganize, and the 2nd Armoured Brigade, which had been refitting at Louviers, was put in to support General de la Laurencie's III Corps which was trying to hold the Seine crossings south of Rouen. It was now apparent that the German armoured units and air force were being employed elsewhere, while three army corps were detached to drive southwest towards Alençon with a view to separating the Tenth French Army from the Armée de Paris.

12. It was at this critical juncture that the 52nd Division was hastily sent put to France. Its leading brigade, the I57th, under an able and cool-headed commander, Brigadier Sir John Laurie, was rushed up and placed under the orders of the Tenth French Army. On the night of I2th/I3th June it took over the right sector of the III Corps front east of Conches, in a very exposed position, with a gap of eight miles on its right, and two newly arrived French battalions on its left west of Evreux.

As none of the 52nd Divisional Artillery had yet arrived, the I57th Brigade was given the support of some French batteries.

13. On 14th June the Germans renewed their pressure on the Tenth French Army front, but most of their tanks and aircraft appeared to have been diverted on a south-easterly axis towards Paris. A fairly sharp infantry attack developed on the left flank of the I57th Infantry Brigade, which suffered some 50 casualties, and the French infantry on their left, as well as the French artillery supporting them, retired hastily, leaving the brigade in the lurch. As a result of this pressure the Tenth

French Army withdrew south-west a distance of 30 miles to the wooded area north-west of Mortagne. As the Armée de Paris was retiring almost due south on the Loire, this divergence of the lines of retreat of the two armies created a gap of some 30 miles on the right flank of the Tenth Army.

14. In conformity with this withdrawal the I57th Brigade moved back and took up a front of eight miles astride the Mortagne-Verneuil road, with the French Cavalry Corps on its right. On the night of the I4th/I5th I was placed by General Brooke in command of all the British troops operating with the Tenth French Army, and was ordered to withdraw them towards Cherbourg for re-embarkation, whilst still co-operating, so far as possible, with the French withdrawal. It had been my intention to leave the I57th Brigade in the line until mid-day on the I9th before withdrawing it, in order to allow General Altmayer to readjust his front. I notified General Altmayer of this intention on the I6th, and he appreciated the respite granted him.

15. On the I6th June, however, the German motorized columns had already followed up swiftly the French withdrawal, and the I57th Brigade was attacked all day. The French units on its right and left retired without making any serious resistance, and the British Brigade was exposed to serious danger by both its flanks being turned. As a result of this enemy pressure, the Tenth Army issued orders for a general retirement on the axis Alençon – Rennes, with a view to withdrawing into Brittany. As co-operation with such a movement would have been contrary to my own instructions, I at once issued orders to Beauman's Force, the 3rd Armoured Brigade (which had once again relieved the 2nd) and the I57th Infantry Brigade, for a withdrawal north-westwards to Cherbourg.

16. In the case of Beauman's Force and the 3rd Armoured Brigade, neither of which were in contact with the enemy, this was a comparatively simple operation, although it involved moving at right angles across the simultaneous line of retreat of the XIV Corps of the Tenth Army. The I57th Brigade, however, was still engaged with the enemy, and it was only due to the cool handling and tactical ability of its Brigadier that it was extricated from its dangerous situation, embussed by midnight on the I6th/I7th, moved 200 miles by roads

encumbered by columns of troops and refugees and embarked 24 hours later at Cherbourg.

17. In order to protect the embarkation at Cherbourg, I had asked for a fresh battalion of the 52nd Division to be left to occupy a covering position some 20 miles to the south. This, combined with the five French battalions of the Cherbourg garrison, ought to have provided ample security, and I had hoped to continue the embarkation until the 21st in order to remove all the stores and mechanized vehicles. The enemy, however, again upset our calculations by the speed with which he followed up our rapid withdrawal. At 9 a.m. on the 18th, a column of 60 lorries, carrying motorized German infantry, reached the covering position near St. Sauveur. Finding resistance there, they turned west to the sector held by French troops, and succeeded in penetrating the position by the coast road. The French made little attempt to resist, and I had to make the decision at 1130 to complete the evacuation by 3 p.m. The covering battalion (5th Bn. K.O.S.B.) was withdrawn between 12 noon and 3 p.m., and the last boat left at 4 p.m. All weapons were removed, except one 3.7 in. A.A. gun, which broke down and was rendered unserviceable, and one static Bofors gun which could not be removed in the time. Two Anti-Tank guns also had to be abandoned during the withdrawal. When the last troopship left, the Germans had penetrated to within three miles of the harbour.

(Sgd.) J.H. MARSHALL-CORNWALL,<br>Lieutenant-General.

*20th June, 1940.*

1. No. 1 Mission, under Major-General Sir Richard Howard-Vyse, represented British interests at the French Army Headquarters (Chief of Staff, General Weygand) in Paris.

2. The Beauman Division was an improvised formation which on 13th June, was organised as follows:-

    *"B" Bde. – Formed of personnel from auxiliary military Pioneer Corps.*

    *"C" Bde. – Formed of personnel from infantry base depots.*

    *4 Provisional Battalion – Formed from reinforcement personnel.*

*"E" Anti-tank Regiment (improvised).*

*"E" Field Battery (improvised).*

*212 Army Troops Company, Royal Engineers.*

*213 Army Troops Company, Royal Engineers.*

3. *General Georges was C.-in-C., North-Eastern Theatre of Operations.*

4. *Norman Force, was an improvised formation which, on 15th June, comprised:-*

   *3rd Armoured Brigade; 157th Brigade Group (157th Infantry Brigade; 71st Field Regiment R.A.; Troop-Carrying Company, 52nd Division).*

   *Beauman Division (see Footnote ²).*

5. *No. 2 Mission had been attached to the Headquarters of General Georges (C.-in-C. North-Eastern Theatre of Operations).*

6. *Eléments Organique Corps d'Armée.*

# ABBREVIATIONS

| | |
|---|---|
| A/S | Anti-Submarine |
| AA | Anti-Aircraft |
| ALC | Assault Landing Craft |
| Bart, Bt | Baronet |
| Bde | Brigade |
| BEF | British Expeditionary Force |
| Bn, Btn, Battn | Battalion |
| BNLO | British Naval Liaison Officer |
| CBE | Commander of the Most Excellent Order of the British Empire |
| Cdr | Commander |
| CGS | Chief of the General Staff |
| CIGS | Chief of the Imperial General Staff |
| CRA | Commander Royal Artillery |
| CRE | Commander Royal Engineers |
| DCLI | The Duke of Cornwall's Light Infantry |
| Div | Division or Divisional |
| DLM | *Division Légère Mécanique* (Mechanised Light Division) |
| DMO | Divisional Medical Officer |
| DSO | Distinguished Service Order |
| EOCA | *Eléments Organique Corps d'Armée* |
| FAA | Fleet Air Arm |
| GHQ | General Headquarters |
| GOC | General Officer Commanding |

| | |
|---|---|
| GSO | General Staff Officer |
| HM | His Majesty |
| HMS | His Majesty's Ship |
| Hon | Honourable |
| I.C. | In Charge |
| KCB | Knight Commander of The Most Honourable Order of the Bath |
| KOSB | King's Own Scottish Borderers |
| L of C | Line(s) of Communication |
| Lt, Lieut | Lieutenant |
| MASB | Motor Anti-Submarine Boat |
| MC | Military Cross |
| MGB | Motor Gun Boat |
| MLC | Mechanised Vehicle Landing Craft |
| MTB | Motor Torpedo Boat |
| MVO | Member of The Royal Victorian Order |
| OC | Officer Commanding |
| QMG | Quartermaster General |
| RA | Royal Artillery |
| RAF | Royal Air Force |
| RASC | Royal Army Service Corps |
| RE | Royal Engineers |
| RN | Royal Navy |
| RNLI | Royal National Lifeboat Institution |
| RNR | Royal Naval Reserve |
| RNVR | Royal Naval Volunteer Reserve |
| RTR | Royal Tank Regiment |
| SNO | Senior Naval Officer |
| TF | Territorial Force |
| TOO | Time of Origin |
| VC | Victoria Cross |

# Index of Persons

Abrial, Admiral Jean-Marie, 65, 74, 79, 84, 87–8, 98–9, 140
Adam, Lieutenant-General Sir Ronald Forbes, 21, 61, 63–4, 67, 73–4, 81, 84, 86, 97
Alexander, Field Marshal Harold Rupert Leofric George, 6, 30, 88, 98–9, 136, 139
Altmeyer, Général de corps d'armée Marie-Robert, 50, 64
Armengeaud, Général Paul, 10

Barker, Lieutenant-General M.G.H., 30, 97
Barratt, Air Chief Marshal Sir Arthur Sheridan, 26, 36, 96, 174
Barthélémy, Général de Brigade, 52, 84
Beckwith-Smith, Major-General Merton B., 98
Bertschi, Général de Brigade, 7, 52
Billotte, Général Gaston-Henri, 29, 32, 35, 38–9, 41–2, 45, 48–9, 54–5, 60
Blanchard, Général Georges, 29, 49–50, 60–1, 64, 67–70, 72, 74–5, 78–80, 87
Blount, Air Vice Marshal Charles Hubert Boulby, 96

Brooke, Field Marshal Sir Alan, 30, 97, 165–76, 182
Brownrigg, Lieutenant-General Sir Douglas, 16

Cave–Browne, Major-General William, 56
Chenevix–Trench, Major-General Ralph, 97
Churchill, Sir Winston Leonard Spencer, 19, 59, 66, 70–1, 168–71
Cole–Hamilton, Air Commodore John Beresford, 173
Corap, Général André Georges, 29
Curtis, Major-General H.O., 26, 52

Daladier, French Prime Minister Édouard, 35
D'Astier d La Vigerie, Général François, 10
De Fonblanque, Major-General Philip, 15, 55, 97, 166, 174
Dill, Field Marshal Sir John Greer, 3, 30, 59, 66–7
Drew, Major General J.S., 173

Eastwood, Lieutenant-General Sir Thomas Ralph, 60, 64, 68
Evans, Major-General R., 44, 180

Fagalde, Général de corps d'armée, 65, 73–5, 79, 98–9
Findlay, Brigadier C.B., 63
Fortune, Major-General Sir Victor Morven, 21
Fox-Pitt, Brigadier W.A.F.L., 56
Franklyn, General Sir Harold Edmund, 9, 31, 49–51

Georges, Général Alphonse Joseph, 4–5, 8, 18, 27–9, 31–2, 34–5, 39–41, 48, 167–8, 176
Gillard, Général de Brigade, 5
Giraud, Général de corps d'armée Henri Honoré, 29, 39
Gort, Field Marshal John Standish Surtees Prendergast Vereker Viscount VC, 1–19, 19–97, 135

Herbert, Major-General W.N., 26
Holmes, Lieutenant-General Sir William George, 21
Howard-Vyse, Major-General Sir Richard Granville Hylton, 166–7

Ironside, General Sir Edmund, 48

Jardine, Brigadier Sir Colin, 97
Jeauneaud, Général, 10
Johnson, Major-General Dudley Graham VC, 6, 30

Karslake, Lieutenant-General Sir Henry, 55, 166, 179
Keyes, Admiral of the Fleet Sir Roger, 71

Laurencie, Général Benoît-Léon Fornel de La, 46, 81, 84, 87–8, 181
Lawson, Brigadier Honourable E.F., 76–7

Leopold III, King of the Belgiums, 33, 35–6, 54, 55, 71, 79
Lindsell, Lieutenant-General W.G., 3, 56, 97
Loyd, Lieutenant-General Henry Charles, 6, 30, 136

Marshall-Cornwall, General Sir James Handyside, 168–73, 178–83
Martel, Lieutenant General Sir Giffard le Quesne, 21, 50
Mason-MacFarlane Lieutenant General Sir Frank Noel, 37, 41, 46–7, 50, 52–3, 62, 64
Michiels, General Chief of the Belgians general staff Oscar, 72
Montgomery, Field Marshal Bernard Law, 6, 30
Mouchard, Général, 10

Nicholson, Brigadier Claude, 63

Osborne, Lieutenant General E.A., 21, 81
Overstraeten, Lieutenant-General Van Raoul, 28, 35–6, 54

Pakenham-Walsh, Major-General Ridley Pakenham, 52, 97
Petre, Major-General R.L., 26, 43, 47, 50–1
Phillimore, Captain W.R., 110
Plunkett-Ernle-Erle-Drax, Admiral the Honourable Sir Reginald A.R., 109
Pownall, Lieutenant General Sir Henry R., 5, 35, 54, 96
Prioux, Général René, 50, 74, 80–1

Ramsay, Admiral Bertram Home, 101–11

Reynaud, French Prime Minister Paul, 59, 70–1
Ritchie, General Sir Neil Methuen, 173

Scott, Major-General J.W.L., 16
Somerville, Admiral of the Fleet Sir James Fownes, 110
Swayne, Lieutenant-General Sir John George des Reaux, 18–19, 166, 173

Tennant, Admiral Sir William George, 96, 99, 110, 126

Thorne, General Sir Augustus Francis Andrew Nicol, 9, 30, 64, 76

Usher, Colonel Charles Milne, 52–3, 61, 65

Voruz, Général de Division, 18, 91

Wake-Walker, Rear-Admiral Sir William Frederick, 110, 127, 133
Wason, Major-General S.R., 74
Weygand, Général d'armée Maxime, 48, 54, 59, 61, 71, 74, 83, 87, 166–9, 177–8, 180

# Index of Naval, Military and Air Force Units

Belgium Army, 28, 30, 33, 35–6, 38, 42, 45, 55, 65–6, 68, 70–4, 79
  1st Corps, 36, 66
British Army,
  1st Corps, 3, 5–7, 9–10, 19, 30–2, 34, 36–9, 42, 44, 46, 53, 62, 69, 73, 76–7, 80–2, 88, 97–9
  2nd Corps, 3, 5–7, 9–10, 21–2, 30–4, 36–9, 42, 44, 53, 62, 66–9, 73, 76–7, 80–2, 87–8, 97, 165–75
  3rd Corps, 21–2, 31, 42, 44, 53, 62–3, 67–8, 73–4, 76–7, 80, 87–8, 97, 120
  Army Educational Corps, 13, 18
  Auxiliary Military Pioneer Corps, 8, 15, 55
  Intelligence Corps, 17
  Royal Army Chaplains Department, 16
  Royal Army Medical Corps, 16
  Royal Army Ordinance Corps, 15
  Royal Army Service Corps (R.A.S.C.), 4, 41, 57, 90, 94, 149
  Royal Artillery, 5, 24–6, 41, 53, 61, 63–4, 68, 74, 77, 82, 84, 89, 99, 181
  Royal Corps of Signals, 17–18, 93
  Royal Engineers, 7, 11, 15, 41, 52, 151
  1st Armoured Division, 21, 24–5, 34, 44, 55, 60, 166, 178–9, 180
  1st Division, 6, 53, 62, 82, 98–9
  2nd Division, 6
  3rd Division, 6, 31, 33, 37, 42, 81, 86
  4th Division, 6, 9, 23, 30–1, 36–7, 42, 49, 53–4, 62–3, 72, 80–2, 85
  5th Division, 9, 21–2, 31–3, 37–8, 42, 49–50, 68, 87
  12th Division, 26, 40, 43–4, 55, 84
  23rd Division, 26, 37, 40, 42–3, 47, 50, 53, 64, 85
  42nd Division, 21–2, 31, 41, 52, 62, 85, 99
  44th Division, 21–2, 30, 42, 49, 53–4, 60, 62, 64, 72, 80–1, 85
  46th Division, 26, 38, 40, 52, 55,

62–4, 81–2, 85, 99
48th Division, 9, 23, 30, 36–7, 42, 54, 60, 64, 66, 73, 76, 80, 85
50th Division, 21–2, 31, 37–8, 42, 47, 49–52, 58, 60–1, 67–8, 71–2, 78, 85, 87, 99
51st Division, 21–3, 55, 178–80
52nd Division, 166, 168–73, 181, 183
20th Guards Brigade, 56
1st Armoured Reconnaissance Brigade, 62
1st Army Tank Brigade, 39, 41, 50
13th Brigade, 9, 50
15th Brigade, 9, 22
17th Brigade, 9
25th Brigade, 9, 47, 52
30th Brigade, 63
36th Brigade, 40, 43, 47
126th Brigade, 85, 99
127th Brigade, 41, 52
138th Brigade, 52
139th Brigade, 52, 62
143rd Brigade, 66
144th Brigade, 23, 64–5
145th Brigade, 64
151st Brigade, 50
157th Brigade, 166, 170, 172, 181
12th Royal Lancers, 30, 32–3, 35, 47–8, 50–1, 66, 82
13th/18th Hussars, 61, 64
Welsh Guards, 41, 48
Royal Tank Regiment, 63
Royal West Kent, 47
Field Security Police, 12–13
Railhead Mechanical Transport Companies, 58

Railway Operating Companies, Royal Engineers, 95

Crested Eagle, 109

Fenella, 125
French Army,
  1st Army Group, 28, 43, 60, 68–9
  1st Army, 7, 29, 31, 34, 38–9, 43, 45–6, 49–50, 53–4, 58–9, 66, 69, 74, 80–1, 90
  7th Army, 28–9, 36, 39, 43, 59
  9th Army, 29, 32, 34, 45
  10th Army, 166–73, 178–82
  Cavalry Corps, 29, 33–6, 46, 50–1, 59–61, 64, 67, 81, 84, 87, 182
  3rd Corps, 53
  4th Corps, 53
  5th Corps, 53
  16th Corps, 6, 65
  1st Light Mechanised Division, 50, 80
  7th Division, 23
  42nd Division, 8
  51st Division, 6, 9
  68th Division, 65, 75, 84

French warships and other vessels employed evacuating troops from Dunkirk, 161–2

Grieve, 104

Isle of Thanet, 118, 158

King Orry, 125, 156

Lydd, 123, 141

Maid of Orleans, 118, 158
Massey Shaw, 151

Index   193

Mona Isle, 115
Mona's Queen, 104

Queen of the Channel, 115, 118

Royal Air Force, 9–11, 17, 26–7, 32, 34–5, 43–4, 70, 84, 93, 95–6, 105–106, 110, 120, 122, 134, 141, 143, 147, 151, 160
   British Expeditionary Force Air Component, 9–10, 22, 26–7, 34, 43, 96, 173–4
   Army Co–operation Wing, 10
   Fighter Wing, 10
   Bomber Reconnaissance Wing, 10
   Advanced Air Striking Force, 43
   Number 11 Group, 106
Royal Navy, 112–54, (*for list of HM Ships, Personnel Ships and Hospital Ships lost or damaged, see pages* 155–8)
   7th Mine Sweeping Flotilla, 119
   8th Mine Sweeping Flotilla, 119
   Royal Navy and associated Vessels,
     Anthony, 127, 155
     Basilisk, 138, 155
     Calcutta, 117, 120, 124, 155
     Cambridgeshire, 174–5
     Canterbury, 124, 133, 156
     Codrington, 127, 156
     Comfort, 122–3, 157
     Esk, 127, 156
     Express, 126, 146, 155
     Gallant, 120, 123, 155
     Gossamer, 123, 156
     Grafton, 120, 122–3, 155
     Grenade, 123, 125, 151, 155
     Harvester, 128, 130, 155
     Havant, 128, 130, 155
     Hebe, 88, 124, 126–8
     Icarus, 128, 130, 156
     Impulsive, 128–9, 130, 155
     Intrepid, 128, 130, 155
     Ivanhoe, 128, 130–1, 155
     Jaguar, 123, 125, 151, 155
     Javelin, 128, 150, 156
     Keith, 127, 138, 155
     Lady Philomena, 136, 157
     Locust, 124, 145–6, 156
     Lynx, 110
     Mackay, 128, 156
     Malcolm, 123, 125–6, 131, 155
     Manxman, 146
     Montrose, 128, 155
     Mosquito, 124, 133, 156
     Nautilus, 123, 157
     Olvina, 137, 157
     Paris, 143, 158
     Royal Daffodil, 144, 158
     Royal Sovereign, 146, 158
     Sabre, 127, 155
     Scimitar, 127, 155
     Shikair, 127, 146, 156
     Skate, 3
     Skipjack, 109
     Vanquisher, 127–8, 156
     Verity, 120, 122, 125–7, 156
     Wakeful, 109, 120, 122–3, 155
     Waverley, 109
     Whitehall, 127, 155
     Winchelsea, 127, 156
     Windsor, 127, 155
     Wolfhound, 115–16
     Worcester, 127, 155
     Worthing, 143, 158
   Royal Marines, 56
R.N.L.I., 151